CLEP* INFORMATION SYSTEMS & COMPUTER APPLICATIONS

Naresh Dhanda, M.S.
Middlesex County College
Edison, New Jersey

Research & Education Association
Visit our website at: www.rea.com/studycenter

Research & Education Association
61 Ethel Road West
Piscataway, New Jersey 08854
E-mail: info@rea.com

CLEP Information Systems and Computer Applications

Library of Congress Control Number 2012933549

ISBN-13: 978-0-7386-1036-8
ISBN-10: 0-7386-1036-4

REA® is a registered trademark of Research & Education Association, Inc.

CONTENTS

CHAPTER 3

Computer Software, Information Systems, and Application Software in Organizations.........................71

CHAPTER 4

Information Systems Software Development...............................127

ABOUT OUR AUTHOR

Naresh Dhanda received his bachelor's degree in Mathematics, Chemistry, and Physics from Panjab University, Chandigarh, India. He holds a master's degree in Chemistry from the University of London, London, England, and a master's degree in Computer Science from Jackson State University, Jackson, Mississippi. For the past twenty-five years, he has taught mathematics and computer science at colleges and universities across the country. He is currently an Associate Professor of Computer Science at Middlesex County College, Edison, New Jersey.

ABOUT RESEARCH & EDUCATION ASSOCIATION

Founded in 1959, Research & Education Association (REA) is dedicated to publishing the finest and most effective educational materials—including software, study guides, and test preps—for students in elementary school, middle school, high school, college, graduate school, and beyond.

Today, REA's wide-ranging catalog is a leading resource for teachers, students, and professionals.

ACKNOWLEDGMENTS

In addition to our author, we would like to thank Larry B. Kling, Vice President, Editorial, for his overall guidance, which brought this publication to completion; Pam Weston, Publisher, for setting the quality standards for production integrity and managing the publication to completion; John Cording, Vice President, Technology, for coordinating the design and development of the REA Study Center; Diane Goldschmidt and Michael Reynolds, Managing Editors, for coordinating development of this edition; Transcend Creative Services for typesetting this edition; and Weymouth Design and Christine Saul, Senior Graphic Artist, for designing our cover.

CHAPTER 1

Passing the CLEP Information Systems and Computer Applications Exam

Passing the CLEP Information Systems and Computer Applications Exam

Congratulations! You're joining the millions of people who have discovered the value and educational advantage offered by the College Board's College-Level Examination Program, or CLEP. This test prep covers everything you need to know about the CLEP Information Systems and Computer Applications exam, and will help you earn the college credit you deserve while reducing your tuition costs.

GETTING STARTED

There are many different ways to prepare for a CLEP exam. What's best for you depends on how much time you have to study and how comfortable you are with the subject matter. To score your highest, you need a system that can be customized to fit you: your schedule, your learning style, and your current level of knowledge.

This book, and the online tools that come with it, allow you to create a personalized study plan through three simple steps: assessment of your knowledge, targeted review of exam content, and reinforcement in the areas where you need the most help.

Let's get started and see how this system works.

Test Yourself & Get Feedback	Score reports from your online diagnostic and practice tests give you a fast way to pinpoint what you already know and where you need to spend more time studying.
Review with the Book	Study the topics tested on the CLEP exam. Targeted review chapters cover everything you need to know.
Improve Your Score	Armed with your score reports, you can personalize your study plan. Review the parts of the book where you're weakest and study the answer explanations for the test questions you answered incorrectly.

THE REA STUDY CENTER

The best way to personalize your study plan and focus on your weaknesses is to get feedback on what you know and what you don't know. At the online REA Study Center, you can access two types of assessment: a diagnostic exam and full-length practice exams. Each of these tools provides true-to-format questions and delivers a detailed score report that follows the topics set by the College Board.

Diagnostic Exam

Before you begin your review with the book, take the online diagnostic exam. Use your score report to help evaluate your overall understanding of the subject, so you can focus your study on the topics where you need the most review.

Full-Length Practice Exams

These practice tests give you the most complete picture of your strengths and weaknesses. After you've finished reviewing with the book, test what you've learned by taking the first of the two online practice exams. Review your score report, then go back and study any topics you missed. Take the second practice test to ensure you have mastered the material and are ready for test day.

If you're studying and don't have Internet access, you can take the printed tests in the book. These are the same practice tests offered at the REA Study Center, but without the added benefits of timed testing conditions and diagnostic score reports. Because the actual exam is computer-based, we recommend you take at least one practice test online to simulate test-day conditions.

AN OVERVIEW OF THE EXAM

The CLEP Information Systems and Computer Applications exam consists of 100 multiple-choice questions, each with five possible answer choices, to be answered in 90 minutes.

The exam covers the material one would find in a college-level introductory business information systems course. The exam emphasizes basic concepts about information systems and the application of that knowledge. References to applications such as word processing or spreadsheets do not require knowledge of a specific product. Instead, the exam focuses on the concepts and techniques applicable to a variety of products and environments. Knowledge of arithmetic and mathematics equivalent to a first-year high school algebra course is assumed.

The approximate breakdown of topics is as follows:

25% Information Systems and Office Application Software in Organizations

20% Hardware and Systems Technology

15% Information Systems Software Development

25% Programming Concepts and Data Management

15% Business, Social, and Ethical Implications and Issues

ALL ABOUT THE CLEP PROGRAMS

What is the CLEP?

CLEP is the most widely accepted credit-by-examination program in North America. CLEP exams are available in 33 subjects and test the material commonly required in an introductory-level college course. Examinees can earn from three to twelve credits at more than 2,900 colleges and universities in the U.S. and Canada. For a complete list of the CLEP subject examinations offered, visit the College Board website: *www.collegeboard.org/clep*.

Who takes CLEP exams?

CLEP exams are typically taken by people who have acquired knowledge outside the classroom and who wish to bypass certain college courses and earn college credit. The CLEP program is designed to reward examinees for learning—no matter where or how that knowledge was acquired.

Although most CLEP examinees are adults returning to college, many graduating high school seniors, enrolled college students, military personnel, veterans, and international students take CLEP exams to earn college credit or to demonstrate their ability to perform at the college level. There are no prerequisites, such as age or educational status, for taking CLEP examinations. However, because policies on granting credits vary among colleges, you should contact the particular institution from which you wish to receive CLEP credit.

Who administers the exam?

CLEP exams are developed by the College Board, administered by Educational Testing Service (ETS), and involve the assistance of educators from throughout the United States. The test development process is designed and implemented to ensure that the content and difficulty level of the test are appropriate.

When and where is the exam given?

CLEP exams are administered year-round at more than 1,200 test centers in the United States and can be arranged for candidates abroad on request. To find the test center nearest you and to register for the exam, contact the CLEP Program:

CLEP Services
P.O. Box 6600
Princeton, NJ 08541-6600
Phone: (800) 257-9558 (8 A.M. to 6 P.M. ET)
Fax: (609) 771-7088
Website: *www.collegeboard.org/clep*

OPTIONS FOR MILITARY PERSONNEL AND VETERANS

CLEP exams are available free of charge to eligible military personnel and eligible civilian employees. All the CLEP exams are available at test centers on college campuses and military bases. Contact your Educational Services Officer or Navy College Education Specialist for more information. Visit the DANTES or College Board websites for details about CLEP opportunities for military personnel.

Eligible U.S. veterans can claim reimbursement for CLEP exams and administration fees pursuant to provisions of the Veterans Benefits Improvement Act of 2004. For details on eligibility and submitting a claim for reimbursement, visit the U.S. Department of Veterans Affairs website at *www. gibill.va.gov/pamphlets/testing.htm*.

CLEP can be used in conjunction with the Post-9/11 GI Bill, which applies to veterans returning from the Iraq and Afghanistan theaters of operation. Because the GI Bill provides tuition for up to 36 months, earning college credits with CLEP exams expedites academic progress and degree completion within the funded timeframe.

SSD ACCOMMODATIONS FOR CANDIDATES WITH DISABILITIES

Many test candidates qualify for extra time to take the CLEP exams, but you must make these arrangements in advance. For information, contact:

College Board Services for Students with Disabilities
P.O. Box 6226
Princeton, NJ 08541-6226
Phone: (609) 771-7137 (Monday through Friday, 8 A.M. to 6 P.M. ET)
TTY: (609) 882-4118
Fax: (609) 771-7944
E-mail: ssd@info.collegeboard.org

6-WEEK STUDY PLAN

Although our study plan is designed to be used in the six weeks before your exam, it can be condensed to three weeks by combining each two-week period into one.

Be sure to set aside enough time—at least two hours each day—to study. The more time you spend studying, the more prepared and relaxed you will feel on the day of the exam.

Week	Activity
1	Take the Diagnostic Exam. The score report will identify topics where you need the most review.
2 – 4	Study the review chapters. Use your diagnostic score report to focus your study.
5	Take Practice Test 1 at the REA Study Center. Review your score report and re-study any topics you missed.
6	Take Practice Test 2 at the REA Study Center to see how much your score has improved. If you still got a few questions wrong, go back to the review and study any topics you may have missed.

TEST-TAKING TIPS

Know the format of the test. CLEP computer-based tests are fixed-length tests. This makes them similar to the paper-and-pencil type of exam because you have the flexibility to go back and review your work in each section.

Learn the test structure, the time allotted for each section of the test, and the directions for each section. By learning this, you will know what is expected of you on test day, and you'll relieve your test anxiety.

Read all the questions—completely. Make sure you understand each question before looking for the right answer. Reread the question if it doesn't make sense.

Annotate the questions. Highlighting the key words in the questions will help you find the right answer choice.

Read all of the answers to a question. Just because you think you found the correct response right away, do not assume that it's the best answer. The last answer choice might be the correct answer.

Work quickly and steadily. You will have 90 minutes to answer 100 questions, so work quickly and steadily. Taking the timed practice tests online will help you learn how to budget your time.

Use the process of elimination. Stumped by a question? Don't make a random guess. Eliminate as many of the answer choices as possible. By eliminating just two answer choices, you give yourself a better chance of getting the item correct, since there will only be three choices left from which to make your guess. Remember, your score is based only on the number of questions you answer correctly.

Don't waste time! Don't spend too much time on any one question. Remember, your time is limited and pacing yourself is very important. Work on the easier questions first. Skip the difficult questions and go back to them if you have the time.

Look for clues to answers in other questions. If you skip a question you don't know the answer to, you might find a clue to the answer elsewhere on the test.

Acquaint yourself with the computer screen. Familiarize yourself with the CLEP computer screen beforehand by logging on to the College Board website. Waiting until test day to see what it looks like in the pretest tutorial risks injecting needless anxiety into your testing experience. Also, familiarizing yourself with the directions and format of the exam will save you valuable time on the day of the actual test.

Be sure that your answer registers before you go to the next item. Look at the screen to see that your mouse-click causes the pointer to darken the proper oval. If your answer doesn't register, you won't get credit for that question.

THE DAY OF THE EXAM

On test day, you should wake up early (after a good night's rest, of course) and have breakfast. Dress comfortably so you are not distracted by being too hot or too cold while taking the test. (Note that "hoodies" are not allowed.) Arrive at the test center early. This will allow you to collect your thoughts and relax before the test, and it will also spare you the anxiety that comes with being late. As an added incentive, keep in mind that no one will be allowed into the test session after the test has begun.

Before you leave for the test center, make sure you have your admission form and another form of identification, which must contain a recent photograph, your name, and signature (i.e., driver's license, student identification card, or current alien registration card). You will not be admitted to the test center if you do not have proper identification.

You may wear a watch to the test center. However, you may not wear one that makes noise, because it may disturb the other test-takers. No cell phones, dictionaries, textbooks, notebooks, briefcases, or packages will be permitted, and drinking, smoking, and eating are prohibited.

Good luck on the CLEP Information Systems and Computer Applications exam!

CHAPTER 2

Computer Hardware and Information Technology

Computer Hardware and Information Technology

2.1 COMPUTERS TODAY

Information technology's ever-increasing development and its powerful influence over today's society has significantly changed the world both on a business level as well as on a personal level.

Business Level

Nowadays, businesses are not able to operate without the use of technology and computers, whether it is in the field of medicine, banking, education, airlines, federal, state, and county governments, music, and so on. Technology is not only a requirement for business survival but also a way to make customers' lives easier.

Cell phones, for example, are computerized devices that can be compared to personal computers as they include similar features, such as a mini-keyboard to type text messages along with a screen to display them; a ROM chip that stores information, similar to a computer's hard drive; a calculator performs some of the functions of a computer's CPU (central processing unit), as well as a variety of generalized daily uses, such as making and receiving calls, sending and receiving text messages and e-mails, checking bank accounts, amongst others.

Personal Level

A human being is surely one of the most intelligent species in the universe, and when it comes to processing information, the computer and the human brain have the following similar characteristics:

13

- **Perform simple and complex tasks**
  Humans can, for example, plan to go on a vacation or construct a bridge. Similarly, computers can perform simple tasks, such as allocating a letter grade to a student based on the calculated average of three test scores received, as well as complex tasks such as installing an engine in an automobile body during manufacturing (robots).

- **Enter, receive, and store information**
  Human brains can receive information and store it in memory. Similarly, computers are used to input data and store it for future use.

- **Give Instructions**
  When executing a task, a human brain gives instructions to another human brain. For example, a supervising engineer responsible for the construction of a bridge gives instructions to subordinate workers. Similarly, in a computer system, a hardware component, known as the control unit, gives operating instructions to other components of the computer system.

- **Short-term vs. long-term memory**
  Human brains have both a short-term and a long-term memory. They can remember a person's name for life, while they may forget another person's name after a few days. Similarly, computer systems have Random Access Memory (RAM), which temporarily stores information that gets deleted once the computer is turned off; and they have a hard disk, where the data that needs to be saved for later retrieval is saved and stored.

In sum, the functioning of the human brain is similar to the functioning of a computer, as it can plan and execute a wide range of simple or complex tasks: it can read data, perform operations on that data, draw conclusions based on the results of those operations, as well as store the data for any period of time. Also, they both operate through an Information Processing Cycle, known as the IPOS cycle (Input, Processing, Output, Storage), which will be discussed later in this chapter.

This chapter will also cover basic computer terminology and technology that will help us understand how computers function.

2.2 THE BASICS OF COMPUTERS

A computer can be simply defined as a programmable, electronic device that performs specific tasks (simple and complex) assigned by a computer program through an IPOS cycle.

Computers and Data

In order to understand the concepts of computers, we need to know terms such as *data* and *information*. While performing tasks, computers store and process data to generate information. Data can, for example, be the number of hours worked as well as the hourly pay rate, which will be used to calculate the gross pay of an employee. Data can also represent the personal information of an employee, such as his name, address, telephone number, number of dependents, etc.

Computer Hardware and Software

A computer is made up of hardware and software. It can be compared to a ready-to-assemble wooden table, in which the package contains an instruction booklet with step-by-step assembly instructions as well as all the parts to be assembled. The instruction booklet can be compared to the computer's software that gives commands to the computer's hardware to perform tasks. The parts to assemble, the nails, the screws, the tabletop, and the legs can be compared to the computer's hardware.

Computer Hardware

Computer hardware is defined by the physical components of a computer system, which include the keyboard and mouse (input devices), the CPU and memory (processing devices), monitors and printers (output devices), the hard disk (storage device), CDs, and flash memory cards (storage media) etc. Most computers also include communication devices (such as a modem) to connect to the Internet and other networks.

Computer Software

Computer software, commonly known as computer programs, allows computers to perform specific tasks or applications. There are two main software categories: system software and application software. When you buy a new computer, it comes with pre-loaded software (system software) known as an operating system, which is required to interface with the computer and manages all the computer hardware and software. It also allows users to run programs and manage files. In addition, computers come with application software packages, such as Microsoft Word, Excel, PowerPoint, and others, that are used for specific applications such as word processing, creating spreadsheets, and designing slide shows.

The IPOS Cycle

The Information Processing Cycle is also known by the acronym IPOS, which stands for the Input/Processing/Output/Storage cycle used by computers.

Input (entering data into the computer)

Data is entered into a computer by using the computer hardware (input devices). For example, if you want to check or access your e-mail, you use the keyboard to enter (input) your user ID and password. Input devices are discussed later in this chapter.

Processing (performing operations on the data)

After the data is entered, the computer processes it and performs operations or tasks. Following the example above, the computer checks whether you entered the correct user ID and password and allows or denies access to your e-mail account. Processing inside a computer is done by a hardware device known as the Central Processing Unit (CPU), which is discussed later in this chapter.

Output (presenting the results)

After the input and processing of operations, the computer generates output through a hardware device such as a monitor. At this point in our example, your e-mail messages are displayed on the computer screen.

Storage (saving data, programs, or output for future use)

All computers store the generated output from a computer system into a storage device such as the computer's internal hard disk or removable flash drive. In the example above, all your received or sent e-mails are stored on the storage devices of your e-mail servicing company such as Yahoo or AOL.

2.3 DIGITAL REPRESENTATION OF DATA IN COMPUTERS

Data

Data is a collection of text, numbers, images, audio, and video that has not yet been processed. For example, the unit price of a t-shirt is one piece of data and the quantity of t-shirts purchased is another piece of data. Data can include text or string (such as a person's name), numbers (such as age), images or pictures (from a digital camera), audio (song), and video (picture and sound together). All businesses store massive amounts of data and information inside the database of their computer system. For example, the IRS stores the yearly income tax returns of all U.S. citizens.

Information

Information is processed data that may aid in making decisions, answering questions, or getting results that take a meaningful form. For example, in order to calculate the total dollar amount to be paid for purchased t-shirts, their unit price is multiplied by the quantity purchased. After calculating the total amount, a decision must be made to pay for the t-shirts using a credit card or cash. In this example, the total amount is the *information*; the unit price and quantity of the t-shirts purchased are the *data*; and the multiplication is the *process*.

Data vs. Information

In order to clarify the difference between *data* and *information*, let's calculate the average of three test scores, labeled T1, T2, and T3, for a student in which each score represents *data* that has not yet been processed. By adding T1 to T2 to T3, a total is obtained. In this case, the addition is the *process,* and the total is the result (*information*) obtained by processing (adding) the three data items labeled T1, T2, and T3. In addition, in order to calculate the average, we divide our total by three. In this further step, the total is now the *data*, the division is the *process*, and the average is the result (*information*). Table 2.1 illustrates the three steps explained above.

Table 2.1   Data vs. Information—Average of Three Test Scores

Example	Data	Processing	Information
1	T1, T2, T3 Scores	Total = T1 + T2 + T3	Total
2	Total	Average = Total / 3	Average of Scores

Data Types

A data type is the value stored in a data item. It is important to determine the data type of any item stored in a computer so it can process and perform the correct type of operations and give the desired results.

The basic data types in computers are text, graphic, audio, video, date/time, amongst others. For example, the number of books in a student's school bag has a data type of number; the name of a person has a data type of text or character (string); the date of birth of a person has a data type of date; and so on. Table 2.2 below illustrates the basic data types in computers.

Table 2.2   Basic Data Types in Computers

Data Type	Description	Example
Text Data (String)	Collection of alphabet letters, numbers, and special characters, such as # or % sign	Memos, letters, addresses, e-mail messages, names
Graphic Data	Photographs, mathematical charts, and drawings	Graphics, charts, house blue prints, sketches, company logo
Audio Data	Sounds, such as music and voice	Voice message left through the use of a microphone, which is stored by a computer in a digital format
Video Data	Moving pictures and images	Video-conferencing, film clip, movie, recording of a movie through the use of a video camera
Date/Time	Date and time of a specific event	Date and time of a child's birth
Multimedia	Combination(s) of text, number, and/or audio/video	Cartoons on TV

Number Systems in Computers

Any character or piece of data typed on a keyboard must be converted to a binary number system, which is interpreted and then processed by a computer. A number system is a systematic way to write or represent any number, whether it is for use in the business world, in our daily lives, or in a computer system.

Base of a number system

In any number system, we must know in advance how many digits will be used to represent a number. This is called the base of a number system. For example, a decimal number system has base 10, because any number is written using a base of 10 in combination with of digits 0 through 9.

Positional values in a number system

Every digit or character used at a particular position in a number system has a positional value that represents the digit at that place raised to the base of a number system. For example, number 312 with base 10 has three digits 3, 1, and 2. The extreme right digit 2 is classified as a unit or 1th digit or ($10^0 = 1$); the middle digit 1 is classified as a tenth digit ($10^1 = 10$); and the extreme left digit 3 is known as a hundredth digit ($10^2 = 100$). The total value stored in a number system is calculated by adding the values of every digit raised to the power of its base. In our example, the total value stored in the number 312 with base 10 is calculated as follows:

$$
\begin{aligned}
312 \quad &= \quad 3 \times 10^2 + 1 \times 10^1 + 2 \times 10^0 \\
&= \quad (3 \times 100) + (1 \times 10) + (2 \times 1) \\
&= \quad 300 + 10 + 2 \\
&= \quad \mathbf{312}
\end{aligned}
$$

Converting a number system into another number system

All characters typed on a computer are first converted to their decimal equivalent and then to a binary code. The decimal equivalent of the alphabet letter "A" is 65, which when converted to binary code yields "1000001." The steps below explain how this conversion takes place.

- The decimal number 65 is first divided by 2, giving a quotient and a remainder

- The quotient from step is 1 divided again by 2, giving another quotient and another remainder

- The division by 2 continues until the quotient is 0 and the remainder is 1

Remainders are always either a digit 1 or a digit 0. In our example and as illustrated in Figure 2.1, they are used to write the binary equivalent of decimal 65. The bottom remainder digit is written first, the second is written next and so on, until all the digits are written.

Computer Machine Language and Binary Numbers

Computers understand only machine language—a language computers use to process data or information that is made solely from two numerical values (or digits)—0 and 1. Machine language uses these two digits, known as binary numbers, to represent data in a computer system. "Bi" means "two," and in computers, the digits 0 and 1 are known as bits—short for binary digits. To represent data in a computer system, any character typed must be converted into an eight bit binary code that is a combination of eight 0s and 1s in ASCII (or Unicode) coding schemes.

Bytes in Computers

As bits, digits 0 and 1, represent the smallest unit of information. Computers use a group of eight bits (known as bytes), a combination of 0s and 1s, to represent any character typed. In a decimal number system, as you move from right to left one digit at a time, each digit is classified as a 1's (units) digit, 10's digit, 100's digit and so on. Similarly, in a binary number system, as you move from right to left one bit at a time, each bit represents a 1's place, 2's place, 4's place, 8's place, and so on. Notice that each digit to the left is twice the number of the digit to its immediate right.

Electrical Switches in Computers

The binary digits 0 and 1 act like an electrical switch, where 0 indicates the OFF state (no current passing) and 1 indicates the ON state (current passing). In the binary number system, if there is a digit 0 in a particular position in an eight bit pattern, that bit does not carry any weight for that position. If there is a

Figure 2.1   Converting a Decimal 65 to Binary Number System

No ÷ 2	Quotient	Remainder (0 or 1)	Use Remainder to write Binary number of a Decimal Number $65_{10} = (1\ 00\ 0\ 001)_2$
65 ÷ 2 =	32	1	Write this remainder digit in 7th (last) position.
32 ÷ 2 =	16	0	Write this remainder digit in 6th position.
16 ÷ 2 =	8	0	Write this remainder digit in 5th position.
8 ÷ 2 =	4	0	Write this remainder digit in 4th position.
4 ÷ 2 =	2	0	Write this remainder digit in 3rd position.
2 ÷ 2 =	1	0	Write this remainder digit in 2nd position.
1 ÷ 2 =	0	1	Write this remainder digit in 1st position.

65_{10} in 8-bit binary code (base 2)	0 1 0 0 0 0 0 1
Written remainder digit from bottom	Added 1st 2nd 3rd 4th 5th 6th 7th
Base 2 positional values =	$0 + 1 \times 2^6 + 0 \times 2^5 + 0 \times 2^4 + 0 \times 2^3 + 0 \times 2^2 + 0 \times 2^1 + 1 \times 2^0$
Decimal equivalent =	0 + 64 + 0 + 0 + 0 + 0 + 0 + 1
Decimal equivalent total =	65

digit 1 in a particular position in an eight-bit pattern, then that bit carries weight for that position. This was shown in Figure 2.1, when decimal number 65 was converted to its equivalent binary number.

Digital Data

Any data that is in computer machine language or binary digit form that is handled by computers and other mobile devices is known as digital data.

ASCII and EBCDIC Code Systems

Both the *ASCII* (American Standard Code for Information Interchange) and the *EBCDIC* (Extended Binary-Coded Decimal Interchange Code) code systems use 8 binary digit patterns consisting of only 0s and 1s, which represent up to 256 (2^8) different characters in computers. They can be any of the following:

- numerical digits 0 through 9
- lower- and upper-case letters of the English alphabet
- special characters such as a comma (,), a question mark (?), a dollar symbol ($), a percentage symbol (%), a pound symbol (#), a period (.), etc.
- control information such as a space return, tab, line feed, etc.

For example, the ASCII code uses the eight-bit pattern 01000001 to represent the letter A. Whenever a user types a particular character, it is transformed into its equivalent integer in the ASCII code, then it is decoded back to its original character by the operating system, and, finally, it is displayed on the screen.

Table 2.3 Decimal and 8-bit ASCII Codes for Symbols Used in PCs

Symbol	Integer	ASCII	Symbol	Integer	ASCII	Symbol	Integer	ASCII
Space	32	100000	A	65	1000001	A	97	1100001
!	33	100001	B	66	1000010	b	98	1100010
"	34	100010	C	67	1000011	c	99	1100011
#	35	100011	D	68	1000100	d	100	1100100
$	36	100100	E	69	1000101	e	101	1100101
%	37	100101	F	70	1000110	f	102	1100110
&	38	100110	G	71	1000111	g	103	1100111
'	39	100111	H	72	1001000	h	104	1101000
(	40	101000	I	73	1001001	i	105	1101001
)	41	101001	J	74	1001010	j	106	1101010
+	42	101010	K	75	1001011	k	107	1101011
/	47	101111	L	76	1001100	l	108	1101100
0	48	110000	M	77	1001101	m	109	1101101
1	49	110001	N	78	1001110	n	110	1101110
2	50	110010	O	79	1001111	o	111	1101111
3	51	110011	P	80	1010000	p	112	1110000
4	52	110100	Q	81	1010001	q	113	1110001
5	53	110101	R	82	1010010	r	114	1110010

(Continued)

Table 2.3 (continued)

Symbol	Integer	ASCII	Symbol	Integer	ASCII	Symbol	Integer	ASCII
6	54	110110	S	83	1010011	s	115	1110011
7	55	110111	T	84	1010100	t	116	1110100
8	56	111000	U	85	1010101	u	117	1110101
9	57	111001	V	86	1010110	v	118	1110110
:	58	111010	W	87	1010111	w	119	1110111
;	59	111011	X	88	1011000	x	120	1111000
<	60	111100	Y	89	1011001	y	121	1111001
=	61	111101	Z	90	1011010	z	122	1111010
>	62	111110	[	91	1011011	{	123	1111011
?	63	111111	\	92	1011100	}	125	1111101
@	64	1000000	]	93	1011101	Del	127	1111111

Unicode Code System

Unlike ASCII and the EBCDIC coding systems, the *Unicode* system is a universal international coding standard that represents characters from other languages such as Chinese, Greek, Hebrew, Russian, Tibetan, Amharic, and Japanese. In addition, it uses 16 binary digit (2 bytes) patterns to represent 65,536 (2^{16}) different characters in computers. The first 256 characters in both the ASCII and the Unicode systems are exactly the same, which makes it easier to incorporate the ASCII coding system into newer operating systems such as Windows Vista and Mac OSX.

Arithmetic and Comparison Operators

Operators are special symbols used to manipulate numeric values and perform operations on one, two, or three operands and return a single result. Examples of arithmetic operators are the +, −, *, and / symbols. Examples of comparison operators are the >, <, >=, <=, and != symbols.

Unary and Binary Operators

Table 2.4 below describes unary and binary operators.

Table 2.4   Unary and Binary Operators

Operator	Description	Example
Unary	Perform operations only on one operand	-5, $-$ is an Unary and negation operator
Binary	Perform operations on two operands	$C = 7 + 5$, $+$ is a binary operator

Operands

The numerical values on which the arithmetic operators perform operations are called operands. When evaluating an expression, a user has to follow the order of precedence of arithmetic operators. For example, in programming language, the mathematical expression "$C = 5 + 8$" can be interpreted as follows:

- The symbol C stores the calculated sum of the numbers 5 and 8.

- The numbers 5 and 8 are called the operands.

- The equal sign ($=$) is called an assignment operator as it assigns the calculated result to the symbol C.

2.4   CATEGORIES OF COMPUTERS

Computers can serve a general purpose of performing a variety of tasks, such as a PC, or a special purpose of performing a specialized task, such as an embedded computer. They are generally classified in one of the six following categories, based on size, capability, and price:

- Supercomputers
- Mainframe computers
- Personal computers (PCs)
- Mobile devices
- Wearable computers
- Embedded computers

Regardless of their classification, all computers go through the IPOS cycle and need hardware, an operating system, and software to perform their operations.

Supercomputers

Supercomputers are designed to perform complex mathematical calculations at extremely high speed. They are used by governments and are also used for scientific research. They are the most expensive type of computers and are very large in size.

Mainframe Computers

Mainframe computers are large, expensive, and powerful computers that allow thousands of users to perform tasks simultaneously. Large companies use these computers, so multiple employees can access computer records at the same time.

Personal Computers (PCs)

Personal computers, often referred to as desktop computers, are compact computers that sit on the top of a computer desk. Usually, they include: a mouse and a keyboard as input devices; a CPU as the processing device; a monitor and printer as output devices; an internal hard disk and flash drives as storage devices; a CD/DVD/Blue-ray disc player for audio and video programs; and a modem and network interface card (NIC) as communication devices. Additional data storage capabilities can be added.

Generally, PCs come with a Windows or a Mac operating system and various software programs. Anti-virus, anti-spam, computer security, and firewall programs can be added to protect the computer system from viruses, spam e-mail, and threats from hackers.

Mobile Devices

Mobile computers are portable and easy-to-carry devices. Cell phones, global positioning systems (GPSs), personal digital assistants (PDAs), portable media players (PMPs), laptop (notebook) computers, and pagers are examples of mobile devices.

Cell Phones

A cell phone is a mobile computing device that has its own operating system (OS), such as Symbian OS or Windows Mobile OS. Similar to a desktop computer, it includes the following:

- An input hardware device in the form of a small keyboard to input numbers for phone calls and write and send text messages. Newer cell phones also have built-in digital cameras to take pictures and videos, a touch-sensitive screen to input data, and a built-in microphone or speaker.

- A built-in processing hardware device (like a CPU) to perform calculations.

- An output hardware device in the form of a liquid crystal display (LCD) screen.

- A storage hardware device in the form of a read-only memory (ROM) chip to store the operating system.

- Network connectivity or access to the Internet by using a wireless Internet Service Provider (ISP).

- Anti-virus software. Computer viruses are programs which, when executed in a computer system, can harm its hardware, software, and stored data; in some cases, they can render a computer useless. Antivirus software for cell phones and other mobile devices is available for added protection.

- A rechargeable battery.

Personal Digital Assistants (PDAs)

Personal digital assistants, or PDAs, are handheld devices that carry information in a digital (binary number) form. Some of the features are outlined below.

- PDAs store contact telephone numbers and addresses, photos, games, and songs; PDAs can be programmed as an appointment book and also have a built-in calculator.

- PDAs can be connected to the Internet.

- PDAs usually come with a built-in mini-keyboard and use a stylus pen to input information.

- PDAs use an LCD display screen.

- PDAs use a ROM chip to store the operating system, programs, and other data.

- PDAs have a RAM chip to hold additional programs.

- To increase storage capability, PDAs come with a slot to insert a flash memory card.

- Data can be transferred to and from a PDA to other devices by placing it on its cradle, and then connecting it to a computer or other device through a USB port.

- In order to connect a PDA to the Internet, there must be a service plan with a wireless ISP in addition to a network card installed in the PDA.

- Similarly to cell phones and other mobile computing devices, when connected to the Internet, PDAs can be affected by computer viruses. In order to protect the PDA, the same precautions taken for cell phones should be applied.

- PDA files can be synchronized with a computer by connecting them through a USB cable, along with appropriate software. File synchronization means that the data stored on the PDA will be exactly the same as the data stored in the computer.

Global Positioning Systems (GPSs)

A global positioning system, or GPS, is a collection of satellites that constantly orbit the earth. Designed, built, and operated by the U.S. military, a GPS provides precise three-dimensional geographic locations to a GPS receiver on the earth by analyzing the signals sent by satellites. Below are some facts about GPS:

- Newer mobile devices, such as cell phones and PDAs, have built-in GPS receivers.

- GPS receivers are convenient to use when traveling. A GPS is also used for navigation by transport systems, to find the location of a lost person, for land surveying, geographical mapping, and other similar purposes.

- When in use, a GPS is powered by connection to a cigarette lighter.

Portable Media Players (PMPs)

A portable media player, or PMP, is a mobile electronic device that stores, plays, and supports digital audio files (such as WMA, WAV, and AAC formats), digital video files (such as MPEG-4, WMV, and AVI formats), and digital images (such as JPEG and GIF formats) on its hard drive or flash memory cards.

- As far as storage hardware is concerned, PMPs come with removable flash memory cards that can be inserted into or removed from a special memory slot. Flash memory cards have non-volatile memory, and its contents are not lost when the PMP is turned off. Secure digital (SD) memory cards are commonly used in PMPs and are faster and more secure than other memory cards.

- Newer expensive PMPs come with a built-in hard drive and can have a storage capacity of up to 160GB.

- PMP players come with a USB cable to charge the battery.

Laptop (Notebook) Computers

Laptop computers are portable, thin, lightweight, and easy-to-carry computers that can have the same power and capabilities as desktop computers.

- Input device: A laptop computer has a full-size keyboard with a built-in mouse and a display screen attached to hinges on the system unit.

- Operating systems and other software: Laptop computers use the same OS and application software as desktop computers.

- Processing device (CPUs): Newer laptop computers use dual-core processors to compensate for processing speed as compared to desktop computers. The CPU speed used in laptop computers is slightly less than the speed on desktop computers.

- Output devices: Laptops have display screens of varying sizes.

- Storage devices: Laptops come with hard disk storage that can have a capacity of 160GB or more.

- Ports and other hardware: Laptop computers have all the ports found on desktop computers. Newer laptops can be equipped with an HDMI port, a video and audio interface used on the latest audio and video

(AV) equipment. Laptops with an HDMI port can be connected to television sets having HDMI connections and show the images that are stored on the computer on the television screen.

- Laptops come with RAM (volatile memory) having a capacity of 4GB or more.

- Power: Laptop computers come with a lithium-ion or nickel-metal hydride rechargeable battery, which uses AHr (Amp hours) or WHr (Watt hours) to indicate the capacity and life of the battery.

Wearable Computers

Wearable computers are worn on some part of a human body. They are used in applications that require people to record or send data via the Internet or to perform computations while doing something else.

Wearable computers come in the form of headsets, watches, jackets, and eyeglasses. The main users of these computers are workers who are moving all the time. For example, in the medical field, an insulin pump is a small battery-operated device that comes with an insulin-filled reservoir as well as an attached microcomputer that controls the delivery of the insulin. It can be attached to a belt or stored inside a pocket of patients.

An eye-tap is another wearable computer device that is worn in front of the eye and is used to capture a picture or a scene to then be sent to another computer for storage.

Embedded Computers

Embedded computers are small computer chips that are built inside another operating product or device and perform a specialized function. They are used in almost every product or appliance we encounter in our daily lives. Embedded computers work independently from other devices and do not require input or instructions. Embedded computers are used in the following:

- household appliances such as microwave and dishwashers

- environmental control devices such as home heating and cooling devices

- other electronic devices

2.5 COMPUTER INPUT DEVICES—HARDWARE

As defined earlier, computer hardware includes all of the physical components of a computer system that can be seen and touched, including the keyboard and mouse (input devices), the CPU and memory (processing devices), display monitors and printers (output devices), the hard disk and RAM (storage device), as well as DVDs, CDs, flash memory cards, etc. (storage media).

Printer and USB cables, modems, and network interface cards (NIC) are other examples of computer hardware. Some hardware, such as a keyboard or a mouse, can be seen on the outside of a computer. Other hardware, such as RAM, an internal hard disk, and the NIC, can be seen only after opening the system unit. Peripheral devices are attached to the computer system in order to perform a variety of tasks. All the hardware devices listed above are also peripheral devices.

Computer hardware devices can be divided into the following six categories:

- input device hardware
- processing device hardware
- output device hardware
- storage device hardware
- communication device hardware
- network device hardware

Input device hardware allows users to input data or instructions into a computer and convert that data or instruction into the binary code a computer uses to process and complete the given task. When using input devices, users also respond to choices and commands. For example, a user can select to print the entire document by clicking "Print all" in a print dialog window.

Examples of input devices include wired and wireless keyboards, wired and wireless mouses, I-Pens, digital pens, point of sale (POS) terminals, digital cameras, microphones, webcams, PC video cameras, touch screens on ATM machines, handheld scanners, and fax machines. Below is a description of each input device.

Keyboard

A wired or wireless keyboard allows the user to input or enter text data (such as a person's name) and/or numerical data (such as a person's age) into a computer.

Mouse

A wired or wireless mouse is a pointing input device that allows the user to make a selection of data or make a choice of operation. For example, to print a document, in the Print dialog box, click the mouse on a command button to print the entire document, the current page, or a range of pages.

A mouse has a left and a right button that activate different functions. For example, we use the left button to save a document, and the right button to highlight a specific portion of a document to cut, copy, or paste.

I-Pen

An I-Pen works in two modes, a "mouse mode" and a "pen mode," which is selected manually by a click of a button. When in "mouse mode," the I-Pen uses the point-and-click method used on a regular mouse; when in "pen mode," the I-Pen acts much like a regular pen. When we write a letter or draw shapes, they are converted using optical character recognition (OCR) software. It is ideal for situations in which workspace is limited.

Digital Pen (Mobile Note Taker)

A digital pen is a portable input device used to capture handwriting and/or drawings that are then converted to computer format by handwritten recognition software. Once uploaded to a computer, the images are stored as a file and can be manipulated just like any other file. Digital pens offer two operational modes: a "mobile mode" for when you are away from your computer and an "online mode" for when you are working online and the device is plugged into a USB port.

Point of Sale (POS) Terminals (Electronic Cash Registers)

These input/output devices are mainly used by retailers. After the completion of a purchase, the POS terminal creates and prints a detailed sales receipt for the customer. POS terminals require the use of general and specialized computer hardware and software, depending on the retailer's needs.

Automatic Teller Machines (ATMs)

ATM machines are computerized telecommunication devices that allow bank customers to manage their bank accounts. ATMs contain both input and output hardware—a CPU; a machine card reader; a keypad; a display screen; a vault that has a mechanism to accept deposits or distribute cash; and security sensors. Most ATM machines use Windows or Linux operating systems.

Audio Devices

Audio input devices create new sounds or capture and store sounds in a computer system. The most common audio input devices are microphones or MIDI keyboards and speech recognition software.

Imaging and Video Devices

These are used to convert images and video into computer language, a process known as digitizing. Examples of video input devices are digital cameras, digital camcorders, PC video cameras, barcode readers, scanners, and web cams.

Sound Card (Audio Card) Devices

Even though a computer has built-in sound capability, some computers may need to use sound expansion cards to provide additional input and output sound signals. This is especially necessary for computer users involved with multimedia—text, sound, images, video, and cartoon animations.

Touch Input Devices

This category includes touch screens, touch sensitive pads, stylus pens for PDAs, and pointing sticks that are used in place of a mouse.

Gaming Input Devices

Games have input devices such as joysticks, game controllers, steering wheels, track balls, game pads and dancing pads.

Biometric Input Devices

Biometrics is a technology that uses special characteristics of the human body (i.e., fingerprints, voice patterns, iris and retinal patterns, facial structure, as well as hand patterns) for identification purposes. Stored in a database system, these characteristics are accessed and used to verify the identity of a person. Biometrics can also be used to stop frauds, scams and counterfeiting of stolen identities and credit cards.

Scanning Devices

Included in this category are the following:

- fax machines;
- page and handheld scanners;
- optical mark readers (OMRs, also known as Scantron machines, after the Eagan, Minn., maker of scannable forms) designed to read specially designed sheets marked with a pencil (such as reading the answers to a multiple-choice questions test);
- magnetic card readers, used to read credit cards, identification cards, ATM cards, and any other card that has a magnetic strip that stores customer information;
- magnetic ink character recognition readers (MICR), a technology used by banks to speed up the clearance of issued checks by reading information such as the bank identifier, check routing number, and a customer's account number;
- bar code readers, which read printed bar code information, translate it into product information on an LCD display, and then prints it on a sales invoice;
- radio frequency identification tags (RFIDs), attached to merchandise or a person, use radio waves to identify and track movements. For example, in a department store, an RFID is attached to an expensive leather jacket. Once the jacket is paid for, the sales associate removes the RFID before it is handed to the customer. If the RFID is not removed, when the customer leaves the store, a loud sound and/or message will be activated by the RFID. RFID tags are used in product tracking, transportation payments (e.g., E-Z Pass), inventory systems, animal and human identification, and in many other areas.

Devices for the Handicapped

There are input devices for physically-challenged computer users. They include:

- Braille keyboards for people with limited hand mobility;
- voice recognition software for people who are blind or visually impaired;
- trackballs that can be used with one finger by people with limited hand mobility;
- mouth pieces for people with mobility impairment. Data and commands are input by blowing through or sucking the mouthpiece. Headsets and microphones also provide hands-free voice input.

Motherboards

A motherboard is the main circuit board of a computer system unit. It has some electronic components built in and others that can be attached. It includes the following:

- a central processing unit (CPU), the brain of the computer, which is composed of an arithmetic logic unit and a control unit;
- memory modules—Random Access Memory (RAM), which is the temporary (volatile) working memory of a computer, whose contents are lost once the computer is turned off, and, therefore, must be saved to storage devices, such as a hard disk or a flash drive. RAM is installed as a pair of chips on the motherboard, and its size is referred to in megabytes (MB). A large RAM, along with a fast CPU, makes the computer run faster;
- a chipset, made up of two parts known as "north bridge" and "south bridge," which is used to connect the CPU to the other parts of the system;
- a set of openings, known as expansions slots, which is used to add expansion cards such as a network interface card, a sound card, and a video card;
- a basic input/output system (BIOS) chip that controls the basic functions of input and output of the computer and that repairs the computer if its system crashes;

- serial and parallel ports to connect peripheral devices, such as the keyboard and the printer;

- a battery-operated chip that acts as a real-time clock to maintain the system's time and the timing of basic functions;

- controllers, which are necessary to control the operation of peripheral devices, such as the monitor, scanners, keyboards, and hard drives; and

- expansion buses to connect expansion cards.

Expansion Slots and Expansion Cards

Expansion Slots

Located on the back of the system unit, expansion slots are openings in the motherboard where you can insert extra expansion cards, such as a network interface card, a sound card, a modem card, and video card.

Expansion Cards (Adapter Cards)

These are added to the computer system in order to provide additional functionality. For example, the motherboard has the capability of providing basic sounds. If you add a sound card, you can expand your sound options for your system.

- A video graphics card is used to show high-quality pictures, text, and images on the computer screen.

- A modem card converts analog signals to digital signals and vice versa so that communication with other computers is available using telephone lines. Computers work with digital signals and telephone lines to transmit analog signals.

- A network interface card (NIC) connects a computer to a network.

Computer Memory Hierarchy

A computer has different types of memory that serve different purposes. They are CPU registers (explained later in this chapter), cache memory, random access memory (RAM), permanent or secondary storage (hard disk, flash drives), virtual memory, and read-only memory (ROM).

Cache Memory

In order to speed up processing, the ALU needs to access certain pieces of data or instructions quickly. These frequently used items are kept in cache memory. There are three levels of cache memory:

- Level 1 Cache (L1 Cache) stores the most frequently used data items or instructions;
- Level 2 Cache (L2 Cache) stores data items or instructions that are less regularly used, but that still need to be accessible; and
- Level 3 Cache (L3 Cache) stores data items or instructions that are used infrequently, but that still need to be readily accessible.

Random Access Memory (RAM)

As described earlier in this chapter, RAM is the volatile, temporary working memory of the computer where all the data, instructions, programs, or documents are stored while the computer is in use. RAM chips are found inside the system unit on the motherboard. All RAM contents are lost once the computer is turned off.

As soon as the computer is turned on, the OS is the first program loaded into RAM and it stays there until the computer is turned off. The OS manages all the operations, including the computer hardware and all programs that are open while the computer is in use. A large RAM size makes the computer run faster. When compared to secondary storage, the RAM is closer to the CPU and its contents are transferred faster to the CPU for processing. Similarly, when the cache memory is closer to the CPU, frequently used data items that are stored in cache memory, enable the CPU to access and process them faster. This is all evident from the memory hierarchy shown in Figure 2.2.

Secondary Storage (Hard Disk)

Secondary storage is discussed later in this chapter.

Virtual Memory

When there is not enough RAM left to store programs that a user is trying to execute, an OS sets aside a certain portion of storage on the hard disk to act as additional RAM and store the data.

To understand the concept of virtual memory, imagine there is a hall with a seating capacity of 500 people. The hall has 10 partitions. Each partition seats 50 people. Think of the hall as a hard disk. One partition of the hall that seats 50 people is reserved and locked. The reserved and locked partition is virtual memory.

Furthermore, imagine that there is another small hall adjoining that partition named virtual memory that can seat a maximum of 40 people. Name this small hall *RAM*. In a situation when RAM needs to seat 50 people, the door of the partition named "virtual memory" is opened and RAM's capacity is expanded to seat a total of 90.

Figure 2.2 below illustrates the computer memory hierarchy.

Figure 2.2   Hierarchy of Computer Memory

Memory Level	
1	**CPU Registers** (Stores items ready to process, being processed and already processed) Fastest of All
2	**Cache Level 1** (Stores most frequently used items by CPU)
3	**Cache Level 2** (Stores medium frequently used items by CPU)
4	**Cache Level 3** (Stores least frequently used items by CPU)
5	**Random Access Memory (RAM)** (Stores Operating System, other programs and files used by a user while computer is on)
6	**Secondary Storage Device (Hard Disk)** ** Virtual Memory (Stores permanently Operating System, other programs, and other user files when computer is off)
** Virtual Memory: A block of hard drive used when RAM runs out of space to store programs.	

Ports on a System Unit

Ports are connectors located on the back or front of a computer system unit and are used to connect various peripheral devices to the system unit, such as printers, scanners, keyboards, mouses, external hard disks, digital cameras, speakers, etc. Different types of ports are described below.

Serial ports send one bit of data at a time, like one car moving on one lane of a highway.

Parallel ports send two or more bits of data at a time and are much faster than serial ports. They are like a multilane highway where four cars can move in one direction.

Universal serial bus (USB) ports are used to connect a wide variety of input, output, or peripheral devices, such as printers, keyboards, mouses, digital cameras, webcams, and external hard disks, to a computer through USB 2.0 cables.

Connectivity ports help a computer communicate with other computers or get access to networks. For example, a modem port will connect an external modem to a computer.

Ethernet ports look similar to phone jacks but are slightly wider. They are used to connect a computer to another computer, a local network, or an external DSL or cable modem.

FireWire ports are digital devices that connect via USB 2.0 or FireWire ports and allow for the fastest transfer of data. Examples include mini digital video recorders, digital cameras, and MP3 players.

Graphics ports or video ports connect a monitor to a computer.

Audio ports connect headphones or microphones to a computer.

Speaker ports connect speakers to a computer.

2.6   CENTRAL PROCESSING UNIT (CPU)—HARDWARE

As introduced earlier, the central processing unit (CPU) of a computer is its "brain." It is a hardware chip mounted on the motherboard that executes the instructions given by a user or a computer program in order to perform specific tasks. The CPU also performs calculations, converts data into information, and oversees the functions performed by other components of a computer. In addition, the CPU contains RAM chips, video cards, and sound cards.

In computers, processing takes place when two numbers are added or subtracted or when two numbers are compared.

Currently, the speed of the CPU is measured in gigahertz (GHz), and the higher the number of gigahertz, the faster the speed of the CPU. Another CPU speed measurement criteria is based on how many instructions per second a CPU can process—millions instructions per second (MIPS), billions instructions per second (BIPS), or trillions instructions per second (TIPS). Furthermore, the number of mathematical calculations a CPU can perform per second also determines its speed. Today's computers come with a speed of about 4 gigahertz.

CPU Components and Architecture

A CPU has three basic components: the arithmetic/logic unit (ALU), the control unit, and the CPU registers.

Arithmetic/Logic Unit (ALU)

The ALU performs all required arithmetical and logical (comparison) operations to complete a particular task in a computer system by executing all the instructions required.

The ALU performs arithmetical operations on two or more numbers using arithmetical operators. For example, if a person works 40 hours a week and receives $10 per hour, the ALU calculates the person's weekly gross pay by multiplying the hours (40) by the hourly pay rate ($10 per hour), and returns a result of $400. Table 2.5 below shows the arithmetic operators used by the ALU.

The ALU also performs comparison operations by using relational operators such as > (greater than), < (less than), or = (equal to). For example, to find the correct letter grade of two test scores, the ALU first adds the two test scores and then finds the average of the scores by dividing it by 2. Then, using the relational operator "greater than" or "equal to," the ALU decides if the average is greater than or equal to 60. If it is "greater than" or "equal to" 60, it returns a result of "student passes"; if it is "less than," it returns a result of "student fails."

Table 2.5   Arithmetical Operators Used in Computers

Arithmetical Operator	Symbol	Example	Result
Addition	+	A = 5 + 6	A = 11
Subtraction	–	B = 78 – 12	B = 66
Multiplication	*	C = 4 * 5	C = 20
Division	/	D = 56/4	D = 14

Table 2.6   Relational Operators Used in Computers

Given A = 5, B = 7, C = 5			
Relational Operator	Symbol	Example	Result
Greater than	>	A > B	False
Less than	<	A < B	True
Greater or Equal to	>=	A >= B	False
Less than or Equal to	<=	A <= B	True
Equal to	=	A = C	True
Equal to	=	A = B	False

Control Unit

The control unit of the CPU manages all the operations of the computer system, including managing the four stages of a CPU Machine Cycle, which will be discussed later in this chapter. The control unit receives every instruction of a computer program in sequence, interprets it, and gives instructions to the appropriate part of a computer system to complete the task.

CPU Registers

CPU registers are special storage areas of the CPU meant for use solely by the CPU. Any data or instruction that needs processing must be present in one of the CPU registers; otherwise, it will not be processed by the ALU. After the ALU processes the data, the result is stored in another register. The ALU uses different types of registers, each with a specific purpose.

- Instruction register (IR): When an instruction begins, the IR holds instructions currently being executed;
- Data register: Holds the data items that are being processed;
- Storage register: Holds the intermediate and the final results of processing;
- Address register: Stores the addresses of each data item or instruction in RAM;
- General purpose register: Holds data as well as addresses of data and instructions;
- Special purpose registers: Hold the status of the computer program.

CPU Machine Cycle

The control unit of the CPU manages all operations taking place in the computer system. The control unit receives every instruction of a computer program in sequence, interprets it, gives instructions to the appropriate part of the computer system to complete the task, and, finally, stores the results (output) obtained.

The control unit manages the following four stages of the CPU machine cycle:

Stage 1: Fetch Instruction

When we want to execute a computer program, the program is brought into the computer's temporary memory (RAM) and it stays there until finished. In addition, all the data and instructions of the program are also stored in RAM at a particular location (known as an address). During this fetch instruction stage of the machine cycle, the control unit requests RAM to provide the first instruction of a program that is stored at a particular address in RAM. The instruction is then placed in an instruction register.

Stage 2: Decode Instruction

After an instruction is brought to the CPU, the control unit decodes that instruction (finds what operation needs to be done) by using an instruction decoder and gives instructions to registers to bring the necessary data into the ALU.

Stage 3: Execute Instruction

The ALU now performs all necessary operations according to the program's instructions, including all arithmetical and logical operations described earlier.

Stage 4: Store Results in CPU Registers

Finally, the generated result is stored in one of the CPU registers.

After stage four, the control unit receives the next instruction of the computer program. One by one, each instruction of the program goes through the CPU machine cycle, until all the instructions have been executed.

2.7   COMPUTER OUTPUT DEVICES—HARDWARE

As introduced earlier, a computer output device is hardware that provides information to one or more people and translates the machine language back to human language. Using output devices we can use, see, read, or hear the information that is generated by the processing of the data that was entered into the computer by input devices.

For example, we can read e-mail on the monitor or print it out using a printer. In this case, the data displayed on the screen is in the form of text. We can listen to music from a CD (sound data) or watch a movie on a DVD (audio/video data) that is playing on the CD/DVD drive of the computer. The sound is coming through speakers that are connected to the speaker port of the computer.

The computer's monitor, printer, and speakers are all output devices that provide the user with different types of information.

Data Types of Output Devices

The following is a description of different data types handled by output devices.

Text

Text data type includes alphabet letters, numerical digits, and special characters to create text data in the form of memos, letters, e-mails, and address labels. The data used in writing an e-mail, creating a resume, or an address label is considered text data because the content of the data is a mixture of alphabet letters and numbers. Text data is never used in arithmetical calculations. For example, we cannot add the names of two people, but we can add two numbers. The name and street address of a person and the description of a person or an object, such as a car, are all examples of text data type.

Numerical

Numerical data is composed of numbers only and can be used to perform arithmetical operations to generate numerical output. The age, height, and weight of a person, the hourly pay rate and number of hours worked for calculating gross pay, a car's speed and distance driven are all examples of numerical data type.

Audio

Audio data involves any kind of sound, such as a human voice or music recorded on CDs. CDs are listened to through speakers connected to the computer. People also listen to songs on their iPod through earpieces or a headset.

Graphics

Graphics are drawings, pictures, and charts that are created on a computer screen using graphical software. A computer with a video card (graphics card) generates an image on a monitor. The video card has VRAM that determines the bit color of an image and is used to create high-resolution pictures. VRAM is separate from RAM inside a computer.

Picture

Examples of picture data type include a digital driver's license or a college student's or employee's identification card with a photo.

Alphanumeric

Alphanumeric data type has a mixture of alphabet letters and numbers. An example is a street address, such as 123 Main Street.

Audio/Video

Video data type consists of moving images. A Web advertisement is an example of video data type. Often, the video data is combined with audio data to make a Web advertisement more appealing. Another example is the recording of a family celebration that can be viewed on a computer.

A LCD monitor can display the output of all data types except sound data. Sound data needs to be handled by devices such as speakers and headsets.

Computer Monitor as an Output Device

Monitors, printers, and speakers are the most common output devices used on a computer.

A monitor connected to a computer is a soft-copy output device that can display words, numbers, graphics, and pictures on its screen, and allows you to work with different programs and applications. There are two types of monitors—CRT and LCD monitors. CRT monitors are considered to be old-fashioned because of their bulky size. LCD monitors, also called flat panel monitors, are commonly used desktop monitors that use a liquid crystal display (LCD) to produce digital images. LCD monitors display clear, sharp images that don't flicker. They take up minimal desk space or can be mounted on a wall. Following are some of the terms used to describe monitors.

Pixel

All the text data or images are created on an LCD monitor by joining a number of pixels. *Pixel* means picture element and is represented by a single point (dot) on any digital image.

Resolution

The resolution of a monitor is described by stating the number of pixels horizontally and the number vertically. A monitor with a resolution of 1600 × 1200 indicates that the monitor has 1600 pixels horizontally and 1200 pixels vertically.

Dot Pitch

Dot pitch is the distance between the centers of two pixels. The lower the dot pitch, the sharper an image is on an LCD monitor.

Printer as an Output Device

A printer is an output device that prints text, drawings, and pictures on paper or transparency film. Once the text, pictures, or graphics are reproduced on paper, it is called "hard copy." Following are some of the terms used to describe printers:

Pixels and Resolution

Pixels and resolution have the same definitions as described earlier for LCD monitors.

Pages Per Minute (PPM)

Printing speed is described by stating how many pages per minute are printed in black-and-white mode and in color mode.

Classification of Printers

Printers can be impact or non-impact. On impact printers, wire pins touch the paper to print the text or images. On non-impact printers, characters and graphics are printed on the paper without actually striking the paper.

Photo Printers

Photo printers are printers that print high-quality black and white or color photos.

Laser Printers

A laser printer is a high-speed, high-quality non-impact printer.

Mobile Printers

A mobile printer is a small, lightweight, battery-powered printer that prints from mobile devices, such as a notebook computer, tablet PC, PDA, or smart phone.

Large-format Printers

Large-format printers accommodate paper with widths up to 60 inches. They are often used by schools and/or professionals to print maps, circuit diagrams, and blueprints.

Fax machines

Fax machines are used as output devices on a computer and can send or receive a faxed document using telephone lines.

Multifunction Office Machines

There are multifunction office machines classified as "3 in 1" or "4 in 1" that are used in homes and offices. The term "4 in 1" means that printing, scanning, copying, and faxing a document can be handled by one machine.

Audio Output Devices

Audio output devices are devices that allow users to listen to speech, music, and other sounds. Two commonly used audio output devices are speakers and headsets. All computers have small internal speakers, but many computer users add surround-sound speakers and/or subwoofers in order to generate higher-quality sounds.

Output Devices for Physically Challenged Computer Users

Computer programs are available that allow hearing impaired computer users to display text on the screen in place of sound. Computer users with limited eye vision can set the colors and size of the text for easier reading, and blind computer users can use voice output devices.

2.8   COMPUTER STORAGE DEVICES—HARDWARE

Storage devices are used to store system software, application programs, data and instructions that can later be retrieved, edited, and saved again. Storage devices also store other types of programs and software such as programming language, graphics, pictures, music, and multimedia applications. The most common storage devices are hard disks, flash drives, and CD/DVD/Blue-ray disks.

After start-up, a computer looks for an operating system (system software) in a storage device and then loads it into memory (RAM). When a user wants to start an application software (program), such as a word processing program, the operating system finds the program in storage and loads it into memory (RAM).

Permanent storage is also known as secondary storage, auxiliary storage, or external storage. As mentioned earlier, storage is the last phase of the IPOS cycle.

Magnetic Storage Devices—Hard Disk

Magnetic storage devices are commonly used to store data, information, instructions, and programs on a disk's surface in the form of a magnetic particle. Electrical charges are applied to iron fillings on the disk's surface. Magnetic particles can exist in two binary states, 0 and 1. Binary state 0 (bit 0) indicates that the magnetic particles are not magnetized and that no data is stored in that bit. Binary state 1 (bit 1) indicates that the magnetic particles are magnetized and that data is stored in that bit.

Every computer requires at least one internal magnetic storage medium, known as a hard disk, to store the operating system, application programs, data, and information. In the case of desktop computers, the hard disk is permanently housed inside a computer system unit, which comes in a vertical tower shape. Advancements in technology have increased the popularity of two types of external hard disk drives: desktop external hard drives and portable external hard drives.

Desktop External Hard Drives

All external hard drives are housed outside the system unit in its own enclosure and are connected to desktops or notebook computers by high-speed interface cables, such as USB or FireWire ports. They are usually placed in very close proximity to the desktop or notebook computer. Once connected to the desktop computer, sending data between the internal hard drive and the external hard drive is easily accomplished.

Computer users might use the internal hard disk to store the OS, application, and other programs and use the external hard disk drive to store personal pictures, documents, and videos. External hard drives are also used to back up the entire internal hard drive. In general, the reasons to use external hard drives are:

- to safeguard files and records in case the computer crashes;

- to protect digital photos, music, and videos;

- to easily recover and restore applications and the operating system.

Portable External Hard Drives

Portable external hard drives, also known as passport hard drives, are also housed outside the system unit in its own enclosure and are connected to desktop or notebook computers by high-speed interface cables. They come in varying capacities starting from 250GB and going up to 750GB. In general, the reasons to use portable external hard drives are that users can

- take their office files home;

- carry thousands of songs or pictures and share them with friends by using their home computer;

- synchronize files between home and office;

- encrypt everything on the drive for added security.

Portable external hard drives are simple to use, and light and easy to carry. They require no power adapter as they are powered using a USB cable connected to a USB port of a home computer.

Formatting a Hard Disk

Formatting a disk is a process that prepares the disk for use by dividing the disk into concentric circles, called tracks, and further dividing each track into a number of pie-shaped arcs, called sectors. Each track and sector has a number, called an address. Once formatted, the disk is ready to store data, information, OS, and other programs. If the disk is not formatted, no data can be stored on it.

File Allocation Tables on a Hard Disk

During the formatting process, a file allocation table (FAT) is also created. The FAT can be compared to the table of contents of a book. The FAT maintains a topics directory. To read about a particular topic in a book, we read the table of contents, select a topic, find its page number, and go to that page and start reading. Similarly, the FAT creates a table of contents to keep track of all the files stored on the disk by specifying the name of each file, its size, and the number of the sector where it begins.

Root Directory on a Hard Disk

During the formatting process, a root directory is also created. All the data on a disk is stored in folders (directory) and filed in a hierarchical form. The root directory is at the top of the hierarchy directory on the hard disk. All other folders or files are created under the root directory. Some areas of the root directory may have folders that store special OS files.

Important Terms Used for Hard Drives

Storage Capacity of a Hard Drive

Nowadays, computers have a storage capacity ranging from 200GB to 2TB.

Table 2.7 illustrates the storage capacities of hard disks.

Table 2.7 Units of Measurement of Memory

Term	Abbreviation	Approximate Number of Bytes	Exact Amount
Byte	B	1	
Kilobyte	KB	1,000	2^{10} or 1,024
Megabyte	MB	1 million	2^{20} or 1,048,576
Gigabyte	GB	1 billion	2^{30} or 1,073,741,824
Terabyte	TB	1 trillion	2^{40} or 1,099,511,627,776
Petabyte	PB	Equals 1,024 Terabytes	2^{50} or 1,125,899,906,842,624

Tracks

During formatting, a hard disk is divided into a number of concentric circles known as tracks. Each track on a disk is numbered (and used in a memory address).

Sector

Each track is further subdivided into a number of pie-shaped arcs called sectors. Like a track, each sector is also numbered (and used in a memory address).

Cluster (Allocation Unit)

A group of sectors forms a cluster, which is the smallest amount of disk space that can store data and information and assign a memory address. A cluster can be made up of two to eight sectors, depending on the OS used in the computer. If the data to be stored is smaller than the size of a cluster, a whole cluster will be allocated to that piece of data.

Hard Disk Platter

A hard disk is made up of a number of platters. Each platter is made from a rigid material, such as aluminum, and is mounted on the same spindle as other platters. Each platter is made up of a number of tracks and sectors. The data on platters is stored magnetically.

Read and Write Heads in a Hard Disk

Similar to a VCR that has a play (read) head and a record (write) head, every hard disk drive has read heads to read (retrieve) data from an opened file and record heads to save (write) data on a disk.

Cylinder

A cylinder is a vertical section of a track that passes through all the platters. A single movement of the read/write head accesses all the platters in a cylinder.

2.9 USB FLASH DRIVES AND CD/DVD/BLU-RAY AS STORAGE DEVICES

USB Flash Drives Storage Devices

USB flash drives are non-volatile portable storage devices. They are electronic (digital), work at high-speed, are small in size, have no moving parts, and are lightweight. Users can perform both read and write operations as well as save and delete files on USB flash drives.

To use a USB flash drive, the device is plugged into one of the USB ports of a computer. After insertion, the drive is recognized by the computer and is assigned an alpha letter, other than A, B, or C to designate its location. The hard drive is always assigned letter C. To check the letter assigned to the flash drive, you can double click on the computer icon on your desktop, which will display the letter drives of all the storage devices on the computer, along with the letter of the flash drive. The letter assigned to the flash drive depends on whether you have a CD/DVD drive, memory flash card, or external hard disk attached to your computer, as any kind of storage drive you attach to your computer is assigned a letter drive. After usage, flash drives can be removed from the computer and inserted in another computer.

Data Types Stored on USB Flash Drives

USB flash drives can store all types of data, including text, numbers, sound (audio), graphics, and video data, provided they have enough space. Files can be exchanged between USB flash drives and other storage devices attached to the computer (with the exception of CDs).

Capacity of USB Flash Drives

Current USB flash drives can store up to 64GB of data.

Care and Precautions

The same basic care and precautions for other storage devices should be taken for flash drives, such as don't open it, drop liquids on it, take it out of the USB port while a file is open or in use, leave it in the car in very cold or very high temperatures, subject the drive to force, and let dust on it.

DVDs/CDs/Blu-ray Disks Storage Devices

Compact disks (CDs) and digital video disks (DVDs) are flat optical disks made from plastic. The disks are usually 12 cm (4.75 inches) in diameter and 1.2 cm (0.05 inches) thick. CDs have storage capacities ranging from 650 MB to 700 MB. DVDs have storage capacities ranging from 4.7 GB to 17 GB. These devices are used for storing music, data, graphics, video, and other types of programs, such as OS and application programs, used in computers.

The sales of these optical disks are gradually dropping as they are being replaced by computer data backup and file transfer storage devices known as USB flash drives. In the music industry, CD players are being replaced by solid-state MP3 players. Table 2.8 shows the common usage and features of these devices.

Technology to Write Data on a CD

The data on an optical disk is stored in the form of Pit (data stored) and Land (no data). Laser beam technology is used to write data on CDs in the form of Land and Pit. Land is a flat area (no Pit) on a disk's surface with no data written on it. Pit has recorded data.

Writing Data on a CD

By burning a flat surface on a disk, a high-intensity laser beam creates a dark spot or indention on that flat surface and writes data on it. The burnt surface is known as a pit.

Table 2.8 Optical Disc Types and Features

CD-ROM	Can be written to only once; used mainly for distributing computer software.
DVD-ROM	Can be written to only once; used to store computer software, text data, or music.
CD-R	Can be written to only once; used to store movies.
DVD-R, DVD+R	Data can be recorded only once; used to store movies.
CD-RW, DVD-RW	Data can be recorded and erased multiple times.
DVD-RAM	RAM (Random Access Memory); can record and erase data multiple times.
DVD-Video	Properly formatted and structured video; used to record movies that are sold or rented.
DVD-Audio	Properly formatted and structured audio; used to store music.

Reading Data from a Disk

A low intensity beam is reflected through the bottom of the disk. The pit that has recorded data will absorb the light and the computer reads the data as binary 0. Land that has no data will reflect the light and is read by the computer as binary 1.

Blu-ray Disks

Blu-ray disks are optical disc storage mediums designed to supersede the standard DVD formats. They are used for storing high-definition videos, for video games, etc. They have the same physical dimensions as standard DVDs and CDs. Blu-ray discs are available in 200GB and 100 GB discs and are readable without extra equipment or modified firmware. Firmware is in-between hardware and software. Firmware contains program instructions (software) that are going to be executed routinely on hardware. In computers, a ROM (read-only memory) chip, which is considered firmware, is installed by the manufacturer. It contains the booting (start-up) instructions whenever the computer is turned on. A blue-violet laser is used to read the disc.

2.10   COMMUNICATIONS USING COMPUTERS

"Communication" via computers means the transferring of data or information from one computer to another. One computer (or mobile device) sends the data and another computer (or mobile device) receives that data. Text messaging, e-mailing, and instant messaging are all examples of communication between computers. The terms *communication* and *transmission* can be used interchangeably.

A communication medium is required to transfer (move) data from one computer to another computer on the same network or between two networks. A telephone is one type of communication medium.

The use of computer hardware and communication software that enables a computer user to send and receive data and information using a communication medium is known as telecommunications.

There are two basic categories of communication media: wired communication media and wireless communication media.

2.11   WIRED COMMUNICATION MEDIA

Many computers use wired communicating technologies in order to communicate with other computers. Wired technologies used for communications include fiber optic cables, twisted-pair cables, coaxial cables, digital subscriber line (DSL), and integrated services digital network (ISDN) lines.

Fiber Optic Cables

Fiber optic cables are made from transparent fiberglass or plastic fibers. Data is sent in the form of light pulses over the fiber optic cables. The sender's data, which is in an electrical pulses form, is converted to light pulses by a light-emitting diode (LED) or a laser device and then travels over the fiber optic cable. When it reaches the receiver's computer, it is converted from light pulses back to electrical pulses so it can be read.

Fiber optic cables are used for local area networks (LAN) and have many advantages. They have the ability to carry a lot of data at one time; they have the ability to operate at high transmission speeds; they have a resistance to noise interference; and they have low maintenance costs.

Twisted-Pair Cables

Twisted-pair cables are comprised of two individual copper wires that are wrapped with an insulation material such as plastic and are twisted to protect against crosstalk. The wires are then wrapped again with an insulation material to protect them from electromagnetic interference (EMI). These cables form a circuit and are used to send data and information.

Unshielded twisted-pair (UTP) cables and shielded twisted-pair (STP) cables are the two basic types of twisted-pair cables and are used mainly in local area networks (LAN) and ethernet networks.

UTP cables are installed using a Registered Jack 45 (RJ-45) connector, which is an eight-wire connector, commonly used to connect computers to a local area network (LAN). Because of their smaller size, UTP cables are easy to install and don't use too much installation space. They are more cost effective compared to other communication media.

STP cables, on the other hand, are expensive and difficult to install. Each pair of STP cables is wrapped in metallic foil. STP cables are commonly used in European countries.

Coaxial Cables

Coaxial cables are made of copper. They have two parallel physical channels separated by an insulation material and each channel can carry a signal.

Coaxial cables are made up of four layers:

- First layer: Electrical copper wire, known as the center core, which conducts AC current. This is one physical channel.

- Second layer: An insulating flexible material, known as dielectric insulator, which insulates the copper wire in the first layer.

- Third layer: The second layer is surrounded by a thin woven copper shield and acts as a conducting layer. Known as the metallic shield, this is the second physical channel.

- Fourth layer (outermost layer): An insulating plastic layer is placed on top of the third layer. It is known as a plastic jacket.

Coaxial cables are used to connect radio networks (transmitters and receivers), televisions, computer networks in consumer devices and military equipment. Cable modems and cable TV connections must use a device called a coaxial cable two-way splitter, in which one wire is connected to the cable modem and the other wire is connected to the television.

Coaxial cables allow cable modems and cable TV services to send and receive large amounts of data at high speeds when compared to other transmission mediums.

Digital Subscriber Line (DSL)

DSL is a transmission medium and high-speed Internet service that transmits digital signals using telephone network cables. DSL sends voice and data signals on separate physical channels, thus enabling users to talk on the telephone and surf the Internet simultaneously. DSL uses a broadband modem technology and download speeds are typically between 3 and 6 Mbps.

Advantages of DSL

In addition to being able to talk on the telephone and surf the Internet simultaneously, DSL transmissions do not require additional wiring. It uses standard telephone wiring and has high data transmission speeds.

Disadvantages of DSL

DSL services are not available everywhere. The strength of the DSL signal reception is dependent on the distance between the DSL service provider's office and the computer using the DSL modem—the larger the distance, the weaker the signal. Thus, data is received more quickly than it is sent.

Integrated Services Digital Network (ISDN) Lines

ISDN is a transmission medium that digitally transmits voice, video, graphics, and text data using a digital telephone network. ISDN digital transmissions are more costly than using a DSL line and, because of that, ISDN has not been widely accepted. An ISDN line requires the use of an ISDN modem. ISDN is a high-speed Internet service with data transmission rates between 64 Kbps and 128 Kbps.

2.12   WIRELESS COMMUNICATION MEDIA

Wireless transmissions use radio waves or infrared light to transmit data through the air. Wireless technologies used for communications include: bluetooth, Wi-Fi, satellite, infrared, cellular, and microwave.

Bluetooth Wireless Transmission Technology transmits voice and data at high speeds using radio waves. Mobile computing devices, such as cell phones, PDAs, digital cameras, fax machines, printers, and garage door openers, use Bluetooth technology. Bluetooth does not require a line of sight between communicating devices. You can talk on a Bluetooth headset even if your device is in another room. Bluetooth works on spread-spectrum frequency hopping technology. This makes it possible for a number of devices to transmit at the same time with no interference because each device transmits on a different frequency. The distance between two devices using Bluetooth communication technology should not exceed 10 meters (about 33 feet).

Wi-Fi Wireless Transmission Technology

Wi-Fi (an abbreviation for Wireless Fidelity) is a wireless local area network (WLAN) technology that uses radio signals to connect wireless computers and other devices through the Internet for data transmission. Wi-Fi follows IEEE 802.11 (standards set by the IEEE organization), which specifies how two wireless devices can communicate with each other over the air.

Wi-Fi cards are installed in many wireless devices such as notebook computers. Wi-Fi technology is also used in home security systems and in telemedicine.

Wireless access point (WAP) provides wireless Internet connections to mobile devices at places such as malls, airports, homes, and schools. A mobile device with a Wi-Fi card must be within 300 feet of the Wireless Access Point. There are two types of WAPs: Hotspots and 3G. A Wi-Fi hotspot provides wireless Internet connections to mobile device users, enabling them to check e-mails and surf the Web. Users may have to pay a fee to use Wi-Fi hotspots. A Wi-Fi 3G network uses cell phone technology for wireless Internet connections.

Communications Satellite Wireless Transmission Technology

Communications satellites, known as space stations, receive microwave-transmitted signals from a station on earth, amplify those signals, and send them back to a number of stations on Earth. Communications satellites are commonly used by GPS devices, Internet connections, video-conferencing, air navigations, and in many more applications.

Microwave Wireless Transmission Technology

Microwave transmission is a technology that uses microwave (radio waves) and integrated technologies for high-speed data transmission. Microwave technology sends signals from one microwave station to another microwave station that has a reflective dish and other equipment. Microwave technology requires line-of-sight and, therefore, to avoid obstructions, they are used in only wide-open areas. Microwave technology is usually installed on the tops of buildings or on mountains.

Cable TV companies, hospitals, colleges, telephone companies as well as other types of businesses use microwave technology for data transmission.

Cellular Wireless Transmission Technology

Cellular technology (CT) allows people to communicate anywhere in the world without being connected via wired phone or cables. The newest cellular technology is Wireless 3G.

Every cell phone belongs to a certain cellular calling area, known as a base station, a cell site, or a cell. Each cell area has its own antenna (communication tower) that covers a certain number of square miles and maintains contact with the cell phones in that area. As the mobile device user changes locations, the signals from the device will be picked up by the closest tower and transmitted to its proper destination.

Cellular communications can handle various data types. A mobile device such as notebook with a cellular modem can access information from anywhere through a wireless Internet connection, provided the user subscribes to the services of a Wireless Internet Service Provider (WISP).

Infrared Wireless Transmission Technology

Infrared Wireless Transmission Technology (IR) uses infrared light waves to transmit data between computers and peripheral devices, such as keyboards, printers, and smart phones. The devices must have an IrDA port that allows the data transmission to use infrared light waves. IR technology requires that the two devices be in line-of-sight to exchange data. IR is used for short- and medium-range communications.

Packets in Data Transmission

A message to be sent over a packet-switched network between two devices is sub-divided into units called *packets*. Each packet stores one unit of binary data. A network may call *packets* by other names such as frame, block, cell, or segment. Routers read the destination address of the packet and decide the most appropriate path on which to send the packets so they can reach their destinations. The typical size of packets may be between 1,000 and 1,500 bytes. All packets sent over the network must conform to the following format:

- The *packet header* provides the destination address (IP address) of the packet as well as information about the length of the packet, the originating IP address, the packet number in the sequence of packets, the protocol to determine the type of packet being transmitted (streaming audio or video, e-mail, Web page, etc.), and information to perform any error checking operations.

- The *packet body (payload)* contains the actual message.

- The *packet footer* (optional) contains a sequence of bits that indicate the end of the message. It may also contain information to perform error-checking operations.

- Once the packet reaches its destination, the receiving device is responsible for reassembling all the packets of the entire message in the correct sequence. Packets are sent over the Internet using Transmission Control Protocol/Internet Protocol (TCP/IP).

- *Packet switching* is the process of sub-dividing the original message into small units or packets and then transmitting them over the Internet to their destination.

2.13   COMMUNICATION DEVICES

A communication device enables one computer user to communicate with another to share data, information, programs, and instructions using a communication medium. Modems, sound cards, MIDIs (musical instrument digital interfaces) and network interface cards (NIC) are types of communication devices.

Modem as a Communication and Analog/Digital Signals

A *modem* is a communication *mo*dulating and *dem*odulating device used in computer networks to convert digital signals to analog signals and vice-versa. Modulating is the conversion of digital signals into analog signals; demodulating is the conversion of analog signals to digital signals. A modem is needed when two computers are communicating over the Internet. Different types of modems include internal modems, external modems, wireless modems, dial-up modems, cable modems, and DSL modems.

Internal modems are inside computer systems and are attached to system boards. They are connected to a telephone and a telephone jack.

Wireless modems are found inside mobile computing devices, such as notebooks, cell phones, or PDAs, and connect wirelessly to the Internet. They are connected to the serial port of computers.

Dial-up modems are electronic devices that convert a digital signal to an analog signal. The converted signal can then be transmitted over an analog communication medium, such as a telephone line. Initially, most computers had dial-up modems, in which a telephone number was dialed to connect to an ISP, which then connected to the Internet. When the telephone connection ended, so did the connection to the Internet. Dial-up modems require one cord to be attached to one port on the modem and the other cord to be plugged into a telephone outlet.

Cable modems are digital modems that allow users to send and receive digital data over the Internet using a cable television network. Cable modems use broadband technology that carries Internet data signals and cable television channels on the same transmission medium. Cable modems send data at much higher speeds than dial-up modems.

ISDN modems are used to send data signals. ISDN modems send and receive digital data using an ISDN data communication medium.

DSL modems also send and receive digital data signals using a DSL data communication medium.

How Modems Work

When computer A sends data to computer B using a telephone line, computer A's modem converts the outgoing digital signal into an analog signal, which then travels over the communication medium (phone line). Computer B's modem receives the signal and converts the incoming analog signal back to a digital signal, which is then displayed on the screen of computer B. This process is shown below in Figure 2.3.

Figure 2.3   Function of a Modem in a Computer as a Communication Device

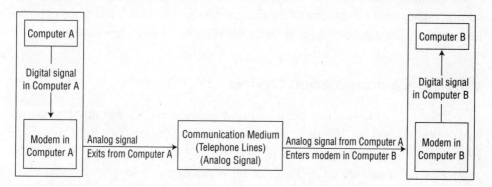

In short, modems convert analog signals to digital signals and vice versa. Computers understand only machine language that is composed of binary 0s and binary 1s. Computers are digital in nature and work with either discrete binary value 0 or discrete binary value 1, but not with values that lie in between 0 and 1.

Modems can transmit and receive signals at speeds up to 33,600 bits per second (bps) or about 4200 bytes (characters) per second.

Analog signals are continuously varying value signals and have values between 0 and 1. Analog watches contain a seconds hand that is continuously moving. The telephone lines transmit information using analog signals.

Digital signals have discrete binary values of 0 or 1. Digital signals can be compared to a light switch, which can be in either the OFF position (binary 0) or in the ON position (binary 1).

Sound Cards as Communication Devices

Sound cards are used for sound input through a microphone and sound output through speakers.

MIDI (Musical Instrument Digital Interface)

MIDI is an industry-standard protocol that enables electronic musical instruments such as keyboard controllers, computers, and any other electronic equipment, to communicate, control, and synchronize with each other.

Network Interface Cards

A network interface card is a hardware device that allows a computer to communicate with other computers on a network. A network interface controller is a hardware device that controls an interface to a computer network.

Wireless Communication Devices

Wireless communication devices allow computers to communicate with each other wirelessly. Wireless devices may use infrared (IR) light, or, more frequently, radio waves (RF), to allow two-way communication. Keyboards, printers, and routers are all available using wireless technology.

2.14   COMPUTER NETWORKING DEVICES

Computer networking devices are electronic devices, such as gateways and switches, that mediate data in a computer network.

A network node is any electronic device that is capable of sending, receiving, or forwarding data in a computer network using a communication medium. A node is the point at which two networks intersect. A printer in a college computer lab is a node, as it outputs data on paper.

The Open System Interconnection Reference Model (OSI Reference Model or OSI Model)

For all network devices to communicate effectively, the network is divided into seven layers, known as the OSI Seven Layer Model. In this model, a layer provides services to the layer above it and receives service from the layer below it.

In a hierarchy from top to bottom, the seven layers are labeled as follows: application, presentation, session, transport, network, data-link, and physical.

Application Layer (Layer 7)

This layer involves programs that respond to a user's request as well as the responses to that request to use the network for applications such as e-mail and file transfer. The service request is initiated by one node in the OSI application layer of one network, and sent to a node in the OSI application layer of another network. In this layer, issues such as "who are the nodes communicating within a network," the processes involved in the communication, and the privacy and security of data are handled. Gateway communication devices handle layer 7.

Presentation Layer (Layer 6)

This layer converts and formats the data into the proper syntax or form so that when sent to another node, it is correctly understood. The formatting may include converting data from one coding system (ASCII) into another coding system (EBCDIC) as well as encryption and decryption of data, among other things. Gateway communication devices also handle layer 6.

Session Layer (Layer 5)

This layer manages all of the aspects that deal with the exchange of data between applications. This includes establishing and ending communication; mode of communication, such as half or full duplex, synchronous and asynchronous transmission; and any problems that occur during transmission. Gateway communication devices handle layer 5.

Transport Layer (Layer 4)

This layer is responsible for completing data transfer between the nodes by placing the data in packets and adding the destination address, header, and other information. Gateway communication devices handle layer 4.

Network Layer (Layer 3)

This layer routes and forwards the packets to their destinations by addressing messages and converting the logical address into the physical address of the receiving node. It also handles how the data is exchanged between two nodes and any congestion that takes place on the network during communication. Routers handle layer 3.

Data-Link Layer (Layer 2)

This layer contains the source and destination addresses. The source address is the address of the sending computer and the destination address is the address of the receiving computer. This layer handles the delivery of data to the receiving computer using the physical layer. Switches and bridges communication devices handle this layer.

Physical Layer (Layer 1)

This layer is responsible for sending bits of data stream from the sending computer to the receiving computer. This layer encodes the data by converting 0s and 1s of data into a physical signal and decodes the data by converting the physical signal into 0s and 1s. Hubs and repeaters handle this layer.

Networking Communication Devices

Computer networking devices are electronic devices in a network, which include gateways, switches, bridges, hubs, repeaters, and routers.

- A gateway interfaces between two networks using different protocols.
- A switch handles and controls the data in transmission to a computer whose destination address appears on the data packet.
- A bridge transmits data between two different LANs.

- A hub connects all the computers in a LAN and enables them to communicate with each other. The hub also handles the exchange of data between the computers in that network.

- A repeater, also called an amplifier, amplifies the strength of the incoming signals (wireless, optical, or electrical) on a network and retransmits them so that they can travel long distances without losing their integrity.

- A network router links two or more networks through wires or radio signals and enables them to deliver data to the destination computer.

Computer Networking Hardware

Computer networks may utilize communication mediums, communication devices, network devices and other hardware.

2.15   COMPONENTS OF A COMPUTER

A computer system is composed of three basic components: a system unit, a monitor, and a keyboard/mouse device.

The system unit is made up of plastic or metal and is the main unit of a desktop computer. It stores all of the physical components of a computer to enable the computer to perform its functions. There are components that are seen and used from outside the unit and others that are installed inside the system unit.

Components that are inside the unit include the following:

- Motherboard
- ROM chip
- RAM chips
- Power supply unit, which regulates the wall voltage required for the electronic components and the cooling fans in order to keep the CPU and other electronic components from getting overheated
- Expansion slots, which are openings in the computer where various types of circuit boards are installed in order to provide added capabilities. Boards inserted into the expansion slots are also known as

expansion boards, or, more simply, cards. Types of expansion cards include:

- A network interface card, which connects a computer to other computers on the network

- A sound card, which provides connections for speakers and a microphone

- A video card, which provides a connection for the monitor

- A modem card, which provides an Internet connection using telephone lines

• Internal disk drives such as a hard disk and CD/DVD/Blu-ray disk drives;

• A system clock, which issues steady high-frequency pulses (signals) that are used by the CPU to control and synchronize the timing of all the operations that are taking place in a computer. The system clock speed is measured in hertz, which represents the number of pulses per second. One hertz is equal to one pulse per second. Today, computers can have a clock speed of more than one gigahertz;

• A bus, which uses electrical connections, known as pathways, to connect various parts of the computer with the CPU and RAM. Bus width represents the number of bits transferred on a bus at one time;

• Expansion buses, which are electrical connections that connect the motherboard to all types of expansion cards;

• Ports—the back and front of the system units include serial and parallel ports, audio and speaker ports, FireWire and Ethernet ports, USB ports, and memory card ports for devices such as digital cameras.

2.16 COMPUTER NETWORKS—LOCAL AREA NETWORKS, WIDE AREA NETWORKS, AND ENTERPRISE NETWORK ARCHITECTURE

A computer network is a particular group of computers and devices that, using communication devices, communication media, and communication protocols, allows the computers on the network to communicate with each other. The networked computers share resources, such as hardware and software, data, information, and much more.

In order for the network to operate, communication software, such as Internet Explorer, and network hardware devices, such as network interface cards, routers, switches, hubs, and modems, must be installed on all the computers involved in the network.

Communication protocols are a set of standard rules that govern how data will be transmitted and received between computers in a network. Communication protocols are managed protocols, such as HTTP, FTP, and TCP/IP.

Some of the rules apply to the following:

- Data formatting—data sent between the sending computer and the receiving computer must be in the same format. For example, all the data must be sent in Unicode or ASCII code.

- Initiating, establishing, maintaining, and governing the communication between two computers.

- Encoding and decoding the data being transmitted.

- Detecting errors and recovering data if the data is corrupted or lost during transmission.

- The rate of transmission in bps.

- Types of transmission—synchronous or asynchronous.

- Mode of transmission—half duplex or full duplex.

- Authentication that establishes the identity of the sending and the receiving computers or devices. The computer users must provide identity in the form of a user ID and password to gain access to the network.

Network Classifications

Computer users who have a desktop and a notebook computer can set up a computer network in their home. A travel agent can have his employees on a computer network to book airline and cruise tickets, hotel rooms, etc. Banks that have branches in different parts of the country have their computers networked. ATM machines are also networked.

These different kinds of networks are classified based on

- the design of the network, also known as network architecture
- their effective distance, that is, the distance they cover
- the number of users using the network

Network Classification by Design

Below are descriptions of some of the basic network designs:

- Internet Peer-to-Peer (P2P) networks—the most common example of locally controlled networks. Each node on the computer can communicate directly with every node on the network. Each computer on the network is a peer and does not have to go through another computer to use the network's resources. For example, when printing, a P2P computer does not have to go through the computer that is connected to the printer. In P2P architecture, computers act as both the client and the server.

- Client/Server Computer Architecture—A client computer is a computer that is searching for data or information on a home computer or a networked computer. A server computer provides that data or information to the client computer.

Network Classification by Distance Covered

Both local area networks (LAN) and wide area networks (WAN) are classified by the distance that is covered.

Local Area Networks (LAN)

A LAN is a computer network in which the connected computers are within a short distance of each other. The computers could be in the same room or in the same building. All the computers on a LAN network share computer hardware, software, data files, Internet connection, and other computer resources. LANs are used by businesses such as travel agents, colleges, and schools.

A LAN network requires the following hardware: a network interface card (NIC), a modem, a router for Internet connection, high-speed connections, and switches for wired LANs.

A LAN has one computer known as a server computer that will store all the computer programs and data files on a storage device so that all the computer users can access them easily.

A LAN has other computers, known as client computers, that access and use the computer programs and data files stored on a server computer.

A LAN can be a wireless network that uses radio waves to communicate or it can be a wired network in which the computers are connected to each other through Ethernet cables.

LANs offer many advantages including the ability to share computer hardware, software and data files. In addition, networked computers can also share a printer, which is controlled by a printer server. LANs allow an administrator to manage the sharing of resources and access to programs or data files.

Wide Area Networks (WAN)—MAN, VAN

Wide area networks are networks that cover large areas. Large companies that have offices citywide, statewide, countrywide, or worldwide usually use them. Like LANs, WANs also share computer hardware, software, data files, Internet connection, and any other computer resources.

Because WANs network computers located in different geographical locations, several types of wired or wireless communication media, such as satellites, high-speed telephone lines, cables, and radio waves, may be used throughout the network.

A metropolitan area network (MAN) is a type of WAN that covers a city or campus of a college.

A value added network (VAN) is a type of WAN in which one company acts as an agent between two parties to provide network connections and some additional services for a fee. The additional services can include online advertising or online shopping, as well as other services.

Enterprise Network Architecture

Enterprise network architecture is the use of collaborative software to enable different departments or people of an organization to access data, share computer resources, and other resources to reduce the number of communication protocols in use. An enterprise network integrates all different computer platforms, such as Windows, Unix, and Apple, and different types of computers, such as mainframes or minicomputers, to communicate and connect computing devices, while maintaining reasonable performance, security, and reliability.

TCP/IP is a unifying Internet protocol that lets organizations tie together workgroups and division LANs and connect with the Internet.

Web protocols (HTTP, HTML, and XML) integrate user interfaces, applications, and data, letting organizations build intranets (internal internets). A Web browser is like a universal client, and Web servers can provide data to any of those clients.

Enterprise network architecture uses both wired and wireless technologies, such as bluetooth, PDAs, and smart phones in its operations.

CHAPTER 3

Computer Software, Information Systems, and Application Software in Organizations

Computer Software, Information Systems, and Application Software in Organizations

3.1 SOFTWARE

A computer program, also known as software, is a sequence of precise instructions given to computer hardware to perform a specific task as well as the correct way to perform it. Programs can do a variety of tasks that can be written, coded, executed, tested, debugged, re-tested, and documented. It can be a simple task, such as finding the average of two test scores, or a complex task, such as designing and manufacturing a robot to assemble cars.

Programming is the act of creating and writing a computer program.

Programming language is a sequence of instructions used to create a program in a selected language (known as programming language), which is used to communicate with a computer's hardware. Just as a student selects a language (English, Spanish, etc.) for writing an essay, a computer programmer selects a computer programming language for writing a computer program.

Syntax of Programming Language

Just as a student of English follows grammar rules to write an essay, computer programming language also has rules that need to be followed. This is known as syntax. For example, in programming languages (C, C++, and Java), each instruction must end with a semicolon (;), the same way that a period (.) ends a sentence in English.

Instruction Set Architecture (ISA)

Each CPU installed in any computer has its own set of machine language instructions known as instruction set architecture (ISA). Each machine language consists of a minimum of two parts that are formed from a group of binary digits, as follows:

1. Operation Code (OpCode), the first set of binary digits in a machine instruction, specifies the type of operation (such as addition or subtraction) to be performed on an operand (in the second part of the instruction).

2. Operands (data to be operated on), the second set of binary digits in a machine instruction, specify the operands on which the operation is to be performed. Operands include values stored in registers and memory addresses where the data is stored.

Desktop System Architecture

Desktop system architecture provides functions such as starting a computer, file management, hardware device management, security management, jobs scheduling, processor management, performance management, and memory management.

Levels of Computer Programming Languages

Computers are only capable of understanding machine language (machine code or object code). A computer reads each program instruction, and interprets it, and the CPU (computer hardware) executes it. Computer programming languages can be classified as low-level languages or high-level languages. Machine languages and assembly languages are two types of low-level languages that are closer to the computer hardware. Table 3.1 shows the hierarchy of programming languages.

Table 3.1 Hierarchy of Programming Languages

High-Level Languages (C++, Java, Fortran, etc.)	similar to human languages
Assembly Language	low-level language that uses symbols to write a program instruction
Machine Language	low-level language that uses binary digits (0 and 1) to write a program instruction

High-Level Computer Languages and Compilers

High-level computer programming languages are not dependent on a specific type of computer. They use keywords that are easy to understand and similar to human languages. Popular high-level computer programming languages include C, C++, Java, COBOL, Visual Basic, UNIX, Shell Programming, Python, and Ruby.

Source code (source program) is a program in which instructions are written by following the syntax of a selected computer language.

A compiler is a program that reads the entire source code of a high-level language and translates it into machine language before any instruction is executed. While translating, the compiler checks and points out the syntax errors found (if any) along with their respective line numbers in the source code. Object code is the translated code from the source code to a machine code.

Assembly Language and Assembler

Assembly language is a low-level programming language that uses a set of symbols or abbreviations, known as mnemonics, to represent machine language instructions (commands). For example, the symbols ADD, SUB, MUL, and DIV represent the arithmetic operations of addition, subtraction, multiplication, and division, respectively. Assembly language is specific to an individual set architecture (ISA).

An assembler is a utility program that translates the assembly language instructions into machine language instructions, one instruction at a time.

Algorithm

An algorithm is a sequence of instructions written in a natural human language that precisely specifies what a computer program must do in order to complete a specific task. In order to write an algorithm, keep in mind the IPOS (Input, Processing, Output, and Storage) cycle discussed in Chapter 1. Once perfected, an algorithm is then used as a base to write the source code of a program. Figure 3.1 shows an example of an algorithm that finds the average of two test scores on a test.

Figure 3.1 Algorithm That Finds the Average of Two Test Scores

1.	Set Score1 to 87 (or Assign integer value 87 to Score1)—Input to a program
2.	Set Score2 to 78 (or Assign integer value 78 to Score2)—Another input to a program
3.	Add Score1 and Score2 giving Total—Processing done in a program
4.	Divide Total by 2 giving Average—Another processing done in a program
5.	Display Score1—First output of a program
6.	Display Score2—Second output of a program
7.	Display Total—Third output of a program
8.	Display Average—Fourth output of a program
9.	Save Score1, Score2, Total, Average, and Average on a disk—Storage operation.

Steps to Solve a Specific Problem Using a Computer Programming Language

In order to solve a particular problem using a selected computer programming language, the following steps must be taken:

1. *Identify the problem to be solved and write its complete description* by stating all main and sub-tasks to be performed. (In Figure 3.1, the task is to find the average of two test scores.)

3. *Write the algorithm for the stated problem* (along with the lines of our example in Figure 3.1).

3. *Coding (process of converting the algorithm into source code).* Type
    the source code in a text editor of the computer programming language
    used to write the program. The text editor resembles the Microsoft
    Word processor screen. For example, Figure 3.2 shows a "TextPad"
    screen used by the text editor to write a Java program. Lines 1 to 13
    display the conversion of the algorithm from Figure 3.1 into Java
    source code.

4. *Save the source code to secondary storage* (hard disk or flash drive)
    using a file name with an extension that is specific to the computer
    programming language that was used to write the program. For ex-
    ample, in Figure 3.2, the file name "SumAvg.java" displayed in the
    title bar of the "TextPad" screen, indicates that the program saved on
    the hard disk is the source code of the Java program with the extension
    ".java"

5. *Compile and debug the source code.* Compilation is the process of
    translating the source code into machine language while finding and
    listing any syntax errors along with their line numbers in the source
    code. Debugging is the process of fixing all the syntax errors flagged
    by the compiler on a line-by-line basis. The source code is compiled,
    debugged, saved, and compiled repeatedly until all the syntax errors
    are removed. After the removal of all syntax errors, the source code is
    translated into machine language (object code). To compile and debug
    the Java source code shown in the "TextPad" screen of Figure 3.2, on
    the drop-down menu select: Tools—External tools—Compile java.

6. *Execute the source code.* After compilation of the source code and by
    using the previously tested sample data, run (execute) the object code
    to test the successful execution of the program. If the program does
    not display the intended results, modify the source code appropriately,
    and then save, compile and execute it again. To execute the compiled
    Java source code shown in the "TextPad" screen of Figure 3.2, on the
    drop-down menu select Tools—External tools—Run Java Application.
    The output of the program is displayed in a separate screen.

7. *Documentation.* Documentation is the process of writing all the details
    of the programming project as follows:

    •   Define and describe the programming project (described in step 1)

    •   Develop an algorithm to solve the problem (described in step 2)

- Write source code (text editor used, program structures and comments to explain important parts of a program [described in steps 3 and 4])
- Compile and debug the program (described in step 5)
- Execute the program using sample data (described in step 6)
- Write a user's manual with all the important details above.

In our example, the algorithm was used as a base to write the Java source code shown in Figure 3.2.

Figure 3.2   Text Editor for Java Program

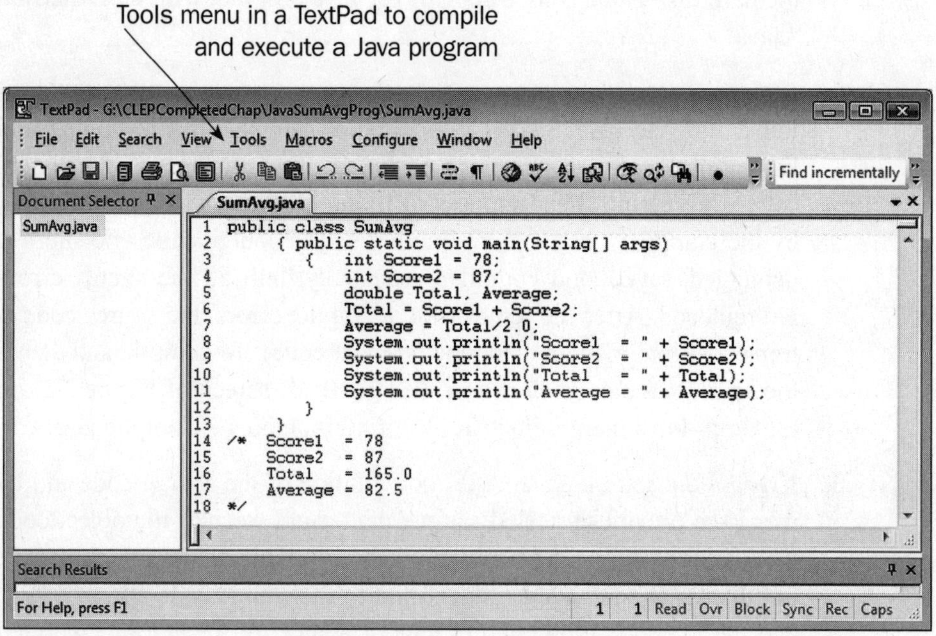

Tools menu in a TextPad to compile and execute a Java program

```
1   public class SumAvg
2       { public static void main(String[] args)
3       {    int Score1 = 78;
4            int Score2 = 87;
5            double Total, Average;
6            Total = Score1 + Score2;
7            Average = Total/2.0;
8            System.out.println("Score1  = " + Score1);
9            System.out.println("Score2  = " + Score2);
10           System.out.println("Total   = " + Total);
11           System.out.println("Average = " + Average);
12      }
13      }
14  /*  Score1  = 78
15      Score2  = 87
16      Total   = 165.0
17      Average = 82.5
18  */
```

Figure 3.3 explains each line of the source code.

Figure 3.3 Java Program to Find the Average of Two Test Scores

Line #	Source Code in Java	Explanation of Source Code Instruction
1	public class SumAvg	Create a java class SumAvg
2	{ public static void main(String[] args)	Function header of function main( )
3	{ int Score1 = 78;	Opening curly brace ({) indicates the start of the body of the java program. Set Score1 to 87 an integer data type variable
4	int Score2 = 87;	Set Score2 to 87 an integer data type variable
5	double Total, Average;	Declare variables Total & Average of double data type
6	Total = Score1 + Score2;	Add Score1 and Score2 and store the result in Total
7	Average = Total/2.0;	Divide Total by 2 giving Average
8	System.out.println("Score1 = " + Score1);	Instruction to display Score1
9	System.out.println("Score2 = " + Score2);	Instruction to display Score2
10	System.out.println("Total = " + Total);	Instruction to display Total
11	System.out.println("Average = " + Average);	Instruction to display Average
12	}	End of body of java program
13	}	End of java program
14	/* Score1 = 78	Displays Score1–Output
15	Score2 = 87	Displays Score2–Output
16	Total = 165.0	Displays Total–Output
17	Average = 82.5 */	Displays Average–Output

3.2 SYSTEM SOFTWARE AND OPERATING SYSTEMS

Below is an outline of important software categories:

- System Software and Operating System
- Network Operating System (NOS)
- Application Software
- Communications Systems
- Web Technology and Programming

System Software

System software consists of a group of programs required to control all the operations that take place in a computer. It manages:

- All the computer's hardware components (e.g., when a user wants to save a document on a flash drive, the system software ensures that there is enough disk space on the flash drive.)
- All the other computer software categories installed in the computer system (e.g., to manage the printing of a document created in Microsoft Word.)
- All the users who are using the hardware and software in the computer system (e.g., if the user wants to log on to the system, the system software checks for proper login ID and password.)

The operating system and the utility programs are two types of system software.

The Operating System (OS)

The operating system (OS) software is the very first software installed on the hard disk of all computer systems; it stays there even when the computer is turned off. When the computer is turned on, the OS is the first software loaded into the RAM of a computer system. Below is an outline of its functions.

- Manages all the programs (except the operating system), such as application software, drawing software and programming language software that are installed on the computer system.

- Manages all the computer hardware and peripheral devices used in the operation of a computer. For example, when a user saves a document on a USB flash drive, the OS ensures that there is enough disk space to save the document. When printing a document, the OS checks if the printer is connected and if there is enough paper in the printer tray.

- Allows users to communicate with the computer hardware when using other programs, such as the application software.

- Manages the starting up (booting) of a computer.

- Manages the device drivers of all the hardware installed in a computer or connected to it. Device drivers are program files on CDs that accompany the newly purchased hardware or devices (such as an external hard drive). When installed in folders on the OS, device drivers enable the OS to recognize all the hardware devices installed in a computer system or connected to it. For example, to use an external hard disk connected to a system unit through a USB cable, its device driver is installed from the CD that accompanied the hard disk package.

- Establishes an Internet connection to surf the Web or send e-mails.

- In order to perform all operations in a computer system, the shell of an operating system allows users to communicate with the OS in one of the following ways:

    1. *A menu-driven interface.* In order to perform any type of operation when using application software, a user clicks on menu choices. For example, the user selects "File," then "Save" to save a file to the computer. (Newer OSs, such as Windows Vista, have tabs instead of menus to issue a command to the operating system.)

    2. *A command-driven interface.* In older computers with MSDOS as the OS, the user typed MS DOS commands on a command prompt of the C drive.

3. *A graphical user interface (GUI)*. The user clicks on an icon that represents a particular operation. For example, clicking on a disk icon starts a save document operation.

4. *Using option buttons and check boxes*. In order to perform certain operations, the user communicates with the OS by checking a box or clicking an option button that appears in a dialog box of the intended operation. For example, in a "Print" dialog box, the user selects the "Print All" option to print the entire document.

Utility Programs

Utility programs perform routine maintenance-type tasks that are usually related to managing computer hardware devices and software programs. The tasks related to hardware could include managing disk drives, printers, and other peripheral devices.

File management utility programs perform operations such as backing up data files stored on a disk and compressing files when they are sent as an attachment to an e-mail. Utility software manages the installing and the uninstalling of software, the scanning and de-fragmenting of disks, the checking for viruses in a computer system, as well as the displaying of screensavers.

Kernel of the Operating System

The kernel part of an operating system is a memory resident program that stays in the RAM while the computer is on. It handles tasks such as file management, peripheral devices management, processor (CPU) management, security and memory management, allocating computer resources (hardware, programs, and data), and maintenance of the computer's clock.

The concept of kernel as a memory resident (RAM) can be compared to a building supervisor who lives in the building and is responsible for its maintenance.

Types of Operating Systems

Windows XP, Windows Vista, Windows 7, Macintosh OS, Linux OS, UNIX, and OS for mobile devices are some of the most popular operating systems. They have all been developed by Microsoft.

Windows XP Operating System

The following versions are available: Embedded, Home Edition, Professional Edition, Media Center for multimedia devices, Tablet PC Edition and Server Edition.

Some Windows XP features include easy and fast user switching; network assistant, remote control for diagnosis (remote assistant); simplified user interface; Windows Media Player; Internet Explorer 6.0; Windows Movie Maker; ASR—Automated System Recovery; creation of offline files; backup/recovery function; file system encrypting (only for NTFS); capability of being used as a Terminal/NetWare-Client; remote connection (desktop sharing); ability to use multiple monitors; electronic file system (EFS) support; sending/receiving of fax support; and SMP (use of more than one processor).

Windows Vista Operating System

Windows Vista is used in all types of computers including notebooks, desktop computers, tablet PCs, and others.

Windows Vista has improved privacy and security as well Internet features. Some of its security and safety mechanisms include user account control (UAC), parental controls, network access protection, a built-in anti-malware tool, as well as new digital content protection mechanisms.

- User account control (UAC) checks the credentials of the user and requires administrative privileges to perform operations such as installing new software or changing the system settings.

- Windows Defender is an anti-spyware utility with the ability to remove ActiveX applications that are installed and block startup programs. Furthermore, Windows Vista features a Spynet network that communicates with Microsoft to check what applications are acceptable.

- An administrator can apply parental control restrictions to other users on the computer, such as Web content blocking, time limitations, as well as restrictions on what kind of games can be played or what programs can be executed.

Some of Windows Vista's improved features include different GUI; multimedia tools such as Windows DVD maker; enhanced communication capabilities on home network computers; use of P2P technology to simplify sharing files and digital media between computers and devices; ability to collapse and expand folders within the main pane of the menu system; and improved versions of Internet Explorer and Windows Media Player.

Windows Vista has some Network Operating System (NOS) capabilities, but NOSs are needed to support the operations of all types of networks, such as LAN and WAN.

Windows 7 Operating System

Windows 7 is the latest released version of Microsoft. Some of its features include: easy creation and sharing of movies; easier devices management; quicker access to data and files; improved PC protection with fewer interruptions; larger support of TV, movies, videos, and music; more efficiency and less waiting; better compatibility for working with a larger set of software and devices; use of touch and tap rather than point and click; and ability to share files, music, photos, and printers among multiple PCs.

Windows 7 has improved and simplified privacy and security to reduce the risk of damage caused by viruses, spyware, and other malware.

- Windows Firewall protects the computer from hackers and malicious software.

- Improved backup and recovery creates copies of the most important files and keeps users' information safe.

- Parental control allows users to put limitations on the games played by their children, to keep them from running specific programs, and, set specific time limits for computer use.

- The new Windows 7 Action Center in the Control Panel makes sure that the computer firewall is on, its antivirus software is up to date, and it is set to install updates automatically.

- Bit locker drive encryption, when turned on, encrypts automatically any file that is saved on the hard drive and thus helps keep documents, passwords, and other important data safe.

- Improved user account control (UAC), a feature that warns when a program wants to make a change on the computer and provides the same level of protection with fewer messages.

- Performance ImprovWindows 7 is designed to improve the performance of the PC, so it's faster, more secure, and more reliable.

Linux Operating System

Linux is a free and open-source operating system based on the UNIX OS. "Free and open source operating system" means that the underlying source code can be used, freely modified, and redistributed, both commercially and non-commercially, by anyone under licenses such as the GNU GL.

Linux is mainly used on servers, but can be installed on other computer hardware such as embedded devices, mobile phones, watches, mainframes, supercomputers, PCs, desktops, laptops, and notebooks, small portable laptops designed for wireless communications and access to the Internet.

- *Linux software packages*—Some of the commercially available Linux packages for personal and business uses are Ubuntu Linux, Red Hat Linux, Debian Linux, Novel Linux, SUSE from Novel Linux, Gentoo, and Fedora.

- *Linux user interface*—it is called GNOME and allows the user to select the display of either a Windows or a Mac desktop appearance on the system. GNOME also includes word processor, database, spreadsheet, and e-mail applications.

- *Linux software equivalency to Windows software*—Linux has application packages that work more or less like the applications designed for Windows OS. Various categories of software that have been designed for applications using Linux OS are office and productivity, desktop publishing, networking, server, multimedia, and education.

Macintosh OS

Mac OS is the trademark name for a series of GUI-based OSs developed by Apple Inc. It is based on the UNIX operating system. Mac computers are recognized for their superior graphics–user interface and processing capabilities. Below are some of Mac OS X main features:

- Aqua GUI with water-like elements.

- Window for users to locate programs and files.

- File-compression capabilities, greater stability, and a Web browser to allow users to send and receive large files.

- In version 10.3, Apple added EXPOSE, a feature to switch between windows and the desktop. EXPOSE instantly displays all open windows as thumbnails for easy navigation of different tasks, as well as hiding all windows.

- Its latest version 10.5, known as the Mac OS X Leopard, includes new features such as the *Time Machine* automatic backup and restore system; a new *Spaces* feature to organize groups of applications and windows; a new *Stacks* feature to store files in a stack; a *Quick Look* feature that shows previews of files; more parental controls; a *Safari* Web browser; improved *Mail* features; *Boot Camp* technology, which allows users to install a purchased copy of Windows on an Intel-based Mac so they can choose between Mac OS X or Windows when the computer boots.

OS for Mobile Devices

All mobile devices, such as mobile computers, cell phones, and PDAs need an OS that resides on a ROM chip. Windows Mobile 6.5 is a compact mobile OS developed by Microsoft for use in smart phones and mobile devices. Windows Mobile for Pocket PC carries the following standard features in most of its versions:

- The Today screen shows the current date, owner information, upcoming appointments, e-mail messages, and tasks.

- The taskbar shows the current time and the volume.

- Internet Explorer Mobile is an Internet browser developed by Microsoft for Pocket PCs and handheld PCs.

- Windows media player is used.

- Internet connections sharing (ICS) allows sharing of an Internet connection on one computer with others.

- Windows NT is used and support for many of the same file types is available.

- Multitasking abilities are possible.

Symbian OS

It is one of the leading open-source, multitasking operating systems designed for smart phones. It is used to make telephone calls, save appointments, browse the Web, send and receive e-mails and faxes, etc. The Symbian OS is compatible with all kinds of devices, mostly removable media file systems.

Windows CE (Embedded Compact)

It is used for devices in entertainment (games), communications, and computing devices with limited storage.

Palm OS

This runs on PDAs and smart phones—the *BlackBerry OS* is designed for BlackBerry devices.

3.3   NETWORK OPERATING SYSTEMS

In the same way that home computers and mobile devices have operating systems, a computer network must have a network operating system (NOS).

The term *NOS* is generally used for software that modifies a basic OS by adding networking features. In another words, a NOS is an OS that connects computers and devices to form a Local Area Network (LAN), and that is specifically designed to implement, manage, and maintain networks.

When installed, a NOS resides on a server. A server-based network operating system provides networking support for multiple users simultaneously, where each has the ability to access the network resources, as well as security and administrative functions. Some operating systems, such as UNIX and MAC OS, have built-in networking functions. Linux, UNIX, Novell Netware, Artisoft's LANtastic, MS Windows Server, and Windows NT are some of the most common NOSs.

Similar to a desktop OS, a NOS manages the use of hardware and peripheral devices on the network. The NOS also manages the flow of information to other computers across the network and the network security using authentication, authorization, login restrictions, and access control features.

The NOS allows users to access data, devices, services, and hardware on the network. It also provides file management, printing, data storage, backup and recovery, and replication services.

NOS architectures include peer-to-peer (P2P) and client/server.

Even though Windows Vista has some NOS capabilities, NOSs are needed to support the operations that are taking place on all types of networks such as LAN and WAN.

UNIX OS

UNIX is a multi-user and multitasking OS, mainly used with mainframes as a network operating system. UNIX is both a stand-alone operating system and a network operating system. Applications for UNIX include software for e-mail, news reading, programming, statistics, and graphics applications.

Because of portability, UNIX OS and the application programs running on UNIX OS can easily be moved from one hardware platform to another.

UNIX allows multitasking with virtual memory support.

UNIX has two types of access security: system access and file access. Access to the system is checked by the login and password of the user, known as User ID (UID). If a user works in a group, then the user is also assigned a Group ID (GID).

UNIX authenticates (login and password) users of the computer system, and files are individually owned. The owner makes the decision on the amount of access and the content of access.

UNIX has a huge amount of different user commands.

With regard to accessing files and directories as well as to Inter Process Communication (IPC), UNIX provides three types of files access—read(r), write(w), and execute(x).

Multitasking and the Operating System

Multitasking is the capability of performing two or more tasks at the same time. In programming terms, multitasking is the capability of running two or more programs at the same time using one CPU. For example, a user can type a document using MS Word and start printing it, and, at the same time, start creating a spreadsheet in Excel.

Multiprocessing

Multiprocessing is the capability of working on two CPU units at the same time and allocating tasks to each CPU. For example, one CPU executes a Word program and the second CPU executes an Excel program. UNIX OS is one of the operating systems used in multiprocessing.

3.4   APPLICATION SOFTWARE

Application software is a set of programs that allows users to perform specific tasks. Application software includes word processor, spreadsheet, presentation, and database packages. Application software is made up of different types of programs as compared to OS software and programming language software.

Before installing application software on a computer system, the user must check whether or not the computer meets the OS and hardware requirements. This is known as compatibility. Each software program specifies the type of OS, hard disk and RAM size, and any other hardware that must exist on a computer system in order to install specific application software.

Standard Office Software Suite Tools

An office suite, also known as an office software suite or a productivity suite, is a bundle of programs that a computer user utilizes on a daily basis. When packaged together, all programs can easily interact with each other and have a common user interface with the OS. For example, all software in the suite uses CTRL+C to copy highlighted text.

Standard office suite tools include word processor, spreadsheet, presentation, and database packages and are very commonly used in businesses and industries because of the portability of documents between programs. Currently, the most popular office suites are Microsoft Office for Microsoft Windows, and Apple's Mac OS X.

Integrated Packages

An integrated package is a large program that contains a word processor, a spreadsheet, a database tool, and other software applications.

Word Processing Application Software

In general, a *word processor* is a program used to manipulate a text document, such as a resume or a memo. Modern word processors can accomplish the following:

- Create, edit, save, and print a document, as well as use a template.
- Insert, edit, delete, move, cut, and copy text in a document.
- Insert a signature line, the date and time, and text in a table format in a document.
- Use a group of icons to format text (boldface, underline, italicize, and set font size, font type, and line spacing).
- Insert bullets, numbers, symbols (special characters), page numbers, headers and footers, images, borders, and shading in a document.
- Set tabs, tabs with dot leaders, page margins, and page style for a document.
- Other features include autocorrect, spell check, thesaurus, mail-merge, grammar check, search and replace, photos and drawings, shapes and lines, mathematical calculations, equations, and macros.

Spreadsheet Application Software

A *spreadsheet* (also known as a worksheet) is a computer program that simulates an accounting ledger book used to record finance-related transactions.

A spreadsheet is a grid of lettered columns and numbered rows. An inter-section of one particular column and one particular row forms a cell, and each cell has an address, such as C4, indicating that data is entered in a cell at the intersection of column C and row 4. In cells, data or information is entered in the form of text or descriptive labels (names of months or days), values (such as sales dollar amounts), formulas, functions (pre-designed formulas in Excel), and charts (graphics) created from data stored in a group or range of cells.

A workbook containing a series of related worksheets is stored on a hard disk drive or USB flash drive within a single Excel file under a name with extension "xls." Each of the worksheets may store specific financial informa-tion. There may be relationships between the data stored in various worksheets so that calculations can be performed among the data stored in the related worksheets.

A spreadsheet has some of the same features used in a word processing program. Below are some features of spreadsheet application software.

- In a spreadsheet, a formula always starts with an equal to (=) symbol followed by a combination of cell addresses, numbers, and arithmetic operators. In formulas, the value in one cell is calculated in terms of values stored in other cells of the worksheet. For example, in a spreadsheet, cell B2 has the value 11, cell B3 has the value 22; cell B4 has the formula (= B2 + B3). Consequently, cell B4 will display the value 33 (= 11 + 22). If the value in cell B2 is changed to 64, then the formula in cell B4 automatically recalculates the result and displays the new value 86 (= 64 + 22).

- In Excel formulas, there are two types of cell addresses (references) known as relative and absolute.

In the relative cell addressing scheme, if we copy the formula (= C3 + C4) from cell C5 into cell D5, then cell D5 will display formula (= D3 + D4). We can write a formula in one cell and copy it into the rest of the cells of that group. Relative cell addressing is used when a group of cells will use the same logic in the formulas for calculations.

In a formula using the absolute cell addressing scheme, one cell has a fixed (absolute) address (such as C8) so when a formula is copied from one cell into another cell, the address of that cell, during copying, remains the same. This is used in cases such as calculating the sales tax paid on purchased merchandise.

- Spreadsheets have pre-defined functions such as statistical functions, date functions, financial functions, and logical IF functions that perform pre-set operations. For example, the function =SUM (A3:A8) when entered in cell (D8) of a spreadsheet will calculate the sum of the values stored in cells A3 through A8 and then store the result in cell D8.

- The edit function key (F2) allows you to edit the contents of a cell.

- Using values stored in a group of cells, different types of charts displaying some business trend can be created. For example, a line chart can be created to display the quarterly sales of an electronics department in a computer store.

- Spreadsheets can format the data stored in cells. For example, place a dollar ($) sign in front of numerical values that represent quarterly sales figures.

PowerPoint Presentation Software

PowerPoint presentation allows users to create their own slides or create slides using a template. Each slide can include text, charts, photographs, sounds, and graphic arts in various combinations. A PowerPoint presentation contains a series of these slides.

The slides can be displayed individually or as a slide show on a projector screen to a variety of audiences. For example, a teacher can design and present lectures using PowerPoint presentation software. Other features that can be used to enhance PowerPoint slides are:

- Create, edit, enhance, insert, rearrange, delete, move, and hide slides
- Create a table
- Insert a text box
- Insert and format a SmartArt Organizational chart and WordArt
- Add sounds and videos
- Draw, copy, and rotate various shapes
- Insert buttons and hyperlinks
- Insert headers and footers
- Perform spell check and use thesaurus
- Format, search, and replace text

- Insert, size, and move an image

- Print a presentation as individual slides and as handouts

- Set timings for a presentation

- Export the presentation to Word

- Link an Excel chart with a Word document and a PowerPoint presentation

3.5   DATABASE PACKAGES

A database (DB) package is an organized way to collect logically related records in files or tables, and then link those tables or files together in a manner that enables a database program to search for a desired piece of information in the database. DB is an electronic filing system. All the information stored is in binary digit form.

Hierarchy of Databases

The building blocks of any DB include characters, fields, records, and tables (file or relation).

- A character in a DB is the smallest unit of information that conveys some meaning to a user of a DB and is the smallest piece of data a computer can process. Suppose, for example, when filling out an application form, you are asked to provide information regarding your marital status (S = single; M = married; D = divorced; and W = widow). In this example, "S," "M," "D," or "W" are all single characters and can be processed by the computer.

- Field (attribute or column) in a DB is a collection of one or more characters in a certain sequence that provides meaningful information to a DB user. For example, "Name" is spelled correctly and can be a field inside a database table, but the word "Nmae" is spelled incorrectly and makes no sense. In a database, field is the smallest piece of data a database user can read from a database table. Full name, street address, city, state, and zip are the fields used to create an "address" table. Field can store information of various data types, such as number, date, and text. Data types are discussed in chapter 2.

- Record (row) in a database is a collection of related fields. For example, full name, street address, city, state, and zip are the only fields required to create an address label. DOB (date of birth) is not a required field when creating an address label.

- Table (file or relation) in a DB is a collection of related or similar records. For example, an address table in a customer DB will store only addresses of customers and nothing else. A relational database (RDB) is a collection of relations (tables) where data in different tables is linked through a common field or attribute. Various data types involved in construction of a table in a database include integers, characters, dates, and numbers.

Types of Keys in a DB

A Primary Key (PK) field in a database table uniquely identifies a record in a table. For example, Table 3.2 below has fields entitled StudentID, Name, Street, City, State, and Zip. StudentID is a Primary Key field as it identifies a unique student in the table.

Table 3.2 "Student" Table

Field-names	StudentID	Name	Street	City	State	Zip
Record 1	345678	John Smith	123 Park Ave	Edison	NJ	08817
Record 2	321456	Roger Moore	456 Wood Ave	South Plainfield	NJ	08876

A Foreign Key (FK) is a field or group of fields in one table (FK table) that matches a field in another table (PK table) where it is a PK. For example, StudentID is a PK in Table 3.2 and a Foreign Key in Table 3.3. PK and FK are used to establish relationships between two tables (a PK table and a FK table).

Table 3.3 "Schedule" Table

Field-names	StudentID	CourseID	Day	RoomNo	Bldg.	Time
Record 1	345678	CSC110	Mondays	121	JLC	9 A.M.
Record 2	321456	CSC121	Tuesdays	134	EH	11 A.M.

A composite PK is formed when two or more keys in the same table uniquely identify a record in a table. For example, in Table 3.3, StudentID and CourseID together can uniquely identify a record in a schedule table.

Types of Relationships in DB

There can be three types of relationships between tables: one-to-one (1:1), one-to-many (1:M), and many-to-many (M:N). A 1:1 relationship exists between two tables A and B if one row in Table A matches one and only one row in Table B and vice versa. A 1:M relationship exists between two tables A and B if one row in Table A matches more than one row in Table B, and only one row from Table B matches at the most one row in Table A. A M:N relationship exists between two tables A and B, if more than one row in Table A matches more than one row in Table B, and vice versa.

Input Masks in Table Design

When creating a table in a database, input masks are created for fields, such as Social Security Numbers (SSNs), so that data can be entered in the table in the proper format. For Social Security Numbers, 111-11-1111 would be the correct format.

Important Operations in Databases

Records are inserted in a table after their creation. New records may be inserted in the table after their creation as well. Changes can be made to a part of a record already stored in a table. For example, in the Student Table above (Table 3.2), if a person moves, changes to the values stored in the street, address, city, state, and zip fields will need to be inserted. This is known as editing a record. In addition, records can be deleted from a table if the information is no longer needed.

Sorting records in a table means to arrange them in ascending or descending order, alphabetically, or numerically. For example, telephone directories are sorted alphabetically in ascending order based on the last name, first name, and middle initial fields.

3.6 WEB BROWSER APPLICATION SOFTWARE

A Web browser (or simply, browser) is an application program that allows users to search, retrieve, and view the information stored on the webpages of various websites. The more commonly used Web browsers are Internet Explorer, Mozilla Firefox, Netscape, Lynx, Opera, and Safari. To browse the Web, users need a computer that is connected to the Internet and has a browser program.

Steps to Use a Browser, Homepage, and Hyperlinks

- Turn on the computer and click on the Internet Explorer desktop icon to start a browser. The homepage of the Web browser appears.

- In the browser window, enter the URL address of the website to visit and press the Enter key.

- The first page of the website appears. This is called the homepage. A common homepage displays the contents or services provided by the website along with hyperlinks. Hyperlinks on a homepage provide a direct connection or link to another webpage that may be of interest. Hyperlinks can be text or image based. A click of the mouse takes a user to a different page. Another click of the mouse can start downloading a file or playing an audio/video clip.

Applications of Browsers

A Web browser allows users to view all the information stored on the World Wide Web. The information can be text, audio, video, images, or other multimedia. Web browsers have other features such as search engine toolbars, spell checker, document download management, form management, and password management. Web browsers are installed also on mobile devices such as cell phones and pocket PCs to view information on websites.

Browser Plug-ins

Browser plug-ins are additional software installed on computing devices to provide additional capabilities and features to a Web browser. These capabilities can include delivery of audio, video, and 3D animations on demand; viewing multimedia files directly on a Web browser; running Java Applets; and accessing PDF files on the Web.

Adobe Acrobat Reader, QuickTime, RealPlayer, and Beatnik are some of the most common plug-in software programs.

Search Engines

A search engine is a program that searches for a specific piece of information on computer networks or databases, and delivers all the pieces of information that matched the specified keywords in the search criteria. The searched information may be in the form of text, audio, video, images, or other multimedia. Internet search engines are tools that search for specific information on the Web. Search engines include Google, Bing, MSN Search, and Yahoo Search.

Google is a crawler-based search engine that has three parts:

- A Web Robot, Bot, Internet Bot, WWW Bot, or Spider (Crawler). Bot is a software application program that automatically searches for new websites on the Web and collects information about that website and also updates information in old websites.

- An Indexer organizes (sorts) the information collected by Spider to make the search easier.

- A search engine program searches for the sorted data and pulls out information that matches the search criteria, which is then displayed on the computer by your Web browser.

In order for a browser to interact with search engines to get the requested information from a website, the following steps need to be taken by the users:

1. Turn on the computer and confirm that it has an Internet connection.

2. Start the Web browser program. The homepage of the Web browser appears.

3. In the IP address window, type the domain name of the search engine such as Google.com, and press Enter.

4. The Web browser now communicates with the server. The server converts the typed domain name into an IP address and sends it to the computer.

5. The Web browser communicates with the Web server whose IP address was sent to the computer and requests it to send the homepage.

6. The Web browser receives the requested homepage from the Web browser and displays it on the computer screen.

Web indexing, also called "Web site A-Z index," creates A-Z style indexes for individual websites or an Intranet. Web indexing is similar to name indexing in a telephone directory.

3.7 COMMUNICATION SYSTEMS— OFFICE SYSTEMS TECHNOLOGY

A system is a collection of physical elements and procedures, entities, or components (software and hardware) that are compatible with each other and function to support the objective(s) of the computer user and accomplish a goal.

Office systems technology is learning the use of the latest word processing, spreadsheet, PowerPoint, desktop publishing, and database management software, office procedures, and Internet usage that are required to work in administrative support and other positions in modern offices.

Skilled office personnel are vital to the smooth, efficient running of a business. Without them, corporations and organizations would come to a standstill. Busy executives rely on office professionals to manage their offices.

Some colleges are offering courses in Office Systems Technology and graduates may become employed as a general office clerk, administrative assistant, office manager, legal office manager, or executive office manager.

Office system technology uses tools such as e-mail, conferencing, and cooperative work environments in a business office.

Office Systems and E-mail

Short for electronic mail, e-mail sends and receives electronic messages and files over electronic networks such as the Internet or any other computer network. E-mail systems use store-and-forward technology, in which an e-mail server system accepts, forwards, delivers, and stores messages on behalf of users.

An e-mail message has two important parts: a message header and a message body. The message header contains the addresses of the sender and the receiver of the e-mail, and an optional subject header. The message body contains the actual message sent. To send and receive an e-mail, a computer needs a modem, a network interface card (NIC), a Web browser, an on-line connection, and an e-mail account with an e-mail service provider such as G-mail, Yahoo, or Hotmail.

One of the fastest growing segments of industry today is e-mail marketing, in which businesses send promotional e-mails directly to existing customers, acquire new customers, and insert advertising messages in e-mails. Furthermore, some credit card companies send monthly e-mail reminders to their customers specifying the total amount due on their credit cards. Due to widespread business applications of e-mail, administrative staffs in offices often have to learn the use of e-mail technology.

Office Systems and Conferencing

Conferencing is having a meeting with company personnel from different geographical locations to discuss critical and important matters affecting the growth, profit, and operations of a company.

Conferencing usually involves one caller and many listeners. Conferencing is becoming popular, because it is an effective way to bring many people from different offices of a company together for discussion without travel involved. Different types of conferencing have emerged in the past few years, and all of them save time, money, and the travel expenses for employees. The most popular types of conferences include audio conferencing, video conferencing, Web conferencing, and telephone conferencing. The type of conferencing chosen is mainly dominated by the availability of the service, the price, and the features required for the conference.

- In audio conferencing, people who are in different locations communicate by talking to each other. A microphone, speaker, electronic equipment, and network systems are required to establish the two-way interactive conference. Audio conferencing is used when people don't need to see each other.

- Video conferencing requires the use of a video camera, microphone, speaker, and audio support. The participants can see each other in real-time. Video conferencing is used in telemedicine and tele-nursing, in student/teacher conferences, and for providing legal testimony in courts.

- In Web conferencing, home or office computers connected to the Internet allow the participants to attend meetings, take part in seminars, and demonstrate products and services. In a Web conference, the participants receive an e-mail invitation that has a link on which to click to join the conference. Web conferencing is used for live questions and answers, for sharing applications and documents, for VoIP (Voice over Internet Protocol), for viewing Webpages, for meetings, recordings, and slide show presentations.

- A teleconference is a conference between participants who are geographically dispersed or live in remote areas, and who communicate by using a telephone or network connection to exchange information. In simplest terms, teleconferencing takes place when participants share a speakerphone. Teleconferencing can also refer to a live event that is transmitted via satellite to various locations simultaneously. Furthermore, it can be used for training people and for networking amongst professionals.

Office Systems and Cooperative Work Environments (CWE)

A Cooperative Work Environment is a group of people working together to attain a common goal. For example, different teachers teach a variety of subjects to the same group of students so they acquire the knowledge required to pass. The teachers are an example of a cooperative work environment.

A Computer Supported Work Environment (CSWE) is a group of people in an office system working together to attain a common goal by using computer technology. The key components of a CSWE used by office personnel are application programs sharing, instant messaging, hardware sharing, audio conferencing, video conferencing, teleconferencing, e-mailing, blogging, and computerized office machines, such as printers and fax machines.

3.8 SPECIALIZED INFORMATION SYSTEMS

A computer-based information system is a collection of computer hardware/ software, procedures, information/data, and networked computers used by people at various levels in organizations. An information system is used to create and collect, store, process, organize, filter, analyze, receive and transmit, share, and distribute data required for the operations of organizations. For example, many pharmacies are computerized and store data about all the people who have their prescriptions at the pharmacy. A person's name, age, telephone number, health insurance carrier, allergies to medications, and any other important health-related information is stored in the pharmacy's computer.

Types of Information Systems

In business, most organizations need to use one or a combination of specialized information systems packages. Data warehousing, statistical analysis, expert systems, decision support systems (DSSs), geographic information systems (GISs), and business intelligence systems (BIs) are kinds of specialized information systems available for business applications.

Statistical Analysis

Statistics is a mathematical science that involves the collection, analysis, interpretation, forecasting, and presentation of data for decision-making in organizations. That data can pertain to people, objects, the stock market, experiments performed in a lab, etc. All types of businesses, including governments, use statistics to create statistical data models, analyze and interpret current data, and forecast future trends.

Meteorologists use computer programs that analyze past statistics and current weather conditions to predict the weather forecast in different areas. Different kinds of computer software programs are used to predict the weather. Each software program collects weather variables, such as wind speed, precipitation, atmospheric pressure, and wave development that are used to produce a weather forecast.

Microsoft Excel has built-in statistical functions such as AutoSum (to find a total), Average (to find an average), Min (to find the minimum value), Max (to find a maximum value), Count (to count the number of items), and Median (to find the midpoint values in a set of values).

Statistics is used in specialized disciplines such as biostatistics, business statistics, engineering statistics, data mining, demography, image processing, political statistics, and sports statistics.

Expert Systems

An expert system is specialized Decision Support Information System software that collects and stores on a computer system the experiences and knowledge of human experts from various professional fields. The collected knowledge is then used to simulate human reasoning and decision making to help solve specific problems.

In computer language, the expert system consists of a large number of "If-Then" decision control structure programming statements. For example, a number of problems in engineering design can be solved by using current expert-system techniques in the field of engineering. After a user inputs the engineering design problems into an expert system, the expert system provides the solutions to the specific problem by using diagnostic techniques programmed in the expert system.

Expert systems have been designed, created, and used to perform tasks in the fields of accounting, medicine, process control and production, financial services, and human resources among others.

Decision Support System (DSS)

A Decision Support System is an information system designed to facilitate the decision making process in business and organization operations. A DSS may include other systems, such as a knowledge-based or a database system, that facilitates the decision making process. DSSs are used in many different business operations such as: bank loan approvals, forest management, clinic diagnoses, etc.

In order to make decisions, a DSS gathers information from internal sources of a company over which they have control as well as from external sources over which they don't have any control. Internal sources for data can include: company documents, assets, raw data, and information about their customers' purchases, etc. External sources can include data warehouse, data marts, relation data sources, and literature searches.

SAP, IBM and Teradata are some of the vendors who supply DSS software.

Geographic Information System (GIS)

Spatial data is the collection of information about earth (real world objects) such as oceans, rivers, roads, lands, parks, and buildings. The information focuses on the geographical location and descriptions of real world objects, and is stored in computers in digital format.

GIS is a computerized system that collects, integrates, stores, interprets, manages, and displays data related to geographical location and a description of an object of interest. GIS collects and stores the following data about earth objects:

- Map data provides the geographic location and the shape of the object.

- Image data, collected using satellite systems and aerial photographs, provides photographs or images of the object.

- Attribute data provides the characteristics or description of the object.

GIS technology can be used for resource management, archaeology, environmental impact assessment, urban planning, criminology, geographic history, mapping, and other purposes. For example, GIS is used for locating underground pipes and cables, developing evacuation plans, and managing agricultural lands. Mapping applications on the web, such as Google Maps and Bing Maps, give the public access to huge amounts of geographic data.

GIS collects a data discrete object, such as a building, or a continuous value object, such as the amount of a snowfall. GIS uses Vector data models for discrete objects and Raster data models for continuous value objects. Vector data models are used to represent the geographical features of objects. GIS using Vectors expresses the objects as follows:

- Points—An object, such as a city, may be shown as a point on a map.

- Lines—An object, like a river or a road, may be shown as a line on a map and can be quantified as distance in miles or kilometers.

- Polygons—Used to specify two-dimensional objects such as a lake, a park, or a building on a map, and can be quantified as perimeter or area.

Cartography is the design and printing of maps, or visual representations of spatial data used in GIS.

GIS uses a *Geo-Coding scheme* to specify the location of an object by specifying X, Y, and Z coordinates, which represent the longitude, latitude, and elevation of the object.

Global Positioning System (GPS) is a real-time location component that uses satellites to show your current position. People also use GPS devices for driving directions to a specific location.

Open source GIS software are GRASS GIS, SAGA GIS, and MapWindow GIS.

Business Intelligence Systems (BIS)

A Business Intelligence System (BIS) is a computerized intelligence system that collects facts about a business, integrates stores, interprets, manages, and generates information and uses it to make sound business decisions. The collected information can relate to a company's market share or a competitors' market share. A BIS monitors all the operations of a company intelligently.

BIS employs a combination of tools such as data warehousing, data mining, decision support systems, data mart and online analytical processing (OLAP) for its operations. BIS uses computer hardware and software as well as people to collect data. It uses various processes to convert the collected data into information, store the generated information, and use the generated information in making business decisions. BIS also manages all the hardware, software, data, people, and processes involved in the system. There are processes to collect data, process data, store data, query data, and more.

Business intelligence systems are used in communications, media and entertainment, energy, financial services, health and life sciences, retail, manufacturing, distribution, and more.

As a result of using BIS, companies such as NASDAQ, Amazon.com and Sega of America have improved their firms by gaining more business, improving their market share, offering more products, and incorporating better data storage techniques.

3.9   ELECTRONIC DATA INTERCHANGE (EDI)

Electronic Data Interchange (EDI) is a set of rules that govern how electronic business is conducted over the network. The electronic business can be an exchange of formatted messages between two computers or EDI can specify the electronic exchange of data related to the purchasing of goods, generating invoices, receiving payments, initiating shipping and delivery of merchandise, tracking shipped merchandise, warranting of merchandise, and more. When a customer places an order on computer that is connected to a vendor's computer, EDI works between the customer and the vendor. A customer can be an end user or another organization. EDI replaces the faxing and mailing of paper documents.

EDI Requirements to Send Messages

The data to be exchanged when using EDI must be in the format the sender and receiver specify. There must be communication software installed on all the computers involved in the exchange of data and all the computers must be networked. The transaction of the document must specify "To" and "From" and the route the transaction has to follow. EDI reduces costs, workforce requirements, and errors associated with retyping orders, invoices, and other documents.

Intranets and Extranets in EDI

An intranet is the internal network of a company that can be accessed only by the employees of the company. Intranets are beneficial when employees work in a group. Web technologies can be used in intranets. Users can create and update webpages that are posted on the intranet similar to webpages posted on the Internet.

Extranets are internal company intranets that allow limited access by outside individuals, such as customers or suppliers, to a certain portion of the intranet. Customers can place orders or make payments using EDI.

How EDI Works

EDI is conducted using a value-added network (VAN) and a virtual private network (VPN). An organization can buy EDI or build their own with their business partners. In order to implement EDI, a business can use the services of a VAN (value-added network) provider for a fee, which provides all the services necessary for the EDI such as data security, transaction services, message formatting, communication protocols, etc. Most VANs can also provide a network on which the data can be transmitted. VAN providers include GE Information Systems, IBM Global Services, and Sterling Commerce. Since most computers have Internet connections, it is better to use the Internet for EDI rather than using a VAN.

A virtual private network (VPN) is a network in which some parts of the network use the Internet, but data is encrypted before it is sent on the Internet indicating that it is a private network. A VPN can secure and give preferential treatment to EDI traffic.

EDI standards for exchanging data are ANSI ASC X12 and UN/EDIFACT.

EDI Methodology

EDI uses the following methodology: FTP, HTTP, Telnet, modems, and e-mails for the exchange of data. FTP and HTTP will be discussed later under the section Communication Protocol. Telnet is a protocol to connect a Telnet client computer and a Telnet server computer and create a command line console session on a telnet server (host) computer. Using a command line window on a Telnet client computer, command line programs run, and shell commands and scripts are connected to a Telnet server locally. Telnet can be thought of as a PC connected to a mainframe computer and the PC is running command line programs, although the programs are stored on a mainframe computer. Telnet is used to troubleshoot remote computers.

Modems are required on all networked computers to convert analog signals to digital signals and vice versa when data is traveling over an analog transmission medium. Both the sender and receiver computers store data digitally and have modems installed. Modems on a sender computer convert the digital signal into an analog signal which then travels over an analog transmission line to the modem at the receiving end, which converts the analog signal back to a digital signal. The digital data can then be viewed on a receiver computer.

Electronic mail (e-mail) involves sending and receiving messages over the Internet. Both the sender and receiver computers must have an e-mail account with an e-mail service provider such as Yahoo, AOL, Gmail, etc.

3.10   ENTERPRISE-WIDE SYSTEMS

An enterprise is a large organization that employs thousands of people countrywide or worldwide and work on networked computers. Enterprise computers generate and collect a massive amount of data and information about their employees, customers, and suppliers.

An Enterprise Information System is a single computing system that combines and coordinates all business operations of a company. The information stored in a single system can be shared by all the departments of that enterprise and by all levels of management such as executive management, middle management, operational management and other non-management employees. The system manages, supports, and stores massive amounts of data. In such systems, the data is stored in one standardized format and in one place as opposed to being stored in fragments.

The enterprise information system consists of software, hardware, people, data, and procedures that operate on data to generate information.

Enterprise Software

Current application software supports transaction processing, management information systems, and decision support systems. Transaction processing systems (TPS) is an information system that collects and processes data based on day-to-day operations. Management information systems (MIS) collect, process, generate, and store accurate information in a timely and organized fashion. An enterprise may use one or a combination of software packages, such as Enterprise Resource Planning (ERP), Customer Resource Management (CRM), and Supply Chain Management (SCM), for the management of its daily operations.

Enterprise Resource Planning (ERP)

Enterprise Resource Planning (ERP) software combines the software of all departments of an enterprise into a single, integrated program, enabling the storage of information in a centralized location. In using this software, the same information can be shared by all departments of an enterprise who are able to communicate with each other. The ERP software installed in a given enterprise must cater to its specific needs. ERP oversees and coordinates all of the company's operations such as finance, sales, accounting, human resources, and manufacturing.

ERP allows businesses to make better business decisions, reduce operational costs, and improve efficiency by delivering the right product at the right time. ERP can be used to manage operations such as manufacturing, inventory management, and so on. ERP is often referred to as "back-office" software. For example, once a salesperson enters an order into the computer system, the shipping department starts making shipping arrangements for the ordered products.

Customer Relationship Management (CRM)

Customer Relationship Management (CRM) manages all the information that a business has about its customers, including each customer's purchasing history and preferred products. CRM can keep records of all customer inquiries and responses. CRM allows businesses to manage accounts and orders efficiently, which leads to increased revenue, satisfied customers, and reduced administrative costs. A wireless CRM is available for mobile devices.

Supply Chain Management (SCM)

Supply Chain Management (SCM) is the management of all interconnected businesses that take part in providing end products or services to end users. Supply chain management involves the acquisition of raw material, conversion to a finished product, transportation, storage, and finally, supplying the goods or services to the end user. Some basic aspects of SCM are:

- Delivery, storage and optimum inventory levels of materials required to make the finished products.
- Decision on processes and location of production.
- Decision on location of storage of finished products and on the optimum amount of inventory.
- Promotion, sales, and delivery of the finished products.
- Timely payments to suppliers of materials and receipt of payments from customers.

Some objectives of SCM are:

- Get continuous supply of materials or services required to make the finished products.

- Find suppliers of materials who are reliable and can supply quality material at competitive prices, in a timely manner, and in the amount needed.

- Maintain optimum level of inventory of materials and finished products, determined from past productions and sales.

- Minimize inventory loss of materials and finished goods.

- Establish cordial relationships with all the suppliers of materials.

- Make timely payments to suppliers.

- All the departments (including customer service) of a company cooperate with each other to maximize efficiency, reduce appropriate costs, and maintain good relationships.

- The company must maintain or improve its competitive edge over other businesses.

3.11   NODE, NETWORK, AND INTERNET

When one person talks to another person, it can be called a people network. If a person talks to another person in the same city, it can be called a local people network. If a person talks to another person in another state or country, it can be called a wide area people network. Each person can be thought of as a node in the people network.

A network node is an electronic device that is capable of sending, receiving, or forwarding data in a computer network using a communication medium. A node is a point where two networks intersect. A node is very similar to a point on a line graph or a point where two lines intersect. A printer that is shared is a node, as it outputs data on paper.

A network is a group of two or more computers that are designed to send and receive information, and share hardware and software. The Internet is a network of networks. For example, in the cell phone industry, if a customer on network A talks to a customer on network B, that would be similar to forming an Internet.

3.12   WORLD WIDE WEB, WEBPAGE, WEBSITE, AND WEBSERVER

The Web or World Wide Web (WWW) is a series of interconnected links that link different websites on the Internet. It can be compared to a series of interconnected highways that link different cities. The Web is a part of the Internet.

A *webpage* is an electronic document on the Web that stores graphic, text, sound, and video data. It is similar to a textbook page that contains text and images. The textbook, however, cannot store sounds or video images. Webpages contain hyperlinks which, when clicked, connect to other webpages on the same website or other websites.

A *website* is a collection of webpages. It is similar to a textbook, which is a collection of textbook pages. Many organizations and companies maintain a website that describes their operations, services, and products. For example, the well-known website Google contains a search engine, which is visited by computer users to get information about a particular topic, by typing in keywords in a search textbox. The homepage of a website is the main or opening page of a company's or organization's website. For example, on Google's website, the homepage shows a simple search textbox in which to type keywords.

A *webmaster* is a person who is responsible for managing a website. The Webmaster's responsibilities include: creating and designing the website, updating the pages of the website, maintaining the website by making certain that the hardware and software on the Web server is working properly, and managing other operations related to the website.

A *webserver* is a computer on the Internet that stores webpages belonging to the website of a particular organization, college, hospital, business, etc. The webserver delivers the requested webpage to a client's computer using HTTP protocol. HTTP is a set of rules or protocols that all computers have to follow when communicating. Every webserver also has software that processes the requests of client computers.

Every webserver has a unique Internet Protocol (IP) address that allows other computers connected to the Internet to locate it. For example, when a user types in the domain name of an organization, the domain name is converted internally to the IP address of the organization and, if found, its homepage is displayed on the client's computer. Generally, all webservers are active 24 hours a day, 365 days a year. But, if the Web server is "down," the server is usually having technical problems or is being updated. Apache HTTP Server and Microsoft's webserver are the two most popular webservers.

A *hypertext link* is text on one page of a website that, with a mouse click, links the user to text on another page of the website. A hypertext link usually appears in a different color on the webpage, is pre-underlined, or is underlined when the mouse moves over it.

Each webpage stores different types of information about the website. For example, on the webpage of the U.S. Department of State there are hypertext links to apply for a U.S. passport, including "First Time Adult Applicant" "Minor Applicants" and "Renew Passport Book by Mail." If a user clicks on the hypertext "Renew Passport Book by Mail," the user will be linked to another page with hypertext "Form DS-82: Application for a U.S. Passport by Mail," which, when clicked on, will allow the user to print the form..

A *hypermedia link* connects an HTML document with a multimedia file. A multimedia file contains text, graphics, sounds, or video data.

Web indexing, also called "Web site A-Z index," creates A-Z style indexes for individual websites or an Intranet.

Communication Protocols

In general, protocols are rules used to perform certain tasks. For example, while driving, there are protocols, such as yield and stop signs, for drivers to follow.

Communication protocols is a set of rules that client and server computers need to follow when communicating with each other over a network or Internet in order to exchange data or a file. For example, when a user wants to log on to a particular website, "http" communication protocol is used between his computer and the Web server of the website. Communication protocols used in a network are FTP, HTTP, SMTP, IMAP, and TCP/IP.

File Transfer Protocol (FTP) is a set of rules that allow files to be transferred from one computer to another. FTP uses a file server to upload and download files from one computer to another. "Uploading a file" means sending a file from a computer to another computer. "Downloading a file" means receiving a file from another computer. FTP protocol is part of the TCP/IP protocol set that states rules to format, order, and check errors in files that are sent over the network. To access some files on the Internet, a user ID and password may be required.

Hypertext Transfer Protocol (HTTP) transfers files from a webserver to a user's computer, which can then be viewed using a Web browser. All HTTP files are stored on a webserver of a particular website. For example, entering *http://www.google.com* in the address window of a computer's Web browser indicates that HTTP is being used between the user's home computer and the webserver of Google's website. "http://" indicates that a file is a webpage.

Collectively, *Transmission Control Protocol/Internet Protocol (TCP/IP)* is a protocol used to route a file from one end of a network to the other end, ensuring that the correct data arrives at the destination computer.

TCP breaks down the message or file to be sent into individual units known as packets. These packets contain information such as the source and the destination address of the packets, as well as the checksum values. Checksum values verify that the packets have reached their destination error free. A damaged packet is resent. IP protocol decides the best route for the packets to reach their destination address.

Simple Mail Transfer Protocol (SMTP) determines which path each e-mail message will follow before it is sent. It is the same as a user deciding which route he will take to get somewhere before he starts driving.

Internet Message Access Protocol (IMAP) is the protocol used to access an e-mail message from an e-mail server to view it.

A *Uniform Resource Locator (URL)* specifies the unique address of a particular website and also specifies the type of transfer protocol to use when transferring the document over the Internet. For example, *http://www.google.com* is the URL, and *www.google.com* is the domain name of the website. A URL has four parts:

- *http://protocol*, which indicates that a file is a webpage.
- *"www,"* which indicates that it is on the World Wide Web (or Web) and is the third level of a domain name.
- *google*, which is the name of the website and the second level of a domain name.

- *.com*, which indicates that it is a commercial organization and is the top level of a domain name.

An *Internet Protocol (IP) address* is the address the computer user enters in the address window of a browser and which is then converted to an IP address. An IP address is made up of four groups of numbers, i.e., 208.177.88.166. If the IP address is located on the Internet, the user's computer is connected to the website; otherwise, he is not connected to the webpage.

3.13   WEB TECHNOLOGY AND PROGRAMMING

Web technology is a combination of multiple technologies, which involves the communication between webservers and webclients. Web technology can be any technology related to the creation of websites and webpages that display the webpage of a client.

A webserver is a computer that acts as a host for any website. It is connected directly to the Internet and sends stored webpages to the client's computer using HTTP. Apache is an open-source webserver that runs on UNIX operating systems, such as Solaris and Linux, and Windows-based servers. A FrontPage Server can create and manage professional-looking websites.

Web technology can involve one or a combination of the following:

- Web server, Web clients, communication protocols, URL and Domain Name System (DNS).
- Use of markup languages, such as HTML, XML, XHTML to create webpages
- Cascading Styling Sheets (CSS) to format webpages
- Client side programming software, such as JavaScript
- Server side programming software, such as Java Servlets
- Representing Web data using XML
- Separating programming and presentations of webpages: JSP technology
- Interfaces and markup languages, and standards for document identification and display.

Markup Languages

Markup languages are used to create a structured document known as a webpage. The structure specifies the elements, attributes, entities, Parsed Character Data (PCData), and Character Data (CData) on the webpage. A markup language is a collection of symbols and special words to specify the elements of a webpage inside tags.

Tags, Elements, and Attributes in a Webpage

Elements are the basic items used to build a webpage. In HTML documents, the elements can be objects (paragraphs, headings, or the page title), various header styles, ordered/unordered listed items, images, text fonts, horizontal rulers, hyperlinks, and background of webpages. Elements are written inside tags that are marked by angled brackets, i.e., <element> and </element>.

There are three types of tags in HTML:

- Tags containing information
- Empty tags (containing no information)
- Comment tags

In HTML, *tags containing information*, are always written inside an opening tag (< >) and a closing tag (< / >) using the following format:

<some element>information</some element>

For example, the "p" element, representing paragraph in an HTML document, may be written as follows:

<p>This is a paragraph.</p>

In this example, "This is a paragraph" is the information contained in the "p" element.

Empty tags contain no information and are written using the following format:

<hr/>

The above tag indicates that a horizontal rule should appear at this point on the webpage.

A *comment tag* is used to write comments describing the action of the HTML code on the webpage and uses the following format:

<!Comments>

Comments are not executed, displayed, or used on a webpage.

Attributes are characteristics that describe the selected element. For example, when inserting an image on a webpage, an HTML tag may appear as:

<image src="C:\Pictures\Clock.gif"/>

In this example, the image is the element, "src" is the source of the image, and the attribute and content of the attribute is "C:\Pictures\Clock.gif," which specifies where the image is stored.

Table 3.4 below shows some elements of a webpage.

Table 3.4   Some Common Elements of a Webpage with their Tags

Element	HTML Statement with Tags	Explanation
HTML	<html> . . . . .</html>	Marks the beginning and end of HTML using <html> tag
Head	<head>.. . . .</head>	Marks the beginning and end of head element using a <head> tag.
Body	<body> . . . </body>	Marks the beginning and end of body element using a <body> tag.
Paragraph	<p>. . .</p>	Marks the beginning and end of paragraph element in a webpage using a <p> tag.
Break	 	Inserts a line break using a tag
Horizontal rule	<hr />	Draws a horizontal rule line across the page using a <hr> tag

(Continued)

Table 3.4 (continued)

Element	HTML Statement with Tags	Explanation
Image	<p img src="C:\Computer.jpg"></p>	Inserts an Inline image of computer object nested inside a paragraph element using a <p> tag and "href."
Anchor	<a href="http://www.a.com/b>A Co.</a>	Anchor element marks a specific location in a webpage using an <a> tag. Creates hyperlink in a webpage.
Title	<title>Webpage Design</title)	Title element assigns title "Webpage Design" to Webpage using a <title> tag.
Heading	<h1>Some Text</h1>	Creates top level (h1) heading element using a <h1> tag. Other heading element tags are <h2> to <h6>, where <h6> tag has the lowest priority.
Ordered list	<ol> <li> One <li> Two </ol>	Creates numbered ordered list using a <li> tag nested inside <ol> tag
Unordered list	<ul> <li> Bulleted List Item 1 <li> Bulleted List Item 2 </ul>	Creates bulleted unordered list using a <li> tag nested inside a <ul> tag
Address	<address> Mr. ABC 123 Street SomeCity, AL 12345 </address>	Adds an address block to a webpage using an <address> tag.
B, U, I	<b><u><i>Text</b></u></i>	Boldfaces, underlines, and italicized text using <b>, <u>, and <i> tags.
Font	<h3>font face="Arial">Text</font></h3>	Sets font face to "Arial" using <font> and <h3> tags
Comments	<!--Header of a Webpage-->	Inserts comments in a Webpage to describe action of a certain HTML code by using <!--. . . --> tags.

Hypertext Markup Language (HTML)

HTML is a markup language used as a tool to create a structured document known as a webpage. HTML creates hypertext documents that resemble an ASCII coded text file. All characters used to write text in a document are defined in an ASCII table and are recognized by almost all computers, except computers using EBCDIC code. Using HTML, forms, tables, and images can be inserted into a webpage.

A webpage is similar to a text file, but with added features, and can be created using a simple text editor such as "Notepad." A webpage is created using the syntax (rules) of HTML.

An HTML document is made from HTML elements. Each element is made up of three parts:

- Tags (described earlier). For example, in the tag Text, the "" indicates the start of boldface text and the "" indicates the end of the boldface text.
- Attribute of the text, such as boldfacing, italicizing, underlining, etc.
- Contents in an attribute—the text itself.

Extensive Markup Language (XML)

XML is markup language used to create structured documents (webpages) by using metadata concepts and by creating user-defined tags. In computers, metadata means data about data. In other words, "metadata" means when using data X, there should be another data Y to explain what attribute X stands for. For example, "December 12, 2009" is a date that does not specify whether it is a date of birth or a date of an appointment. In XML, a tag such as <DOB>December 12, 2009</DOB> would be used that identifies the date as a date of birth. XML documents may include text, e-commerce transactions, graphics, and mathematical equations.

Almost every character appearing in Unicode can be represented in an XML document. XML can be used to develop custom markup languages. A number of applications are being developed that make use of XML documents. XML is actually a useful data storage structure for PHP programmers.

XML allows users to create their own tags and define how they interact with each other. HTML uses only fixed tags and can't create new tags. HTML has some empty tags, such as <br>. In XML, the same empty tag can be written as <br /> or
</br>. In HTML, almost every item is not case sensitive, but in XML all attribute names and elements are case sensitive.

Extensive Hypertext Markup Language (XHTML)

XHTML is an application of XML, a stricter version of HTML, that integrates XML and HTML. Because XHTML documents need to be well-formed, they can be parsed using standard XML parsers.

Cascading Styling Sheets (CSS)

CSS is a language that helps users to separate the content of a webpage from its formatting. CSS is an advanced technique used to format webpages, as follows:

- Allows Web developers to apply typographic styles such as font size and font type.

- Allows Web developers to set line spacing, letter spacing, margins and indentations.

- Stores style in a separate document. All formatting of text and colors on a page can be saved in a separate file and linked from the webpage CSS.

- Allows for easy website maintenance. For example, in order to change the styles, Web developers simply need to change the style sheet.

Client-Side and Server-Side Programming Languages in a Webpage

When surfing the Web, some operations are done on the client side computer, while others are done on the server-side computer. When users request a particular page from a website, the server-side computer sends the requested webpage to the computer Web browser, which then displays it on the computer screen. To deliver a webpage to the computer, some programming languages interface with client-side computers and others interface with server side computers.

Client-side programming languages make it easier to create webpages. Cascading Styling Sheets (CSS) and JavaScript are used on the client side of a webpage. Cascading Styling Sheets (CSS) make it easier to format images in a webpage. JavaScript codes can be placed directly into HTML code. Elements such as links, images, and forms can all be manipulated using JavaScript. JavaScript helps create dynamic menus and transitional effects, such as fading and sliding animation. JavaScript code is written in text editor and saved in a file with a .js extension. JavaScript codes can also be placed on server side computers, and be called from a webpage by linking it to a file with a .js extension.

Server-side programming languages in a webpage are used to create executable scripts on the server and to deliver the webpage. Such languages are JavaScript, Java Server Pages (JSP), Active Server Pages (ASPs), and ASP.net. JavaServer Pages (JSPs) technology allows for easy creation of Web content that has both static and dynamic components.

Representing Web Data—DTDs (XML Document Type Definitions)

XML focuses on the structure of data rather than on the presentation of the data. XML integrates and manipulates Web data through a common data model, such as DTDs (XML Document Type Definitions). DTDs provide syntax to explain which elements may appear in the XML document and which are the element contents and attributes.

3.14   WEBPAGE DEVELOPMENT

Figure 3.4 shows the general structure of an HTML document with some basic elements (and a brief description) of a webpage. (Remember that <element>…</element> are the start and end tags of the same element.)

- The **<html>** in the first line is the opening tag of an "html" element and </html> in the last line of the webpage is the closing tag of the "html" element. The "html" element indicates creation of the webpage using HTML markup language.

- **<head><title>. . .</title</head>** has the "title" element nested inside the "head" element.

- **<body>. . . </body>** is the "body" element containing the body of the webpage and is usually started after the end of the "head" element.

- **<p>. . . </p>** is the start/end tag of a "p" element containing the text of paragraph(s) in a webpage.

- **<h1>. . . </h1>, <h2>. . . </h2>, and <h3>. . . </h3>** are tags of different "heading-level" elements. There are six heading level elements (h1 to h6), with h1 being the largest and h6 being the smallest. Headings also provide section headers when a webpage is divided into sections with different levels of importance.

- **<ol> <li>. . .</ol>** is a numbered "ordered list" element tags starting from number 1. Each listed item is written after the "li" element tag on its own line and the listed items are nested inside the <ol>. . .</ol> element.

- **<ul> <li>. . .</ul>** is a bulleted "unordered list" element. Each listed item is written after the "li" element tag on its own line and the listed items are nested inside the <ul>…</ul> element.

- **<a> ... </a>** is an "anchor" element using a "<a>" tag, which creates a text hyperlink to a website by using "href" and specifying the URL of the website.

- **<img src="SomeImage.gif">** is an "img" element to place an image inside the webpage.

Figure 3.4   General Structure of a Simple Webpage

Explanation of Element	HTML Statement with Tags
Start of html element	<html>
Start of head element	<head>
Start/End of title element	<title> Title of Webpage</title>
End of head element	</head>
Start of body element	<body>
Start/End of "h1" heading element	<h1> h1 Level Heading</h1>
Start of "p" element	<p>
Text in paragraph	Text in Paragraph
End of "p" element	</p>

(Continued)

Figure 3.4 *(Continued)*

Explanation of Element	HTML Statement with Tags
Start/End of "h2" heading element	\<h2\> h2 Level heading\</h2\>
Start of "ol" element	\<ol\>
Numbered list item 1 using "li" element	\<li\> Numbered Ordered List Item 1
Numbered list item 2 using "li" element	\<li\> Numbered Ordered List Item 2
End of "ol" element	\</ol\>
Start/End of "hr" element	\<hr\>
Create a link to a Web site using \<a\> element	\<a href="http://www.SomeWebSite.com/File\>TextforHyperlink\</a\>
Start/End of "h3" heading element	\<h3\> h3 Level Heading\</h3\>
Start of another "p" element	\<p\>
Text in paragraph	Text in paragraph
End of another "p" element	\</p\>
Insert centered image in a "p" element	\<p\> align="center"\<img src="SomeImage.gif"\>\</p\>
Start of bullet "ul" element—unordered list	\<ul\>
Bullet list item 1 using "li" element	\<li\>Bulleted Unordered List Item
Bullet list item 2 using "li" element	\<li\>Bulleted Unordered List Item
End of "ul" bullet unordered list	\</ul\>
End of "body" element	\</body\>
End of html element	\</html\>

Steps to Create a Webpage

Use Text Editor to Create a HTML Document

For the purpose of this example, Notepad text editor is used to create, edit, and save the HTML document. In a text editor such as Notepad, the HTML document is saved as an ASCII text file by adding the extension ".html" to the file name, indicating that the saved document is an HTML document. We can enter any simple text in a text editor with its default settings, but the entered text cannot be formatted in any way, which means no boldface, underline, or italics, changing the font size, highlighting, or performing any other similar operation on the text.

The following elements are added to an HTML document to create a webpage.

- html element using <html> tag
- Body element using <body> tag
- Title element using <title> tag
- Heading elements h1, h2, h3 using <h1>, <h2> and <h3> tags
- Create an ordered number list with the "li" element nested inside the "ol" element, and the <li> tag nested inside the <ol> tag
- Create a bullet unordered list with the "li" element nested inside the "ul" element, and the <li> tag nested inside the <ul> tag
- Create a hyperlink using an anchor and an <a> tag
- Insert an image inside a paragraph using a <p> tag
- Insert comments using <!-- --> tags. Comments are not executed as HTML code
- Insert address element using the <address> tag.

For example, here are the steps needed to create and execute the webpage shown in Figure 3.5.

1. Turn on the computer.

2. In the lower left corner of the task bar on the desktop, click on Start—All Programs—Accessories—Notepad.

3. A blank Notepad document appears on the screen.

4. In Notepad, select File and New—a new notepad document opens and type the HTML code for creating a webpage.

5. Enter the entire HTML code (shown in Figure 3.4)

6. When finished with the text, save the file—on the drop down menu, select File and Save.

7. In the Filename text box, enter C:\LessonOne.html as the file name, and click Save. An HTML document can be saved in any folder on your hard disk.

8. Minimize the Notepad text editor window containing the HTML document.

9. To view your newly created HTML document as a Webpage, open Internet Explorer

10. On the drop down menu of Internet Explorer, select File and Open.

11. In the "Open" dialogue window, click Browse.

12. Navigate to the C drive and highlight "LessonOne.html" file, and click Open.

13. If there are no syntax errors in the HTML code, the webpage is displayed in Internet Explorer.

14. If there are syntax errors in HTML code, they are listed in an Internet Explorer window explaining the error type and its line number in the HTML code. To remove errors, minimize the Internet Explorer window and maximize the Notepad window. Make the necessary corrections by reading and correcting each error listed. Save the HTML document again.

15. Minimize the Notepad window, and maximize the Internet Explorer window. Select View and Refresh. The corrected webpage is displayed.

16. The webpage of the HTML document is shown in Figure 3.6.

Figure 3.5 HTML Code to Create a Webpage.
Filename: LessonOne.html

```html
<html>
<head>
<!--Header of the Webpage-->
<title>Computer Science Department at MCC</title>
</head>
<body>
<p align="center"><img src="C:\Computer.jpg"></p>
<h1 align="center">Computer Science Majors at MCC</h1>
<a href="http://www.middlesexcc.edu/future/academics/control.cfm/ID/2390/
        program/11">
Computer Science at Middlesex County College, Edison, NJ</a>
<h2><b>Computer Science Associate Degree and Computer Science Certificate
        Programs at MCC</b></h2>
<h3>Associate Degree Programs</h3>
<ol>
    <li>Computer Science Transfer
    <li>Computers and Information Systems - General Option
    <li>Computers and Information Systems - Network Administration and Support
        Option
</ol>
<hr />
<h3 align="center"> Computer Science Certificate Programs</h3>
<ul>
    <li>Computer Programming
    <li>Network Administration and Support
    <li>Java and Web Programming
    <li>Technical Certificate in Windows NT/Novel Netware
    <li>Technical Certificate in Computers and Information Systems
    <li>Network Administration Certificate
    <li>Technical Certificate in Computer Desk Help Administration
    <li>Information Systems Security Certificate and Achievement
</ul>
<hr>
<p>For additional information, please contact:<br>
<address>
Prof. Francis Burke, Chair Computer Science<br>
Middlesex County College<br>
2600 Woodbridge Ave, Edison, NJ 08818<br>
Tel: 732.906.2526<br>
</address>
</p>
</body>
</html>
```

Figure 3.6   Webpage of HTML Document

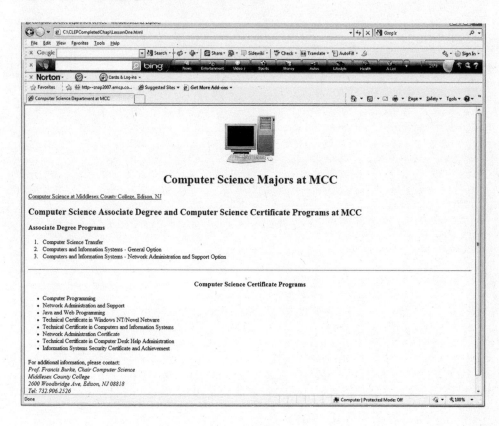

CHAPTER 4

Information Systems Software Development

CHAPTER 4

Information Systems Software Development

4.1   BASIC CONCEPTS IN INFORMATION SYSTEMS

Data

As described in chapter 1, data consists of text, numbers, images, audio, or video that has not been processed yet.

- Text data contains text-only data, such as a person's name or a city's name. Arithmetical operations cannot be performed on text data.

- Numerical data consists of numbers, which can include a person's date of birth or, say, a student's SAT score. Arithmetical and comparison operations can be performed on numerical data. The numbers can be written as integers (whole numbers) or as decimals, such as 1.23.

- Alphanumeric data is a mixture of text and numerical data, such as a street address (123 Park Ave.).

- Image data can be a picture of a person or scenery.

- Audio or sound data can be a song or a human voice.

- Video data is a combination of sound and image data, such as a movie.

- Multimedia is formed when text, audio, video, animation, and still images are combined into one.

Information

Information is data that has been processed. Information can help users make decisions or can simply be used for future needs. For example, when a user purchases a number of books and adds up the cost of the books, a total amount for the purchase is tallied. That total is information and the user decides how to pay for the purchase.

All businesses store large amounts of data and information in the database of their computer information systems. For example, the Internal Revenue Service stores the yearly income tax returns of all U.S. citizens who file a return.

Information System

An information system (IS) is composed of a group of people, computer hardware, computer software, procedures, and data that work together to collect, organize, process, filter, and store data systematically. The collected information is then analyzed by decision makers who make decisions about the day-to-day, short-term, and long-term operations of a business. In today's world, an information system, for the most part, operates in a computer networking environment.

Different types of people, such as data entry operators, system administrators, computer programmers, computer engineers, and network engineers, are needed to operate an information system.

Computer hardware, as discussed earlier, is any physical component, such as a monitor or a hard disk, that can be seen or touched. The keyboard allows the input of data/information, the CPU processes it, the monitor displays it, the hard disk stores it, and the printer prints it.

Computer software can be a series of programs, such as an operating system, an application software program, or a database management program, that are required to perform day-to-day operations on computers.

A *procedure*-like program is a sequence of instructions that instructs the computer to perform a specific task. For example, a procedure can be written to calculate the average of three test scores and allocate a letter grade based on the average of those scores.

Processing data or information means to convert the data or information from one form to another form by following a series of steps. For example, boiling water is the process of converting water from a liquid to a gas (steam).

In computers, *process* is a program that follows a series of instructions to perform a specific task such as generating and printing a payroll check.

Organizing data or information means to sort (arrange) the data alphabetically or numerically, or into groups. For example, a doctor's computer sorts and stores patients' records based on patient ID numbers.

Filtering information is the process of removing redundant (duplicate) data or unwanted information from a pool of information. Filtering extracts a specific type of information. For example, a credit card company might identify late-paying customers in order to send a payment reminder.

Storing data is the process of saving collected data/information on a hard disk or other storage device, such as a flash drive.

Information Technology

Information technology enables computers to handle large amounts of information, perform complex calculations, and control many simultaneous processes.

4.2 INFORMATION SYSTEM DEVELOPMENT: METHODS AND TOOLS

Information system or software development is the act of writing instructions which, when followed by a computer, will solve a specific problem or a number of problems for a specific type of business.

System Development Methods

System (or software) development methods are guidelines used to initiate, organize, plan, construct, and regulate the development of an information system or software.

Purpose of System Development

A newly-developed business system can improve the efficiency of a business in many areas such as standardizing business operations and practices, automating tedious tasks, and increasing productivity.

The Systems Development Life Cycle (SDLC)

The Systems Development Life Cycle (SDLC) is a systematic and organized way to develop an information system (IS) by specifying problem analysis, design, implementation, testing, and support (maintenance) of the information system. The information system requires upgrades from time to time and needs to be maintained continuously.

The basic steps in SDLC are as follows:

1. **Feasibility studies, also known as preliminary investigations**
   A feasibility study is done to determine whether it would be best to modify an existing system (which might involve purchasing new hardware or software) or to install a new one. In most instances, cost will determine the path to be taken.

2. **Requirement analysis or system analysis**
   The objectives of the organization must be analyzed so that the new or modified system will meet those objectives.

3. **System design**
   The selection of programs for the new system is decided as well as how the programs will work together in the new system. If the programs needed to meet the requirements of the new system are not readily available, then developing the design of custom programs may be necessary. Tools such as algorithms, structured flow charts, and pseudo codes may be used in designing the logic of the new system.

4. **System acquisition**
   Upon management approval of the design, the systems analyst decides which vendors to use and acquires the needed hardware and software.

5. **System implementation**
   The actual code of the new system is written. Programming languages such as C++ and Java may be used to write the code.

6. **System testing**

   All of the acquired and installed software is tested completely. When tested, each individual function or module of a single program needs to work correctly on its own. Then the functions or modules are collectively tested. Finally, if a system has more than one program installed, all programs are tested collectively to determine if they work together correctly.

7. **System installation**

   The new system is delivered to the user and installed.

8. **Training**

   The people who are going to use the new system are trained. A user manual for the system is generated.

9. **System maintenance**

   As the needs of the organization change, the modules of the programs are updated or changed to meet those needs.

Approaches in System Development

System development models use different approaches to software development. Basic approaches include linear (sequential), repetitive (iterative), prototyping, rapid application development (RAD), and an object-oriented programming (OOP) approach. A waterfall model uses a linear (sequential) approach, while prototyping uses a sequential approach in system development. Rapid application development uses the repetitive approach and object oriented programming treats everything as an object.

Model Structure Design—Software Development

Model structure design divides a program (software) into smaller sub-programs (modules, functions, or sub-routines) in a hierarchical form by using a top-down approach. Each module has a specific name and set of instructions to perform a specific subtask according to the syntax (regulations or rules) and the guidelines of the intended program.

Waterfall Model or Traditional Approach— Software Development

In software engineering, the Waterfall Model is a sequential development process that employs a "top down" approach in the Software Development Life Cycle (SDLC). The different phases in system development using the Waterfall Model are shown in Figure 4.1. The documentation of every detail in each phase of system development is very important in order to compare the intended outcomes with achieved outcomes, so that necessary adjustments can be made. The model states that each phase must be completed before proceeding to the next stage.

Figure 4.1 Waterfall System Development Model

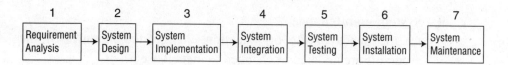

1. **System Requirement Analysis**

   In this phase, the end user must analyze and clearly state the problem to be solved, specify functionalities in the new system and what the end product should be. When gathering requirements, all the users of the system are consulted. Finally, a document stating all the requirements of the new system is created. The requirement analysis document acts as a guideline for the next phase.

2. **System and Software Design**

   The requirement analysis document created in phase1 is studied in detail and what the system is going to do is decided. Then, software and hardware requirements for the system are designed. Development of all of the details of the information system takes place. In software development, the writing of instructions is dependent on project inputs, various processing to be done on input data, all desired outputs, what information needs to be stored, and other necessary details. Algorithms, flow charts, and any other tools that help in completing the project are designed. The system design specifications serve as input for the next phase of the model.

3. **System Implementation**

   The actual program instructions for the solution to the project are coded. The system may use a number of individual programs.

Each individual program may be divided into a number of modules (functions). To start, the code for each individual module of a single program is written. Then, the code for all of the individual units of the single program to work collectively is written. Finally, the code needed for all the programs to work collectively in a system is written. When coding the solution to a problem, the following must be kept in mind:

- The project inputs, all processing to be done on the input data, all desired outputs, what information needs to be stored, etc.

- If the project is subdivided into smaller modules or functions, then all the functions or modules must be coded also.

- Use of decision statements or any other type of statements.

4. **System Integration**
   The written codes for all the modules and programs in the system implementation phase are integrated into a single complete system that will be ready for testing in the next phase.

5. **System Testing**
   In general, each individual component of a system, as well as the whole system, is tested. The code for each individual function or module of a single program is also tested. Then, a unit test on each individual program is done. After that, a complete system test is conducted to check that all the programs in a system collectively work correctly. Finally, all the parts of written code are tested many times to make sure that there are no logical errors, runtime errors, or any other flaws in the code.

6. **System Installation (Deployment)**
   The system is delivered to the user and is installed. All the programs and hardware are also installed.

7. **System Maintenance**
   After installation and use, the system needs to be maintained continuously. Some problems that were not revealed during the testing phase may be revealed during the normal operation of a system. The parts of the system program with problems are modified as required. Parts of the program may need modification (because of changes in state or federal laws or changes in a state's sales tax rate). These types of modifications are considered maintenance of the system.

Prototype Incremental Model—System Development

A prototype is a small working model of a system that is built before building a large system. Prototypes are built and evaluated. In the traditional SDLC model, all steps are planned well in advance and are written by system developers. SDLC models do not keep the user in mind.

A new concept in software engineering, known as the incremental model, is being used in system development. In the incremental model, a system is built with basic functionalities. Once this starting version is perfected, more functionality is added, tested, and perfected. The process continues until the complete system is built.

The prototype model focuses on the users of the system from the beginning. When the prototype is built, the user can decide whether or not he likes the system. If the user likes it, then more functionality can be added to the prototype. If the user does not like it, then the current prototype is modified before proceeding. The advantage of the prototype model is that the user can test the system as it is being built and the developer can make necessary modifications. The system is created using user feedback.

Extreme Programming (XP)—System Development

In the extreme programming (XP) model, a group of individuals works together to develop a system. They freely share ideas and suggestions at each stage of development. At every stage, all steps of the SDLC are applied.

Object-Oriented System Analysis and Design—
System Development

The object oriented modeling technique is used to identify objects in a system and the relationships between them. When applying system concepts for object oriented modeling, objects, attributes, and methods that are applied to study the behavior of an object are discussed.

- Objects are nouns, which can be a place, a person, an event, or a thing. In object-oriented programming (OOP), an object is an item containing both data and methods (procedures) that operate on data.

- Attributes are the characteristics of an object. For example, a student object can have attributes such as a name, a student ID, major course of study, GPA, credits completed, etc.

- The behavior of an object describes the type of actions an object can do. For example, a student (object) can think, go to school, study, play games, etc. Methods in object oriented programming are used to control the behavior of an object. For example, method "calculate GPA" will calculate the GPA of a student.

Object-oriented analysis and design (OOAD) is a software engineering approach that models a system as a group of interacting objects. Each object represents an entity in the system, and can be described by its class, its state (data elements), and its behavior.

Object-oriented analysis (OOA) analyzes the functional requirements of a system. This technique is used to study current objects to determine if they can be reused or to add new objects to create a new application. Object-oriented design (OOD) uses OOA models to produce implementation specifications. OOD concentrates on *how* the system does it. OOA finds what the system *does*.

Unified Modeling Language (UML) is used to model an Object Oriented System, which describes a system in terms of objects. The UML is a very important part of developing object oriented software and the software development process. UML diagrams show both static and dynamic views of a system model.

A static (structural) UML view provides a static view of the system using objects, their attributes, operations that can be performed on those objects and the relationships between classes in a system. Class diagrams are used to show the structural view of objects by listing classes of system, their attributes and the relationships between different classes.

A dynamic (behavioral) UML shows the dynamic behavior of the system by showing collaborations among objects and changes to the internal states of objects.

Rapid Application Development (RAD)—
Software Development Methodology

Rapid Application Development (RAD) is a system development methodology that uses an iterative process and incorporates prototype methodology to develop a system one segment at a time. It is a Joint Application Development (JAD) process, in which developers and end users are involved in all stages of system development until it is delivered. Using re-use concept, RAD uses already-developed software or tools or their segments in building a new system.

RAD re-uses prebuilt components from other programming languages (such as Java and C++) by including them along with other programs in building a new system. RAD uses already developed software or tools such as Graphic User Interface (GUI) builders, Computer Aided Software Engineering (CASE) tools, Database Management Systems (DBMS), Object Oriented techniques and flexible management in system development. RAD is an *iterative* process:

- After finding the initial end-user requirements, the developers build a prototype.

- The end users try the prototype.

- The end users and developers jointly meet to review the prototype against the original requirements.

- The requirements are redefined and changes in the prototype are made and then retested.

- The process requirement changes as the prototype is tested and change requests are "TimeBoxed." The "TimeBoxed" concept in RAD means that the project is divided into a number of parts, and each part must be completed by its deadline date. For example, part 1 must be finished first, part 2 next, and so on. Each part has its own deadline date to finish certain selected items (known as deliverables) within budget.

- The above process is repeated until the system is finally ready to be installed on the end-user's computer, thus making it an iterative process.

RAD phases are as follows.

1. Requirement (Prototype) Phase
   With the involvement of the user, the requirements of the new system are established.

2. Design Phase

   The requirements of the new system are examined and a prototype is built by incorporating the features from components of ready-made software or tools. Consideration must be given to screens, forms, reports, and user-interfaces that are to be added to the new system. Usually, the more iterations that are done in this phase, the better the system is built.

3. Implementation Phase

   The actual code for the new system is written and linked with the code from other software. Many iterations are done in this phase.

4. Testing Phase

   The system is tested and, based on customer feedback, improvements are made and bugs are removed.

5. Deployment Phase (Turnover)

   The system is installed at the user's site and is ready to use.

6. Training the User

   The end users are trained to use the new system, and user manuals are generated.

7. Maintenance Phase

   The system is maintained continuously.

Advantages of RAD are as follows:

- The system is built one segment at a time and is tested while being built. It is easy to change portions of a segment during the development process. Because of prototyping, it is easier to find out if the project is working properly during the earlier stages.

- It saves time and money, and reduces manual coding when ready-made software is purchased.

- Since it uses tools such as GUI builders and CASE tools, a high quality system can be built rapidly and at relatively low cost.

- Due to the use of pre-tested ready-made software, there will be fewer defects in the system.

- RAD can produce documentation of the development process that can be used in future development.

- RAD is a Joint Application Development (JAD) as end users are involved in all stages of development.

Disadvantages of RAD are as follows:

- Some unwanted features may be added to the new system or some features may be ignored because they did not exist in the ready-made software or tools.

- The code in the new system may not execute as efficiently as it should.

- Because of JAD and conflicts of interest among the people involved in the project, it may take a long time to establish the requirements of the system.

- Deadline dates in TimeBoxing may cause some of the required features of the new system to be ignored.

- RAD is not suitable for mathematical or computationally oriented applications.

System Development Tools

System development tools, in layman terms, are aids, devices, or things that make it easier to do other jobs. A system development tool or programming tool can also be called a software development kit (SDK). This is a program used by system developers as an aid when creating new systems or supporting other programs or writing application programs.

Computer Aided Software Engineering (CASE) is software consisting of automated tools and methods used to support various activities in the System Development Life Cycle (SDLC). CASE uses structured methods and GUI to build high-quality systems. The term CASE can apply to any type of software development environment in many fields. CASE functions include support for analysis, design, implementation, and maintenance phases of SDLC and generating programming code.

Some typical CASE tools are configuration management tools, data modeling tools, model transformation tools, source code generation tools, and UML.

Data modeling tools are used during the development of an information system and define and format data. These tools are also used to decide how data is represented and accessed.

Source code generation tools build source codes. Microsoft Visual Studio has an advanced form of code generation where the user can interactively select and customize a source code from choices of predefined pieces of source codes.

Microsoft Office Visio is a diagramming tool for Microsoft Windows that uses vector graphics to create diagrams such as business process flow-charts, network diagrams, workflow diagrams, database models, and software diagrams.

4.3   PROJECT MANAGEMENT

Project

A *project* is a specific task undertaken to create or build something new, such as an information system, a retail product, a building, or a bridge, etc. Every project has goals and objectives that must be met. A project has a beginning and an end. The project is completed when its goals and objectives are accomplished. A project can have constraints, such as a time limit, a budget, and limited resources (machinery, equipment, people, and materials). A project must deliver something at the end. It can be the installation of an information system, completion of a new building or bridge, etc.

Project Management

Project management is a scientific approach to initiate, plan, organize, manage, staff, and complete the intended objectives of the project successfully. The project must be completed within the given time frame, with allocated resources and allocated budget.

Resources in a Project

Resources in a project include:

- Finances—All the finances needed to pay for the project.
- People—All the people who are involved in the project—programmers, system designers, office staff, contractors, builders, etc.

- Real Estate—A building, office, or warehouse space that is needed for the project.

- Machinery and Equipment—Computer hardware/software, office machines/equipment, etc.

- Services—Any services that must be paid for during the course of the project.

- Office Supplies—Stationery, toners for printing machines, etc.

Project Manager—Functions and Responsibilities

Below are the main functions and responsibilities of a project manager.

- Clearly defining the goals and objectives of the project.

- Defining all the tasks needed to complete the project.

- Establishing a time schedule for each task, including the start and end dates.

- Estimating the cost of the project.

- Selecting members of the project team.

- Assigning duties to members of the team, based on their area of expertise and experience.

- Coordinating and supervising the members of the team in order to finish the project on time.

- Monitoring the project for completion of goals, tasks, costs, and any other elements necessary to complete the project.

- Finishing the project.

Once the project is completed, all the activities of the project members are ended. Any contracts in place must be settled with the customer. A report can be written documenting both good and bad work practices for future projects.

The duties of a project manager may be divided into three categories: task needs, team needs, and individual needs.

- Task needs involve attaining team objectives, planning work, allocating resources, defining tasks, assigning responsibility, controlling and monitoring quality, scrutinizing progress, and checking performance.

- Team needs include: appointing secondary leaders, building and upholding team spirit, setting standards and maintaining regulations, training the team, setting up systems to facilitate communication with the team, developing work methods to craft team function cohesiveness.

- Individual needs include helping individuals develop to the best of their abilities, balancing team needs and individual needs, performance appreciation and rewards, helping with team members' personal problems.

Project Management Software

Project Management Software is used to help project managers deal with all aspects of project management, including planning, scheduling, monitoring, organizing, controlling costs, etc. Project management software is used in all types of industries and is usually a combination of many types of software. Microsoft Project plans, manages, and communicates project information quickly and effectively. It supports PERT and Gantt Charts.

4.4 INFORMATION (DATA) PROCESSING: TYPES AND METHODS

Information, or data, processing converts data into useful information. To process data, the four steps of the Information Processing (IPOS) Cycle (Input, Process, Output, and Storage) must be followed. There are three types of information processing methods:

- Batch processing
- Real-time processing
- Transaction processing

Batch Processing

In batch processing, data is first collected until the end of a specified time period. The time period chosen depends on how the data needs to be used and can range from an hour per day to once a year. The collected data is then processed all at once.

For example, if an hourly employee receives a weekly paycheck, his total number of hours worked and pay rate are processed once a week to generate his paycheck. Utility bills are usually processed once a month, while data for a W2 form is processed once a year. Batch processing is useful for operations that are not time sensitive.

Real-Time Processing System

In real-time processing systems, the data is processed the moment the data is generated. Supermarkets and department stores use real-time processing.

Transaction Processing System (TPS)

A Transaction Processing System (TPS) is an information system that collects business data and processes it based on day-to-day activities. For example, when purchasing an airline ticket online and using a credit card to pay, the moment the "submit" button is pressed, a seat is reserved. This is known as Online Transaction Processing (OLTP).

4.5   USER INTERFACE DESIGN

Interface in Human Language

In human language, *interface* means two people talking using human language, such as English, Spanish, Hindi, German, etc. Using natural languages, human interface is in written text or spoken form. When communicating in any language, speaking or writing requires the use of grammatically correct sentences. Similarly, people have to interface with computers.

Computer-User Interface

Computer-user interface allows people to use computer hardware and/or computer software to communicate with other computers. The part of the operating system or other software that allows the user to communicate with the computer is called the *user interface*. The interface may also include two independent systems interacting with each other to communicate and perform operations, such as importing or exporting a document.

The user interface can also be an input to manipulate the system. Check boxes, option buttons, command buttons, and input text dialog boxes that appear in various windows of an application program or other programs are also user interfaces.

The output from the system may be a user interface allowing the system to indicate the effects of the user's manipulation of the system. For example, if a user clicks on the "Save" command button in a Save dialog window, the net effect is that the document is saved.

Interfaces in Computer Technology

All of the following are types of user interfaces:

- **Mouse/Keyboard User Interface**
  This user interface allows the user to interact with the operating system using the keyboard, mouse, menu bars or tabs, and graphical user interface (GUI). The user interfaces with the operating system to perform tasks such as defragmenting the hard disk, managing system resources, troubleshooting network connections, etc.

- **Command Line Interface**
  In command line interface, the user types commands, data, or instructions on a DOS prompt using the keyboard. The user must type those commands using correct syntax and spelling. It can be difficult to use a command line interface if the user doesn't remember the correct syntax of commands. The command line interface was more popular in the early days of computer technology when computers used MS DOS as the operating system.

- **GUI Interface**
  In GUI technology, the user interacts with graphical icons, images, and/or menus to perform various operations on a computer. For example, when a user clicks on the printer icon in an application window program, a print dialogue window opens enabling the printing of a document.

- **Hardware Interface**
  Network interface cards, modems, routers, hubs, switches, wires, and sockets are hardware devices required for computers to communicate with each other.

- **Software Interface**

  In many instances, a software program may have to communicate with another software program. This requires software interface. For example, copying data from a Microsoft Excel document and pasting it into a Microsoft Word document requires the software programs to interface.

- **Hyperlinks in Web-Based Applications**

  While surfing the Internet, users may have to click on hyperlinks in web-based applications to move to different webpages of a website.

- **Check/Text Boxes, Option/Command Buttons in Dialog Windows** (Figure 4.2)

  In many application programs, such as Microsoft Word, there are user interface objects that appear in dialogue windows when certain operations are performed. The user interface objects are:

  - Check boxes in which the user places a check mark to select one or more operations. If all check boxes are left unchecked, the user has not selected any operation. If one or more boxes are checked, the user has chosen to perform those desired operations. For example, the user can place a check mark in a bold-facing text check box as well as an underlining text check box and both operations will be performed.

  - Option buttons allow a user to select only one option button or no option button from a number of buttons. For example, if there are two option buttons marked as "Yes" or "No" to indicate whether you are a U.S. Veteran, then you must select either "Yes" or "No," not both.

  - Dialog boxes allow users to type text or select a mode of operation. For example, in a "Print" dialog box, users can select a printer from the list of printers displayed in "Printer Name" dialog box.

  - Command buttons, such as "Save," "OK," and "Cancel," when clicked, will execute a certain command such as saving a document or printing a document.

Figure 4.2 **"Print" Dialog Window with Check Boxes, Option Buttons, Dialog Boxes, Command Buttons and Text Boxes as User Interface**

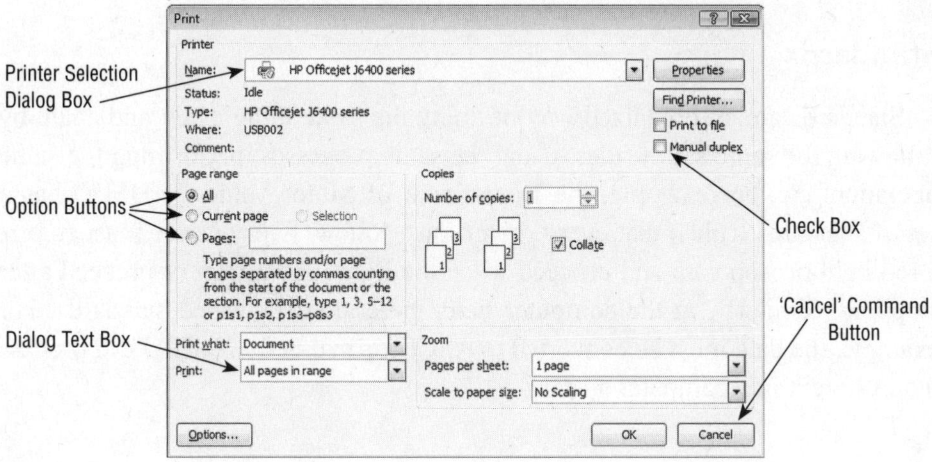

User Interface Design

User interface design is a process used to design how a user is able to interface with an information system, operating system, other programs, computer hardware or a website. The designed interface must meet the user's goals and objectives, and should make the user's interface as easy, simple and efficient as possible. User interface is used in computer systems, automobiles, commercial planes, home appliances, mobile computing devices, ATM machines, parking garages, and many more everyday items.

An efficient user interface design requires minimal input to achieve the desired output, and the system minimizes undesired outputs. Designing a user interface with the system may require creating menus, dialog boxes, check boxes, option buttons, command buttons, hyperlinks for Web pages, and constructing system prototypes.

When designing a user interface, it is important to be aware that there are different levels of users using the system. There are users who have only limited or no experience with the system, users who have experience in the basic functions of the system, and users who have experience in using almost all the functions of a system. The user interface must be able to adapt to all users.

4.6 DEVELOPMENT AND PURPOSES OF INFORMATION STANDARDS

Standards

Standards are an organized way of doing the same thing again and again by following the same set of rules, using the same processes, performing the same operation, etc. For example, the Department of Motor Vehicles (DMV) has a set of standards (rules) that every driver must follow. Every driver must stop at a red light or stop sign and proceed when the light turns green or proceed after stopping. Similarly, in the computer field, there are established standards. For example, the data must be converted to ASCII format before a CPU can process it and store it in a computer system.

Standards in Computer Technology

Standards in computer technology are sets of rules, conditions, and guidelines that enable organizations to use combinations of computer hardware/software from different manufacturers so they can communicate with each other. If standards are not set, then only hardware and software from the same company could be used together.

Standards in computer technology are set by a group of people or some organizations. Standards are set so that computers using hardware/software from different vendors are able to communicate with each other when sending, receiving, and exchanging data and information.

For example, a body known as the Institute of Electrical and Electronic Engineers (IEEE) sets the standards for all types of hardware used in the computer industry. IEEE not only sets standards for hardware used in computer technology, but it also sets standards for small sizes to large sizes all types of household appliances such as toasters, washing machines, and dryers, etc.

A body known as the American National Standards Institute (ANSI) is responsible for software used in computer. ANSI has set standards for a number of programming languages such as C, C++, and FORTRAN that are used in writing computer programs.

Information Standards

To send and receive information between different types of computers, standards have been set for programming languages, operating systems, data formats, hardware interfaces, and communication protocols. If these standards are not set, computers assembled by different vendors will not be able to communicate with each other to transfer data and information.

Programming Languages

Programming languages used in computers are C, C++, COBOL, FORTRAN, Java, Ada, Visual Basic.Net, etc. For processing of data, all programming language instructions must be converted to the machine language of particular computers. Current programming language software can be installed and executed on various types of platforms.

Operating Systems

The platform of a computer specifies the operating system and hardware used in assembling a computer. Various operating systems used in computers are Windows XP, Windows Vista, Windows 7, MAC, UNIX, and Linux. Various types of operating systems used on computers are multiuser, multiprocessing, real-time, multithreading, and multitasking.

Data Formats

Various important data types used in computers are text, number, audio, video, and Boolean. When combined, various data types form multimedia data. Data can be stored as a machine binary code file or a textual human readable file. Data files store binary data and text files store ASCII data. Multimedia files store a mixture of data types such as text, sound and images (pictures). In DBMS, data files store database information that can be queried, and other types of files, such as index files, are used to organize data and store administrative data.

Data Format Standards are set to write names, states, countries, dates, SSNs, etc. in a particular format. For example, a date must be written in mm/dd/yyyy format, and a SSN must be written in 012-34-5678 format.

Hardware Interface

Hardware interface is involved when different hardware devices are able to communicate with each other to exchange data and information.

Communication Protocols

When communicating, the sending and receiving devices must agree on the formats of the data involved. The set of rules defining the format of data is known as protocols. HTTP protocol defines how information pages are transferred from a host computer to a client computer when communicating over the Internet. FTP protocol defines the uploading and downloading of files between two computers over the Internet.

Internet Markup Languages Standards

W3 consortium has specification standards for Internet markup languages such as HTML, XHTML, CSS, and XML. These markup languages are used in webpage design.

Information System Development Standards

Development standards are a detailed and specific set of rules that describe all the activities that must take place for successful, efficient, and reliable development of an information system. Development standards include the following:

- Computer languages standards: Specify the computer languages that will be used to develop, use, and maintain the system.

- Computer platform standards: Specify the platform to be used to develop, use and maintain the system. The platform specifies the desktop and network operating systems, the peripheral devices, type of network, the user interfaces, and all other hardware or software.

- System management tools (such as CASE) standards: Tools used to develop, produce documentation, use, and maintain the system.

- Processes standards: The processes used to process data in the information system.

- Documentation standards: Documents all the standards listed above and all activities that are taking place in the development of the system.

- Quality Standards: Quality standards are set for all the standards listed above and any other activity that takes place in system development to meet business goals and hardware and software expectations.

Standards to Use Information System

Standards are used when a user wants to access and use an information system. The identity of the user must be established. Common ways of establishing the identity of the user include a User ID and password, fingerprints, or an iris scan. The system administrator can also give permission to a user to access and process information. Standards must be set for the use of operating systems, programming languages, and software tools in a system.

CHAPTER 5

Programming Concepts and Data Management

Programming Concepts and Data Management

5.1 ALGORITHM, SEMANTICS, AND PSEUDOCODE IN PROGRAMMING

Algorithm in Programming

Most people need to solve a simple or a complex problem daily. For example, a family going on vacation might systematically plan their daily activities for their entire vacation.

In computer terms, this type of planning is called an *algorithm*, which can be defined as a detailed and finite sequence of instructions or steps, written in a natural human language through the drawing of charts or the writing of pseudocode, to precisely specify what a computer program must do in order to complete a specific task or problem. As described and explained in Chapter 2, an algorithm is used to perform calculations to solve a particular problem in a systematic and simplified fashion.

Algorithms are implemented as computer programs, and every field of study has its own concept of creating and using algorithms.

Semantics in Programming

Semantics is the study of the meaning of a word or the interpretation of a written or spoken sentence or statement.

For example, in computer language, we write an assignment statement by saying "Assign value 12.99 to variable Price" or "Set the value of variable Price to 12.99." The semantics (meaning) of the assignment statement is that we are copying the value "12.99" to the variable called "Price," i.e., wherever the word "Price" appears, it will use the value 12.99.

Pseudocode in Programming

Pseudocode is a way of writing a computer algorithm in readable form, which can then be used as a basis to write an actual computer program. The pseudocode is, however, more structured and simpler than human language. A short, precise definition is "a program design tool that uses English-like statements to outline the logic of a program."

Figure 5.1 below represents an example of a pseudocode, in which the gross pay of an employee is calculated when the number of hours and the hourly pay rate are entered as input.

Figure 5.1   Pseudocode to Calculate Gross Pay of an Employee

1. Using the keyboard, input "number of hours worked this week."

2. Using the keyboard, input "hourly pay rate."

3. Multiply "hours worked" by "hourly pay rate," storing the result in "Gross Pay."

4. Print "hours worked," "hourly pay rate," and "Gross Pay."

5.2   PROGRAMMING LANGUAGE SYNTAX AND STRUCTURES (PSEUDOCODE)

As defined earlier in Chapter 2, a computer program (or software) is composed of a sequence of precise instructions that instructs the computer's hardware to perform a specific task and how to perform it. It can be a simple task, such as finding the average of two test scores, or a complex task, such as designing and manufacturing a robot used to assemble cars.

Programming is the act of creating and writing a computer program to perform a particular task, such as generating and printing an employee's payroll check.

5.3   PROGRAMMING LOGIC—SEQUENTIAL, LOOPING, AND DECISION PROGRAMMING

Programming logic involves human thinking to give correct and valid mathematical reasons (logic) in a step-by-step manner when writing a computer program that will perform a particular task or solve a particular problem.

Programming logic may involve making decisions during the execution of a computer program. For example, when deciding whether a student has passed or failed a test based on a test condition, the test condition would be "if the test score was greater than or equal to sixty, the student passes the test; otherwise, the student fails the test."

Types of programming logic used in writing a computer program may involve sequential, looping, decision, and event-driven control structures.

Sequential Programming

Sequential programming logic is a set of statements that is executed only once. The pseudocode written to find the gross pay in Figure 5.1 is an example of sequential programming logic, as the sequence of statements is executed only once.

Looping Programming

In *looping programming logic*, the same sets of statements are repeated a certain number of times. Looping programming logic is also known as repetition or iterative programming logic.

Using the syntax of programming language, we can add a few statements to the pseudocode written in Figure 5.1 to make the programming logic run (execute) five times as shown in Figure 5.2. Let's imagine that we want the LoopCount to start at 1 and end at 5. "Increment LoopCount by 1" means that 1 is added to the LoopCount each time four statements in our programming logic are executed once. In Figure 5.2, the statements written inside a pair of brackets{} forms the body of the loop (sequence of statements) to be executed every time the loop is run. The word "for" is a keyword used in C++ programming language to implement looping programming logic.

Figure 5.2   Pseudocode to Calculate Gross Pay Using Looping Programming Logic

```
            for (LoopCount = 1; LoopCount <= 5; LoopCount ++)

            {
            1. Input "number of hours worked this week."
Body        2. Input "hourly pay rate."
of   ───▶   3. Multiply "hours worked" by "hourly pay rate" storing the result
Loop           in "Gross Pay."
            4. Print "hours worked", "hourly pay rate" and "Gross Pay".
            }
```

The pseudocode in Figure 5.3 shows three different ways to display numbers 1 to 5 using looping programming logic. In the example, the word "SET" means to assign a value to the variable NUMBER.

Figure 5.3   Pseudocode to Display Numbers 1 to 5 Using Looping Programming Logic—Three Ways

1	2	3
SET NUMBER TO 1	SET NUMBER TO 1	NUMBER = 1
WHILE NUMBER < 5	WHILE NUMBER < 5	WHILE NUMBER < 5
PRINT NUMBER	PRINT NUMBER	PRINT NUMBER
SET NUMBER TO NUMBER + 1	INCREMENT NUMBER BY 1	NUMBER = NUMBER + 1
END WHILE	END WHILE	END WHILE

Decision Programming

Decision programming logic, also known as selection programming logic, selects one choice from a number of different operations that can be performed based on the outcome of some test condition applied to a variable such as a test score.

Different programming languages use special keywords or reserved words to implement the selection programming language logic. For example, the decision programming logic to allocate a letter grade based on the outcome of a test score using multiple "If" statements is shown below.

The variable "Score" stores the value of a test score, and the variable "LetterGrade" stores the assigned letter grade based on the value of the test score. Words such as "If" and "AND" are reserved words used in many programming languages to apply decision programming logic. The word "AND" indicates that the conditions specified on its left and right sides must be satisfied for the entire operation to be true. The semicolon (;) is used to mark the end of a programming language statement, the same way a period (.) is used to mark the end of a sentence in the English language.

If (Score >= 90 AND Score <=100) LetterGrade = 'A';

If (Score >= 80 AND Score <=89) LetterGrade = 'B';

If (Score >= 70 AND Score <=79) LetterGrade = 'C';

If (Score >= 60 AND Score <= 69) LetterGrade = 'D';

If (Score >= 00 AND Score <=59) LetterGrade = 'F';

The following pseudocode (Figure 5.4) shows the logic in a section of a computer program to assign a letter grade based on the input test score. In our example, the word "SET" means to assign value 'F' to LetterGrade. In many programming languages, single alphabet characters such as, F (for fail) or P (for pass), are written inside a pair of single quotes as shown by the pseudocode in Figure 5.4.

Figure 5.4   Pseudocode to Display Letter Grade
Using Decision Programming Logic—Three Ways

1	2	3
IF SCORE <60	IF SCORE <60	IF SCORE >=60
SET LetterGrade TO 'F'	LetterGrade = 'F'	LetterGrade = 'P'
END IF	END IF	ELSE
IF SCORE >=60	IF SCORE >=60	LetterGrade = 'F'
SET LetterGrade TO 'P'	LetterGrade = 'P'	END IF
END IF	END IF	

Event-Driven Programming

An *event* is a signal to a program that something has happened or occurred and the program must perform some operation to deal with the occurrence of that event. Various events in programming languages or application programs are "mouse single click," "mouse double click," and mouse movement when performing an operation. For example, a user highlights the file name in a file name list box and double-clicks the left mouse button to open the selected file.

Programming languages, such as Visual Basic and Java, are event-driven programming languages and use graphical user interfaces to start an event. Figure 5.5 shows the event concept using an example from Visual Basic Programming language. In this example, two numbers will be added when we click the "Click to Add 2 Numbers" command button.

Figure 5.5   VB Program to Add Two Numbers—Describing Event Concept

Label 1 Object	→ Number 1	12	← Text Box to input Number 1
Label 2 Object	→ Number 2	13	← Text Box to input Number 2
Label 3 Object	→ Sum of 2 Numbers	25	← Label displaying the Sum of 2 numbers.

Command Button Object "Clidk to add 2 Numbers" → [Click to Add 2 Numbers] [Exit] ← Exit command button to exit application.

VBProgFig4.5 - Add Two Numbers

The Visual Basic Code to Add 2 Numbers Application Program is as follows:

```
Public Class FrmVBProg45
    Private Sub BtnExit_Click(ByVal sender As System.Object, ByVal e As System.
    EventArgs) Handles BtnExit.Click
        Me.Close()
    End Sub
        Private Sub BtnAdd2Nums_Click(ByVal sender As System.Object, ByVal e As
        System.EventArgs) Handles BtnAdd2Nums.Click
            Dim Num1 As Integer, Num2 As Integer, Sum As Integer
            Num1 = Val(TxtOne.Text)
            Num2 = Val(TxtTwo.Text)
            Sum = Num1 + Num2
            LblSum.Text = Sum
        End Sub
    End Class
```

5.4   OBJECT-ORIENTED PROGRAMMING AND OBJECT-ORIENTED METHODS

Object-Oriented Programming (OOP)

OOP perceives everything as an object, where every object has a unique identity, displays some state, and exhibits some behavior. An object is a noun representing an entity that exists distinctly in the world. For example, a place, a thing, a real person, a geometrical shape (e.g., a circle), a city, a student, a book, and a bank account are considered to be objects in object-oriented programming languages.

In short, OOP can be defined as an approach to program design in which a program consists of a collection of objects that contain data and methods to be used with that data.

Unique Identity of an Object

Every object created has a unique identity. For example, every person employed or living in the U.S. has a unique Social Security Number; every manufactured car has a unique vehicle identification number (VIN); every student attending a college has a unique student ID number; every patient admitted to a hospital has a unique patient ID number, and so on.

State of Objects

Every object exhibits a certain state, which is described by the characteristics (data fields) having certain current values. For example, every student object in a class has a unique student ID, has a current semester GPA, is enrolled in certain subjects every semester, is of a certain age in the current semester, belongs to certain student clubs in the current semester, and so on.

Behavior of an Object

The behavior of an object is controlled by a set of methods. When called, methods ask the object to perform some task or an operation. We will discuss methods in more detail later in this chapter. For example, we write methods for how to calculate the GPA of a student, how to enroll a student in a particular course, how to display a letter grade in a particular course for a particular student, and so on.

Classes in OOP

A class in OOP is data structure that defines the data fields and the methods to operate on those data fields in the same unit. Furthermore, in OOP, objects of the same type are treated as belonging to one class. For example, when discussing a student as an object, a group of students that are registered in the same course (i.e., Math131) is a group of students belonging to the same class of Math131. The class is a collection of similar types of objects. All the students in this particular class of Math131 are taught by the same teacher; all the students are studying the same course material; all the students meet in the same room every day of the week for the same number of hours, etc. When creating a class of similar objects, we specify the name of the class, the data fields, and methods that will operate on the data fields to change the state of a particular object.

Object Instantiation

An object of a class is known as an instance of a class, and the process of creating an object is known as instantiation. It means that the terms *object* and *instance* are synonyms. A *class* is a collection of similar or identical objects. Once a class is defined, one can create as many objects as desired. In our example of the Math131 course, we can create one class or a section of 25 students. But if more students are trying to enroll in the Math131 course, we can create more sections of the same course. No matter how many sections of the Math131 course we have, each object (student) in each section is controlled by the same concept of OOP; that is, each object has a unique ID, has the same number of data fields, and is manipulated (operated upon) by the same methods.

Encapsulation in OOP

In the OOP approach, all objects of the same class are associated with the same data fields and the same methods. The details of how the method works are hidden from the user or client who calls the method. This process is known as encapsulation or data hiding.

Object-Oriented Methods in a Class of Objects

A *method*, also known as a sub-routine, consists of a set of programming statements that can perform some action on the data fields of an object in order to change the state of that object; input values in data fields when creating a new object; and display the current value stored in the data fields of a particular object. Object-oriented methods include static methods, instance methods, accessor method, constructor methods, destructor methods, mutator methods, and dummy codes.

Static Method or Class Method

When a method has an association with a class as a whole, it is called a static or class method. For example, a method that keeps track of the total number of objects created in a class.

Instance Method

When a method is related to an object or an instance of a class, it is known as an instance method. Instance methods are passed a hidden reference (such as "Me" and "this") of an object in OOP. For example, in Figure 5.5 in a VB program, in order to add two numbers, the statement 'Me.Close()' is passing a reference of the current form (Me) object to Close() method that stops the execution of the current VB project.

Accessor Method

The accessor method provides a way to access a particular state of the object from another part of the program. For example, if there is the method "getGPA" for a student class, then "getGPA" will access and retrieve the current GPA of the student in question.

Constructor Method

Constructor methods are special methods in OOP that are called upon automatically when an object of a class is created. In programming languages such as C++, the constructor methods have the same name as the name of the class itself. The main purpose of the constructor methods is to provide initial values of data fields when an object is created. In the event a programmer does not provide a constructor method when writing an object-oriented program, then the compiler provides a default constructor.

Destructor Method

Destructor methods are special methods in OOP that are called upon automatically when an object of a class goes out of existence. In programming languages such as C++, the destructor methods have the same name as the name of the class itself preceded by a special character called a tilde (~).

Mutator Method (Modifier or Update Method)

The mutator method is a method that changes or modifies the state of an object. For example, the "setGPA" method will assign a new value to the GPA datafield of a student when the GPA of a course the student has recently passed is included.

Dummy Codes

Dummy codes are inserted in a program skeleton to simulate processing and avoid compilation error messages. They may involve empty method declarations.

5.5   DATA TYPES

To store data in a computer system and to achieve efficient data management, data type must be understood as well as the data types used to store data in each column of a table inside a database. As mentioned earlier, a database table contains columns (field-names) and rows (records or tuples). In Chapter 2, the terms *data, information*, and *data type* were defined. Also introduced were basic data types used for storing data in a computer information system. Below is a brief review on data types in computers.

Data type specifies the kind of value that can be stored in each column of a database table and the type of operations that can be performed on those values. For example, to count the number of students present in a class, integer (whole number) data type for a column (named "StudentCount") in a table that represents the number of students in a particular class must be used. Character data type would be used in a column (named "StudentName") in a table that describes the name of a student.

Operations Performed on Values Stored in a Column

An addition operation can be performed on a column (named "Student-Count") to count the number of students registered in a specific school of a college. An addition operation cannot be performed on a column named "StudentName" because the column contains character data type.

Selecting Data Type for a Column

Data is selected for each column in a table for three reasons.

First, a table structure needs to be created in order to store data in a table. A database program such as Oracle requires specification of the column names and the data types for each column (field names) in a table.

Second, all the computer programs perform error checking when a value is entered for the selected column in a table. For example, if the name of a student is entered in the "StudentCount" column, the computer program generates an error, and we cannot proceed until we enter the correct data type (integer) for the "StudentCount" column.

Third, all database programs allocate and use storage space more efficiently when the data type of columns is specified. For example, an integer data type column occupies 2 bytes of memory space, and floating point numbers may occupy 4 bytes of memory space. If we select floating point numbers as the data type for integer data type values, the program will work correctly as both are number data types. But the execution of the computer program will slow down because the computer has to read more memory spaces as compared to required memory spaces.

Data Types

Programming languages use different data types in their programs. For example, an Oracle database uses four basic data types: number, character (or string), date and time, and Boolean (see Table 5.1).

Table 5.1   Basic Data Types for Columns in a Table of Oracle Databases

Data Type	Syntax	Description	Example
Number	Integer Numbers ColName Number(N);	Stores whole number by specifying N number of digits used to store values	CityPopulation Number (10);
	Fixed Point Numbers ColName Number (M,N);	Contains a fixed N number of digits after the decimal point	Price Number(5,2);
	Floating Point Numbers ColName Number;	Contains a variable number of digits after the decimal point	InterestRate Number;
Character	ColName VARCHAR2(Size);	Stores variable-length characters, where values for a particular column in different rows will have a different number of characters.	FirstName VarChar2(20);
	ColName CHAR(Size);	Stores a fixed number of characters	SSN Char(9);
Date & Time	ColName Date;	Stores date and time. Stores date in DD-MON-YY format. Stores time in HH:MI:SS format	DOB Date;
Boolean	ColName Boolean;	Stores true/false values T for true and F for false	USVeteran Boolean;

Integer Data Types

Integer data types are whole number values. Examples include the population of a city, the number of students in a class, the number of books sold in a bookstore, etc.

Real Number (Floating) Data Types

Real number data types hold values such as the GPA of a student or the selling price of a shirt.

Single Character Data Types

When a single alphabet character needs to be stored as a value in a data field, the value to be stored is written within single quotes. For example, the middle initial of a person's name would be stored as 'D.'

String Data Types

A string is a data type that stores a sequence of data values, usually bytes. The elements of the string represent characters which adhere to a specific encoding. String data allows values, such as street addresses and names of cities, states, or diseases, to be stored. Many programming languages have "string" data type built into them. Some programming languages treat string data as an array (a collection or sequence) of characters. Other programming languages, such as Java and C++, treat string data as an object and provide a string class for storing and processing string objects. String data, depending on the language, can be either mutable or immutable. If a string is immutable, its contents cannot be changed once it is created.

In the example below, the first statement creates a string object with the value "one" stored in the memory reference "Any." In the second statement, a new string object is created with the value "two" stored in the memory reference "Any," thus replacing the old value "one" with a new value "two" and making it impossible to reference the old value "one." String objects are immutable, that is, they cannot be changed once they are created.

String Any = "one";

String Any = "two";

GIF, JPEG Files

Animated images are GIF files in computers. JPEG/Exif and JPEG/JFIF are the most common formats for storing and transmitting photographic images on the Web.

Boolean Data Type

Boolean data type, also known as logical data type, is used in computers to represent the concept of True (number 1) and False (number 0). Boolean data type is used to test an expression that is then used to control the programming structures such as a selection control structure (using if /then/else construct in C++) or in a looping control structure (using "for," "while," or "do" while in C++).

In C++, "bool" is a reserved word to represent Boolean data type values "true" and "false," which are also reserved words in C++ and are used as values in expressions. In C++, the following syntax (see Figure 5.6) is used to test an expression using selection control structure, in which the "if" part represents operation 1 to be performed when the "test expression" yields the "true" value, and the "else" part represents operation 2 to be performed when the "test expression" yields the "false" value.

**Figure 5.6 Boolean Data Type in C++, Its Syntax
and Example of Use of Selection Control Structure**

C++ Syntax	C++ Example	Explanation of C++ statement in example

if (test expression) //true
    Do operation 1;
else   //false
    Do operation 2;
	int TestScore;
	cout <<"\nEnter Test Score? ";
	cin >> TestScore;
	if (TestScore >= 60)
	    cout <<"\nYou passed the exam.";
	else
	    cout <<"\nSorry, you failed the exam.";
		—Declares TestScore as integer variable
		—Message to input TestScore
		—User enters the TestScore
		—Test expression—if TestScore is >= 60
		    —true value, prints "You passed the exam."
		    —else part of test expression
		—Else prints "Sorry, you failed the exam."

Binary (Machine-Readable) Data Type

The data stored in a binary file is stored in binary form and designed to be read by computer programs. Many classes created in programming languages, such as Java, are stored in binary files and are read by a Java Virtual Machine (JVM). The data stored in a binary file is an exact replica of the data stored internally within the computer system and is also referred to as an unformatted file. It is faster to process a binary file than a text file (formatted file), in which data is stored in a human-readable form.

Enumerated Data Type

Programming languages such as C++ have built-in (pre-defined) data types such as integer, float, Boolean, character, and string. These data types are declared and represented using keywords specific to each data type. For example, in C++, integer data type is declared using the keyword "int."

Programmers encounter situations where it is more efficient to execute a program if a programming language allows programmers to create user-defined data types. Some programming languages, such as C++, use the keyword "enum" to allow the user to create user-defined data type along with a list of acceptable values in the newly created data type. Enumerated data types don't exist as known or built-in data type in a programming language, but once defined, they are recognized as data type in the programs of that programming language. For example, the following C++ statement allows the user to create user-defined data type: "Months" having "Jan," "Feb" . . ., "Nov", and "Dec" as acceptable values, that is, any variable that is declared as "Months" data type can only accept "Jan," "Feb," . . . , "Nov," or "Dec" as valid values.

enum Months {Jan, Feb, Mar, Apr, May, Jun, Jul, Aug, Sep, Oct, Nov, Dec};

Furthermore, the statement below declares the variables "Birth" and "New-Year" as "Month" data type and will be accepted as valid user-defined data type in C++ programs:

enum Month Birth, NewYear;

5.6 DATA STRUCTURES

In computer programming language, *structure* refers to how data or information is stored in a computer system. *Data structure* is a scheme to structure (arrange or organize) data so that data of varied types can be entered, stored, sorted, retrieved, and manipulated by a computer program efficiently. Data structure provides different ways of storing and using all the varying data type values discussed above in a computer system.

In programming languages, data structures are implemented as data types, the relationship between data types, and the operations that can be performed on them. Oracle SQL is one of the computer programs used to structure data.

In the business world, computers store data in the form of records in table form, and the relational database design offers a powerful approach to store data in tables. In relational databases, tables are linked and operations can be performed such as querying a database, or adding, deleting, updating, and sorting records in a table of a database.

For example, to store data about a book, the title of the book is needed, as well as the subject it deals with, the name of the author, information about the author, the number of pages, the ISBN, the year of publication, etc. In order to create a data structure for a book, an object-oriented programming concept is used by creating Abstract Data Types (ADT), which is done by simply storing a number of built-in data types under one programmer-selected group name.

Abstract Data Type (ADT)

In OOP, Abstract Data Type (ADT) is used to create user-defined data type (known as ADT) by collecting a number of data fields of built-in data types of programming language and methods to perform operations on those data fields as one unit. ADT is used to deal with a particular type of object such as "Date" and "Time."

Creating ADT for "Date"

Businesses deal with all kinds of dates on a regular basis. Dates of arrivals and departure, birth dates, appointment date, shipping dates, and hiring dates of employees are some basic examples. In OOP, "Date" is created as an ADT by grouping three built-in integer data type data fields to represent the month, day, and year and the function to operate on these data fields.

The C++ programming language creates "Date" as ADT by using the keyword "class." The created "Date" ADT can be used for many instances (objects) such as date of birth, date of employment, etc. For example, "DOB" and "Employment" are instances (objects) of the "Date" class. The data members (month, day, and year) of the "Date" class are listed as private so that they are only visible to functions of the Date class only. C++ uses // (two forward slashes) to insert comments in a program, which are not executed in the program.

In the C++ programming language, "GetDate," "DisplayDate," and "Date" are three member functions of the "Date" class and are used to operate on three data members (month, day, and year) of the "Date" class. The member functions are listed as public so that they can be used by other classes if the "Date" class is included in another class.

Figure 5.7   Create a "Date" Object (ADT) in C++

Line #	
1	#include<iostream.h>
2	#include<iomanip.h>
3	// Class declaration section—Lines 4 to 11
4	class Date // class is used to create ADT—the ADT name is class
5	{ private:
6	int Month, Day, Year; // Three built-in int data fields of Date ADT—Data Members
7	public:
8	Date(int = 03, int = 25, int = 2010); // a constructor—Member function
9	int GetDate(); // a function to input data members from keyboard—Member function
10	int DisplayDate(); // a function to display date—Member function
11	};
12	// Class Implementation section—Lines 13 to 27—to provide the definition of member functions
13	Date::Date(int NMonth, int NDay, int NYear) // Constructor member function
14	{ Month = NMonth;
15	Day = NDay;
16	Year = NYear;
17	}
18	int Date::GetDate() // GetDate member function to input data members from the keyboard
19	{ cout<<"\nEnter Month: "; cin>>Month;
20	cout<<"\nEnter Day: "; cin>> Day;
21	cout<<"\nEnter Year: "; cin>> Year;
22	}
23	int Date::DisplayDate() // DisplayDate member function to display data members

(Continued)

Figure 5.7 (continued)

Line #	
24	{ cout <<setfill('0');
25	cout << setw(2) << Month <<'/'<< setw(2) << Day << '/' << Year << "\n";
26	return 0;
27	}
28	main() // main( ) function controls the execution of program
29	{ Date DOB(12,26,1989); // Declare and initialize 'DOB' object in 'Date' class (ADT)
30	Date Employment; // Declare Employment object in 'Date' class (ADT)
31	Employment.GetDate(); // 'GetDate' function is called to input data members for Employment object
32	, cout <<"\nDate of Birth is : "; DOB.DisplayDate(); // Display data members of DOB object
33	cout <<"\nDate of Employment is : ";Employment.DisplayDate(); // Display data members of Employment object
34	system("pause");
35	}
36	/*
37	Enter Month: 12
38	Enter Day: 13
39	Enter Year: 1958
40	Date of Birth is : 12/26/1989
41	Date of Employment is : 12/13/1958
42	*/

Table 5.2   Line-by-Line Explanation of C++ program in Figure 5.7

Line #	Explanation
1 and 2	Header files required to input data and format data before displaying
4 to 11	Class declaration section to select ADT name, the data fields (members), and member functions names that will perform operations on data fields.
13 to 27	Describe class implementation section to provide the working details of each member function of Date class. Lines 13 to 17 describe a constructor member function 'Date' used to provide values of data members at the time of creation of an object. For example, in line 29 at the time of creation of DOB object, the data members are set to 12/26/1989 indicating the date of birth is 12/26/1989.
	Lines 18 to 22 describe a member function 'GetDate' that allows a user to input data members during the execution of a program. This member function is called in line 31 for employment object, and data member values 12, 13, and 1958 were input in lines 37, 38, and 39 for this object. Employment object was declared on line 30.
	Lines 23 to 27 describe a member function 'DisplayDate' that displays the data members of the 'Date' class. Lines 32 and 33 call 'DisplayDate' function to display DOB and Employment objects.

(Continued)

Table 5.2 (continued)

Line #	Explanation
28 to 35	They belong to main ( ) function of a C++ program. The main ( ) function controls the execution of the entire C++ program. All the statements (lines 29 to 35) written inside a pair of { } forms the body of main () function. · Line 28 is the function header line of the main () function. · Line 29 declares and initializes the data members to 12, 26, and 1989 for the"DOB" object in "Date" class. In other words, DOB is 12/26/1989. · Line 30 declares 'Employment' object of 'Date' class. · Line 31 calls 'GetDate" function to input data members of Employment object from the keyboard during the execution of program. The input values for data members were 12 for Month (line 37), 13 for day (line 38), and 1958 for year (line 38)
28 to 35	· Line 32 displays the data members of the DOB object in date format as 12/26/1989. · Line 33 displays the data members of the Employment object in date format as 12/13/1958. · Line 34 is only used when you type and execute the C++ program using 'Dev-C++' as a text editor.
36 to 42	They are not typed as part of the program. They are the output of the C++ program and are copied and pasted as comments (written between /* . . . */) from the output screen of a C++ program.

Inheritance in OOP

Further in ADT, a newly-created ADT can inherit data members and member functions from previously created ADTs, the same way a child can inherit property or money from his parents, as well as his grandparents.

5.7 TYPES OF DATA STRUCTURES

Types of data structures include files, strings, linked lists, lists (one dimensional array), tables (two-dimensional arrays), records, heterogeneous array (structs and classes), stacks and queues, and trees. Each of these basic structures has many variations and allows different operations to be performed on the data stored in a computer.

Files and File Types

A file collects data or information as one unit. It has a name, known as a filename, and is stored (saved) on secondary storage devices such as a hard disk or a flash drive of a computer. The file can be opened by highlighting the name of the file in a file open option of the program used to create the file.

Program files, data files, text files, and binary files are all types of files used in computers. The type of program used to create the file and the data stored in the file is indicated by the extension part of the filename. Some of the common extensions used in a filename along with the data stored in them are listed in Table 5.3 below.

Table 5.3   Extension in Filenames and their Corresponding Program

Extension	Program Used to Create a File
.doc	Microsoft Word—Office 2003, a Word Processor
.docx	Microsoft Word—Office 2007, a Word Processor
.xls	Microsoft Excel—Office 2003, a spreadsheet
.xlsx	Microsoft Excel—Office 2007, a spreadsheet
.ppt	Microsoft PowerPoint—Office 2003, PowerPoint presentation
.pptx	Microsoft PowerPoint—Office 2007, PowerPoint presentation
.CPP	Dev-C++, or Turbo C++, a C++ program,
.VB	Microsoft Visual Studio, a Visual Basic program
.eml	E-mail message
.psb	Photoshop's Large Document Format
.wmv	Windows Media Video
.vob	DVD video object file
.bin	Binary file
.mp4	MP4—MPEG-4 video file format
.dat	Data files
.txt	Any program that can read text files
.pdf	Adobe Acrobat Reader—portable document file
.htm or .html	Hypertext Markup Language, Web page design
.bmp	Windows, a Bitmap image
.zip	WinZip, a compressed file
.bak	backup file—used by many applications and often created automatically

Program Files

Program files are stored as a folder in an operating system, where all of the application programs that are not part of the operating system are installed and stored by default. Each program is placed in its own subfolder where all of the related binary files of the program are also stored. The user can select the name of the program subfolder, but usually the default subfolder name suggested by the program is chosen. For example, to go to a particular program's subfolder, at the task bar the user clicks Start, All Programs, and the subfolder of the desired program. To open Microsoft Word, at the task bar, the user clicks Start, All Programs, Microsoft Office, Microsoft Word.

Binary Files

A binary file or unformatted file stores data in a file format that is an exact representation of the data stored internally within a computer. The data stored in a binary file is not formatted. The data that is underlined, boldfaced, etc., is considered formatted data. Binary files are usually not able to be edited with a word-processing program.

Text Files

Text files or formatted files are files that store formatted data. Such files store their data in ASCII code. Data in a text file is stored as continuous lines and the end of file (EOF) is marked by an end of file character at the end of the last line. Text files are used to store information. Text files are given ".txt" extensions and can be read by any program that reads text. Text files are considered platform independent. ASCII file formats can usually be inspected and modified with an appropriate text or word-processing program.

Data Files

Data files store data that is read and processed by a program file. As shown below in Figure 5.8, data files may hold a number of records. Each part of the data field (First Name, Last Name, etc.) in a record is separated by a space. In almost all computer programming languages, a program can be written to write data to an empty data file. Another program can be written to read the data stored in a data file and process it to generate information. The data stored in the data file shown in Figure 5.8 is used to print payroll checks of employees.

Figure 5.8   Records Stored in a Data File

First Name	Last Name	Hours Worked	Pay Rate	Federal Tax Rate	State Tax Rate
John	Smith	40	10.99	0.15	0.08
Allisa	Jones	38	12.50	0.18	0.10
. . .	. . .	. . .	. . .	. . .	. . .

Random Access and Sequential Access Files

Sequential Access Files

Text files are sequential access files as the data stored in them has to be read sequentially.

Random Access Files

Files stored in a storage medium such as a hard disk, are called random access files. The files can be directly accessed without opening other files.

Digital Files

Digital files are files that store data in two discrete states: on (1) and off (0). Digital 0 represents the "off" state indicating an absence of an electronic charge, and digital 1 represents the "on" state indicating the presence of an electronic charge.

Computers use a binary system made up of two digits, 0 and 1, known as bits (short for "binary digits"). A *bit* is the smallest unit of data a computer can process. All characters typed from the keyboard are represented in a group of eight bits, known as a byte. One byte can display 256 (2^8) combinations of 0s and 1s.

Digital files are used extensively for transferring data. For example, a digital camera stores photographic images in digital form on a card or a strip. Those images can then be transferred to a computer by connecting the digital camera to a computer via a USB cable. In fact, a user can directly insert the card into a computer slot to view the digital images on a computer screen.

In the entertainment industry, video, gaming, audio, recording, and computing can be shared seamlessly. Songs are recorded in digital format. Items such as televisions, MP3 players, and iPods can be connected to a home computer to transfer or view data. For example, a user can view digital images on a television screen by connecting a computer to the television with an HDMI cable. Various digital image file types are JPG, GIF, TIFF, PNG, and BMP.

Audio Files

Audio files provide sound when you listen to downloaded MP3 files or live broadcasts through Internet radio.

Video Files

Video files are video clips displayed on a computer when it is connected to the website of a particular company. Movies and television shows can also be watched over the Internet for free. For example, if a user visits a website of a major league baseball team, he can watch highlights of a game in video clips.

File-Naming Conventions

Every file stored is given a name according to file-naming conventions. A file name is a name assigned to a file in order to secure a storage location in the computer's memory.

According to the 8.3 file-naming convention, file names have eight characters, optionally followed by a period (.) and a file name extension of three characters. This convention was used for MS-DOS computers before Windows 95 and Windows 98 were introduced. For example, for a file named "Resume.doc," "Resume" represents the file name and ".doc" represents the three letter extension.

Windows supports file names of up to 255 characters in length. Windows also generates an MS-DOS-compatible (short) file name in 8.3 format, to allow MS-DOS-based or 16-bit Windows-based programs to access the files.

Extensions in a File Name

When saving a file created in Windows OS, adding the extension to a file name is not necessary as the application program used automatically adds a three- or four-letter extension. The extension part of the full filename allows the OS to identify the file type as well as the program that was used to create the file.

File Path

The location of a file is specified in its file path, which starts with the letter of the drive it is stored in, followed by the folders and subfolders it is stored in. The file path creates a tree, like a hierarchical structure, to access a file. In the file path name, the backslash character (\), known as a delimiting character, separates folder and subfolder names. Depending on which operating system is used, other delimiting characters include the colon (:) and the forward slash (/). File paths are also used when a user visits the website of a company as well as in the construction of Uniform Resource Locators (URLs).

In the example below, the path for the location of the file Resume.doc is shown. In this path, the folder "Jones" is at the root directory level (drive C); "JobApplications" is a subfolder under the "Jones" folder; and the "Resume. doc" file is located under the subfolder "JobApplications."

C:\Jones\JobApplications\Resume.doc

5.8 FILE STRUCTURES

A file structure is a description of the way in which data is stored in a file. The computer organizes files so that the data and information stored in the files can be retrieved and used easily. File structure is basically a computerized filing system.

How Files Are Stored

Named files are stored on the storage devices of a computer system, such as a hard disk or a file server (known as server computer) on a computer network. Each of them enables user access to the data stored in those files. The hard drive is made up of platters, tracks, sectors, etc., as discussed in previous chapters. Every hard disk has a root directory (folder), and a user creates a hierarchy of file folders (folders, subfolders, files) on the hard drive to store the files and allow easy access to the data in the files. Each file name on a hard disk is usually connected to an index in a file allocation table, such as the FAT in a DOS file system, or an inode in a Unix-like file system.

A database is a kind of file structure used for the storage, organization, manipulation, and retrieval of data stored in tables (equivalent to files). Database concepts will be discussed later in this chapter.

Types of File Structures

The following file structures are used in computer systems: hierarchical, network, sequential, indexed, and hash.

Hierarchical File Structure

In the hierarchical file structure, the folders are arranged in a scheme that resembles a family tree with folders related to one another, from top to bottom, where the file at the bottom of the hierarchy stores the actual data or information. Figure 5.9 shows a hierarchical file structure with the following characteristics:

- C:\ is the root directory on the hard disk and is called a parent node.

- "Engineering" and "Business" are Level 1 folders and are created directly below the root directory C:\ . These are known as child nodes (folders).

- The "Electrical" and "Chemical" subfolders are also child nodes and are created at Level 2 below the "Engineering" folder (which becomes the parent folder).

- The "Finance" and "Marketing" subfolders are known as child nodes and are created at Level 2 below the "Business" folder (which becomes the parent folder).

- "Richard" (child) and "Alice" (child) are two Level 3 files below the "Electrical" (parent) subfolder and store the data or information.

In the hierarchical file structure, there is a parent-child relationship between the folders at the current level and the level above. Every child folder can have one *and only one* parent folder, except the root directory, which does not have any parent folder.

Figure 5.9 Hierarchical File Structure

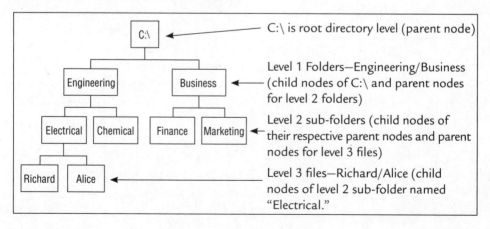

Network File Structure

In network file structure, the records are arranged in groups, and each group is known as a set. These sets are connected to each other in a number of ways. A network file system is a computer file system that supports the sharing of files, printers, and other resources as persistent storage over a computer network.

In network file structure, a particular file at one level can have more than one parent file. Also, a child file can have content from more than one parent file. In OOP, when creating a new class (ADT), it can include ADTs from many other previously created ADTs. For example, the "Child" ADT can have data members such as "DateOfBirth" and "TimeOfBirth," where "DateOfBirth" is an object of a previously created ADT "Date," and "TimeOfBirth" is an object of a previously created ADT "Time."

Figure 5.10 shows what a network file structure might look like using the OOP concept. It has the following characteristics:

- Imagine that A through G each are ADTs in OOP.
- ADTs B, C, and D each contain an object from previously created ADT "A."
- ADTs B, C, and D are child ADTs and A is a parent ADT.
- ADT "E" contains objects from previously created ADTs "B" and "C"
- ADT "F" contains objects from previously created ADTs "C" and "D"
- ADT "G" contains objects from previously created ADTs "E" and "F"

Figure 5.10   Network File Structure

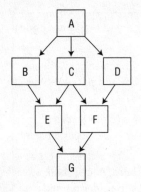

Sequential File Structure

A sequential file structure is a structure in which the data in a file is accessed and processed in a serial manner from beginning to end, in the order that the data was written during the creation of a file. The data file created in Figure 5.8 is an example of a sequential file structure, because the date fields were stored and read in the order of First Name, Last Name, Hours Worked, Pay Rate, Federal Tax Rate, and State Tax Rate.

Indexed File Structure

In sequential files, data is accessed and processed only in the order in which it was written to a file.

In the event access was needed for a particular record without reading other records, the solution would be to create an index for a file that stores data. The index for a file is created by selecting a primary key (PK) from a list of data fields in a file. An index file contains the index to a data file based on a selected primary key that allows quick access to a particular record in the data file. The index to a data file is stored in a separate file and contains a list of the ordered PK values and the corresponding recording number in a data file. An index file works exactly like an index in the back of a book. Listing topics in ascending alphabetical order creates the index.

Social Security Number (SSN) and the Vehicle Identification Number (VIN) of a car are good examples of data fields that can be used to create an index. As mentioned earlier, the PK identifies a unique record in a data file. The concept of indexing in databases will be discussed later in this chapter.

Hash Files, Hash Tables, and Hash Function

Hashing finds the location of a data item or record stored in the memory directly from the PK value, rather than looking for a PK value in the index table and then searching for the corresponding record in a data file. When a hash function is applied to records stored in permanent storage such as a hard drive, a file known as a hash file is created.

Hash table

When a hash function is applied to records stored in RAM, a hash table is created.

Buckets and Hash Function in a Hashing Scheme

In a hashing scheme, storage is divided into a number of partitions, known as buckets, where each bucket can store a number of records. Using an algorithm, a hash function converts the key value of each record into a bucket number and then stores that record in the calculated bucket number. To access a record using a hash function, the key value is converted to a bucket number, and then the contents of the calculated bucket number are retrieved in order to search for the desired record.

The steps in a hashing scheme are as follows:

1. Decide how many buckets are needed to store all the records. If 15 buckets are needed, they are numbered as 0 to 14.

2. Divide the key value of the record by the number of buckets and find the remainder.

3. Store that record in a bucket number equivalent to the remainder value obtained in step 2.

4. When steps 1, 2, and 3 are applied to each key value of a record, a file known as hash file is created.

Figure 5.11 shows how to apply a hashing scheme to find the bucket number of records using their key values, imagining that we want to create 25 buckets to store records.

Figure 5.11   Example of a Hashing Scheme

Record #	Key Value	Key Value ÷ 25	Remainder	Bucket Number
1	145	145 ÷ 25	20	20
2	56	56 ÷ 25	6	6
3	134	134 ÷ 25	9	9
4	26	26 ÷ 25	1	1
5	50	50 ÷ 25	0	0

5.9 OTHER DATA STRUCTURES

One-Dimensional Array

A one-dimensional array data structure, also known as a list, is a collection of data items of the same data type, under one group name, and stored in continuous locations of a computer's memory. Such a list is called a contiguous list of data items and is used to store data items when the size (number of data items) in the list is fixed. In computers, a list of the same data type items is known as a "homogenous array."

A list can contain the names of persons, cities, employees, books, or other groups of the same data items. The start of the list is called the head and the end of the list is called the tail. Figure 5.12 shows a list of names of cities. Each item in the list is known as an element.

Figure 5.12 A List of Names of Cities

New York
London
Sydney
Bombay
Toronto
Madrid

In C++ programming language, the list of prices (float data type) of four elements (any item can be an element) is declared and assigned values using the statement shown below in Figure 5.13. Using the list, one can search for a particular element or sort the elements in ascending or descending order. Many other operations can be performed on elements in the list as well.

Figure 5.13 One-Dimensional Array (List) of Prices

Declare and Initialize Array (list) : float Prices[4] = {22.99, 45.99, 23.79, 12.49};				
Subscript of Elements	0	1	2	3
Element Accessed as	Price[0]	Price[1]	Price[2]	Price[3]
Value Stored in Element	22.99	45.99	23.79	12.49

In a one-dimensional array structure, each element is accessed by its own position with respect to its start position, known as "subscript." In many programming languages, the subscript starts from 0 (zero) and the last subscript is always one less than the actual size (number of elements). In our example on the prices of four shirts, the subscripts are 0, 1, 2, and 3. The elements are accessed as Price[0], Price[1], Price[2], and Price[3]. One-dimensional array structures use only one subscript to access each element.

A one-dimensional array (list) of prices when stored in a computer's memory is shown in Figure 5.14. Imagine that each value requires one block of memory space and the starting memory address is 123.

Figure 5.14 Storage of Array Prices in a Computer's Memory

Element Stored	Price[0]	Price[1]	Price[2]	Price[3]
Memory Address	123	124	125	126

Heterogeneous Array

A collection of items of different data types is known as a *heterogeneous array*. Heterogeneous arrays are better dealt as ADTs (classes), discussed earlier in this chapter. For example, information about a child can be stored in the form of a heterogeneous array by collecting data fields such as "Name" (string data type), "DateOfBirth" (date data type), "Age" (integer data type), "Weight" (float data type), "Height" (float data type), and so on.

String Data Structure

A *string* is a collection or a sequence of characters in which each character occupies one byte of memory space. In many programming languages, such as C++ and Visual Basic, there is a built-in "string" data type. For example, "Roger Smith" is a string representing the name of a person; "012-23-4567" is a string representing the social security number of a person; and "2600 Park Ave." is a string representing a street address. In C++, you can declare and assign value to a string data type variable as follows:

String Name = "Roger Smith";

Two-Dimensional Array (Tables) Data Structure

A *homogenous two-dimensional array* is a collection of data items of the same data type that are stored in a rows and columns format. It uses two subscripts, namely row subscript and column subscript, to access each of the elements in the array. A two-dimensional array is also known as a table, because a table is made up of data stored in a number of rows, and each row has a certain number of columns.

Figure 5.15 shows a two-dimensional array to store three test scores for each of three students, using syntax of a C++ program. This array has a total of 9 (number of rows multiplied by number of columns) elements. The figure shows the row subscript followed by the column subscript, written inside a pair of opening and closing square brackets ([ ]) for each of the test scores using the two-dimensional array name "Score." In C++, both the row and the column subscript start from zero (0).

In a two-dimensional array structure using different computer programming languages, computer programs are written to find the sum and average of each row and each column and the sum and average of the entire array. After finding the average scores for each row, a letter grade can also be allocated.

Figure 5.15   A Two-dimensional Array of 3 Test Scores for 3 Students

Declaring and Initializing Two-dimensional Array of integer data type
int Score[3][3] = { {56, 89, 67}, ◄——— Row 1 (Row Subscript 0) with 3 scores in column format
                    {89, 78, 99}, ◄——— Row 2 (Row Subscript 1) with 3 scores in column format
                    {75, 87, 65} ◄——— Row 3 (Row Subscript 2) with 3 scores in column format
                    };

Number   Number
of Rows   of Columns

	Column Subscripts		
	0	**1**	**2**
· Value of Element · Accessed Element · Row Subscript 0	56 Score[0][0]	89 Score[0][1]	67 Score[0][2]
· Value of Element · Accessed Element · Row Subscript 1	89 Score[1][0]	78 Score[1][1]	99 Score[1][2]
· Value of Element · Accessed Element · Row Subscript 2	75 Score[2][0]	87 Score[2][1]	65 Score[2][2]

Stack Data Structure

A *stack* is a data structure in which the data items are removed from the top of a list and inserted only at the top of a list. It is just like stacking a number of boxes on top of each other. Remove a box from the top and insert a box at the top of a stack. The stack structure works on a concept known as "Last In, First Out" (LIFO). For example, when passengers board a plane, the seats with higher-numbered rows are filled before the seats with lower-numbered rows, and when they get out of the plane, the ones with lower-numbered rows leave the plane first and the ones with higher-numbered rows leave the plane last.

Queue Data Structure

A *queue* is a data structure in which new data items are added at the end of the list while other items are removed from the beginning of the list. It is similar to students standing in a queue in a cafeteria. An incoming student joins at the end of the queue, while the student at the front of the queue is served and leaves the queue. The front of the queue is called the *head* and the end of the queue is called the *tail*. Queue data works on a concept known as "First In, First Out" (FIFO).

In computers, when printing, every document to be printed has to join a queue. The document that joined the queue first will be printed first, and the document that joined the queue second will be printed second, and so on.

Tree Data Structure

A tree is a data structure in which data items are stored in the form of a hierarchical organization chart, similar to the organizational chart of a company. In any company, the president is at the top (first level) of the hierarchy and the vice presidents are at the second level, directly below the president. Each vice-president may have a number of managers working directly below them as subordinates, at the third level. Each manager may have a number of supervisors working directly below them, at the fourth level. Finally, each supervisor may have a number of floor workers working directly below them, at the fifth level.

With tree data structures, terms such as node, root node, parent node, child node, siblings, leaf (terminal) node, subtree (branch) of tree, and depth of a tree are used. Figure 5.16 shows a tree data structure.

Figure 5.16   Tree Data Structure

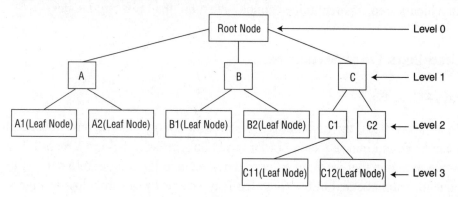

In Figure 5.16, each location in a tree is called a *node* of a tree. The node at the top of a tree is called a root node, at Level 0, also known as a *parent node*. This tree is an inverted tree, because the "root" is at the top and the "leaves" are at the bottom. In the figure, the root node (parent node) has three child nodes

(A, B, and C) at level 1, indicating that there is a parent-child relationship between the root node and these three nodes.

Node A at level 1 has two child nodes (A1 and A2), at level 2. Now node A is considered the parent node and there is a parent-child relationship between node A and the two child nodes, A1 and A2. Since nodes A1 and A2 are the last nodes under node A, they are known as leaf nodes, the same way leaves are last on any branch of a tree. Leaf nodes are also known as terminal nodes. Nodes A1 and A2 are known as *siblings* since both of them have the same parent.

Just like node A, node B at level 1 has two child leaf nodes, B1 and B2, at level 2, and there is a parent-child relationship between node B and the two sibling nodes, B1 and B2.

Also like node A, node C at level 2 has two leaf child nodes, C1 and C2, forming the parent-child relationship. At level 3, there is a parent-child relationship between node C1 and the two sibling nodes, C11 and C12. Node C2 does not have any child node, and, therefore, it is a leaf node.

The entire side of node C with child nodes C1 and C2 and, in turn, node C1 with two child nodes, C11 and C12, is known as a *branch* of a tree or a *sub-tree*.

Binary tree

In a binary tree, a parent node cannot have more than two child nodes.

Linked Lists Data Structure

Arrays—Drawbacks

In an array (list), the data items are stored in contiguous memory locations and can be stored in a sequential order based on a selected field in a record. For example, imagine that we want to store the name and ID number of a student in a sequential alphabetical order. Such list may appear as shown below in Figure 5.17. To add a new student to this list and maintain the sequential order, the records need to be shifted physically forward.

For example, to insert (add) a new student Magda Michael and maintain the sequential order, we need to shift the records of students Moore Roger,

Roque Alice, and Wong Sin forward first, and then insert the record of Magda Michael. Similarly, to delete the student Chaplin Charlie's record from the list and maintain the sequential order, after deleting the student Chaplin Charlie's record from the list, we must shift the other student's record backward.

Figure 5.17   Students' Records in Alphabetical Order

Arenas Maryam	45567
Chaplin Charlie	34789
Moore Roger	52341
Roque Alice	34123
Wong Sin	43267

Linked Lists

As seen above, to insert and delete records in an array is a cumbersome process. A linked list data structure solves the cumbersome process of arrays. A linked list is used in place of an array in situations where inserting or deleting data items from a list occurs frequently.

A *linked list* is a data structure that, when storing records or data items, uses an additional field (known as a pointer) in a record to store the link (reference or address) to the next data item or record in the list. In a linked list, it is not necessary that data items be stored in contiguous memory locations as required in the case of arrays. Each data item in the list is called a *node*.

Pointer

A *pointer* is an added data field in a record (data item) that points to the location of the next record in the list. A pointer is like a detour sign placed on roads to guide motorists when roads are closed for repairs. When a new record is added to the list, the pointers are adjusted to the added new record and then the pointer of the newly added record is set to the next record in the list.

Head and Tail

The *head* points to the first data item in a list and the *tail* pointer indicates the end of data items in a list.

Figure 5.18 below shows the linked list data structure to store the test scores of students. The head points to the first 6 score (56) in the list. Each horizontal arrow in the figure indicates it is a pointer to the next score in the list. Tail indicates that 99 was the last score in the list.

Figure 5.18   Linked List Data Structure

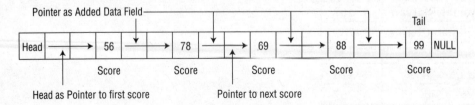

Adding Data to a Linked List

Data can be added to a linked list at the beginning of the list, at the end of the list, or at any location between the beginning and the end of the list. In the example above, a score can be added before the first score 56, after the last score 99, or between any other scores in the list between 56 and 99. When a new record is added to the list, the pointers are adjusted to record before the added new record and to set the pointer of the newly added record to point to the next record in the list.

Adding Data at the Beginning of a List

If a new score (76) is added at the beginning of the list (before the current first score 56), then the head pointer should be set to point to the newly added score 76, and pointer to score 76 should be set to point to score 56, which is now the second score in the list.

Adding Data at the End of a List

If a score is added to the end of the list, then after insertion of the new score, the pointer to score 99 is set to point to the score of the newly added score and the pointer to the newly added last score is set to NULL.

Lists come in three forms: singly linked list, doubly linked list, and trees.

Singly linked list—Each data item points to the next data item in the list without pointing backward. The search for a data item takes place by starting from the first data item and by moving forward one data item at a time until the last data item is reached.

Doubly linked list—In a doubly linked list, each data item has one backward pointer to point to the previous data item and one forward pointer to point to next data item in the list.

Trees —Tree data structures were discussed earlier in this chapter.

5.10   DATABASE MANAGEMENT SYSTEM (DBMS)

A *Database Management System* (DBMS), also called database software, is a program that allows the user to create, maintain, and access a computerized database structure, while doing operations such as inserting, editing, and deleting data or records; querying (retrieving) data; sorting records; and creating forms and reports from the records stored in the database. In short, DBMS is a program that performs all the actual operations inside a database.

Data Management

The same way that a computer is dependent upon the existence of hardware and software, an organization is dependent on the existence of data.

Data management is the technique used to manage data that is stored in a computer's memory as a resource for an organization. The main objective of data management is to make quality business decisions. Data management is a very broad topic and encompasses many other topics such as data browsing, data modeling, data maintenance, database administration, data mining, data warehousing, and database management systems. All these terms are discussed briefly.

Data Browsing

Data browsing is the process of going through various files of a database and reading each record in a file to search for a particular kind of information.

Data Modeling

Data modeling is the technique used to create a database structure that allows data to be collected at its point of origin; organizes that data in a manner that stores it efficiently and with easy accessibility to make business decisions and produce reports; and allows data to be manipulated (inserted, updated, deleted, and organized).

In a database management system, the data is collected and stored in tables. A database is a collection of tables (entities), where each entity is an object (a noun, person, place, or thing) and the data about each entity is collected and stored as attributes (columns in a table). Then, relationships are created between the tables to access data stored in two or more tables in a single SQL statement for making business decisions.

Data modeling involves the selection of meaningful names of entities -(tables) and attributes in each entity, creating table structures and relationships between the tables. The concept of data structure that involves data modeling is discussed later in this chapter.

Data Maintenance

Data maintenance is a technology that allows information or data to be kept accurate and up-to-date. It is also used to determine the percentage of errors an organization can tolerate in a database.

Database Administration

Database administration is an important part of data management in an organization and is performed by a database administrator (DBA). The DBA performs the following tasks:

- Provides support services to the end users regarding data and information usage. This includes: managing the training, teaching database standards and procedures to collect quality data, as well as how to access and manipulate data efficiently.

- Handles the procedures for backup and recovery of data stored in a computer's memory in case a computer system crashes.

- Provides data integrity, data security, and privacy of data stored in a computer system.

  —Data integrity (data quality) means that data should be available when needed and it should be current, accurate, and complete.

  —Data security means that data must be protected against unauthorized access and modification. Presently, identity theft is a big concern in the business industry. All the users of a database are given a user identification and password by the DBA to control unauthorized access to the database. The DBA sets the rule for the creation of passwords and user IDs. Usually, a user sends a written request to the DBA for the issuance of a user ID and password.

  —Data privacy means that an individual or an organization determines "who can see their data," "what part of data can be seen," "how the data will be used," and "where the data will be used."

Data Mining

Data mining is an automatic process that searches and analyzes data stored in a database from different angles and converts it into useful information. Data mining uncovers any flaws, problems, and opportunities that may exist in stored data that the end user is not aware of such as finding problems in the relationships of tables. The data mining process does not require initiation on the part of the end user.

Effects of Data Mining

The analyzed data may increase revenue, cut operations cost, or increase market share of an organization.

Applications of Data Mining

Data mining is used in areas such as hiring of employees, fraud detection, determining sales trends, increasing or reducing inventories based on buying preferences of customers, reducing loss of inventory from theft, performing computer forensics, and improving quality control to find defective items, etc.

Because of the decreasing costs of computer hardware, software, and other computer technology, data mining is becoming more popular with many organizations.

Data Mining Tasks

- *Creating a class of data*—Data mining will divide data items into classes by date or by predetermined groups. For example, sports fans may be divided into groups of baseball, football, or hockey fans based on their likings.

- *Creating clusters of data*—Creating clusters is similar to creating a class of data, but the groups are not predefined. Data mining will try to create groups.

- *Creating associations between data*—For example, many people arrange social functions for a Saturday because it is usually a nonworking day. Therefore, they are willing to pay a higher rental fee for a hall. Fewer people arrange social functions for a Friday because it is usually a working day. They usually pay a lower rental fee.

- *Establishing sequential patterns*—Data mining may establish future trends and patterns. For example, if a customer purchases a digital camera, he may buy an additional memory card to take more pictures and a bag in which to store the camera's accessories.

Data Warehousing

A *data warehouse* is a place where data that has been collected (integrated) from various databases is housed. The data is stored for archival and security purposes.

Warehouse Architecture

There are two types of warehouse architectures: a *centralized data warehouse*, which stores all the company's data in one centralized location; and a *decentralized data warehouse*, which stores data in regionally based warehouses. For example, a company can store its data in five different regional warehouses based in the north, south, east, west, and central regions of a country.

The stored data can be subject oriented (i.e., sales or inventory), formatted, or raw data. It can be collected on a daily, weekly, monthly, or a yearly basis. The data stored in a warehouse can also be updated in a timely manner to reflect the latest value. When data in a data warehouse is updated, all the values stored in various fields are recalculated. For example, when employees are paid weekly, the payroll information is updated every week to show current total gross pay, current net pay, and so on. At the end of the year, the data is used to generate W2 forms used for filing income tax returns.

The data stored in a data warehouse is never removed. There is always a computer system in operation that can access the data easily and quickly to meet the day-to-day operations of an organization.

A data mart is a small sub-set of a data warehouse that is subject oriented and is usually used by a particular group of people. For example, if a sales department wants to view their sales data for the previous five years, they would receive their information from a data mart and not the data for the rest of the company. A data warehouse is made up of a number of data marts.

Metadata

Metadata is the storage of information that provides a detailed explanation of the characteristics of the data and the set of relationships between data stored inside the database. For example, for data stored in a table, metadata stores the name of each attribute in that table, the data type of each attribute, the relationship (e.g., 1:M) with the same attribute in another table, any constraints (entity/ referential integrity constraints) used to store data for that attribute, and so on. In short, metadata provides information about the usage of data in a database.

Data Integrity

Data integrity ensures that data stored in a database is accurate (no inconsistencies) and that, when processed, it yields the same results all the time. Accurate means that for the same piece of data item, there should not be different values stored in different tables of the database.

For example, the address and telephone number of an employee should be identical in human resources files and in the file of the department the employee works in. The companies should not list items in their sales catalog if items are out of stock or discontinued.

Data Consistency

Data consistency means that the same value for a particular piece of data appears in different places in a database. For example, the date of birth of an individual should be the same on all data referring to that individual.

Data Corruption and Data Loss

Data corruption means that stored data has been damaged and is unreadable.

Data loss means that data that was input and is stored on a storage medium can no longer be retrieved. Data loss can take place because of human error, natural disasters (fire, earthquake, tornados, etc.) at locations where data is stored, or because of hardware failures and file corruption.

Data Indexing

An *index* is an arrangement to sort or arrange data used to access the records in a data file (table).

An *index key* is a sorted data field in a table that is used to access data in a data file.

A *unique index* is an index key that points to a unique row in a data file.

Data indexing creates a separate file containing the field used for indexing a file and the address or record number of the corresponding record in a data file.

Data indexing is a flexible and commonly used method to reduce the number of times a user accesses a database when searching for data. B-tree is one form of index structure that is used to store data in a relational database. Indexing uses pointers to point to the record number in a data file.

Data indexing is shown in Figure 5.19, which assumes that a writer writes a number of books for the same publisher. The "Index to Writer Table" stores the "WriterID" in ascending order, and for each "WriterID's" corresponding record, numbers are stored in the "Record No. in Writer Table" column to match the "WriterID" column in the Writer Table.

Figure 5.19   Data Indexing—Writer Table

Index to Writer Table		Writer Table			
Writer ID	Record No. in Writer Table	Record No.	Writer ID	Book Title	ISBN Number
1456	1, 3	1	1456	C++ Programming	123-45-6781
1469	4	2	1478	Java Programming	123-67-8901
1470	5	3	1456	Computer Concepts	123-45-6782
1478	2	4	1469	C Sharp Programming	123-45-6764
		5	1470	Artificial Intelligence	123-45-7632

5.11   DATABASE MODELS

A database model describes nouns and relationships among different nouns using components such as entities, attributes, relationships between entities, instances of an entity, and constraints (discussed earlier in this chapter).

An instance of an entity, also known as an identifier, identifies a unique row in a table using one or more attributes. Usually, the PK or composite PK uniquely identifies a record in a table.

Hierarchical Data Model

A hierarchical data model is organized in a tree-like structure, showing parent-child relationships. One parent can have more than one child, but one child cannot have more than one parent. The parent-child relationship is shown by links called "pointers," where one parent can have more than one pointer to link all its children. This type of structure shows a 1:M type of relationship. The hierarchical model in Figure 5.20 shows the hierarchical relationship between various types of students. Each box in the model is called a node, indicating that there is a parent node and a child node.

Parent "Student" has two children: "Business" and "Computer Science."

Parent "Business" has two children: "Finance" and "Accounts."

Parent "Computer Science" has two children: "DBA" and "Programmer."

Figure 5.20   Hierarchical Data Model

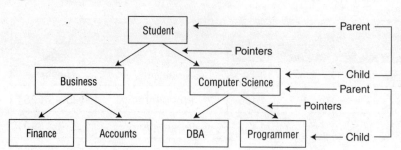

A hierarchical data model shows many types of relationships in the business world. It is used to create tables of contents, recipes, and any nested information.

A hierarchical data model is not suitable to show redundant data. Redundant data means that one piece of data exists in many rows in the database. If the same piece of data is to be modified, then it has to be modified in all the rows in the database, thus avoiding inconsistencies inside a database. For example, if an employee's address appears in many rows of a database and the person moves, then his address has to be changed in all rows of the database. It is quite possible that while changing the address, we may fail to change the address in some rows, which would lead to inconsistencies in the address of that person.

Network Data Model

In a *network data model*, the database can be seen as a group of records that are joined in a 1:M relationship and one record can have more than one parent. The network data model resembles the hierarchical data model with one exception: one child can have more than one parent.

For example, before a student's class schedule is generated, a student is admitted to the college by the college admissions office. The admissions office can admit many students to the college, thus showing 1:M relationship between the admissions office and the students. Once admitted to college, the registrar's office registers the student in a class and generates a tuition payment invoice. The registrar's office can generate more invoices for more than one student, thus showing a 1:M relationship between the registrar's office and the students.

The student then takes the invoice to the college's accounting office to pay the tuition fees. The accounting office can accept payment from more than one student, thus showing a 1:M relationship between the accounting office (1) and a student (M).

In short, in the example above, before a student can register and take a class, she has to touch base with three parent entities—the admissions office, the registrar's office, and the accounting office. Then the student (one entity) is taught by a teacher (another entity). The teacher (entity) tests the students (entity) and generates a letter grade. The registrar's office (entity) enters the student's grades in various subjects into the computer system and generates a transcript.

Relational Database Model (RDBMS)

E.F. Codd introduced the relational data model, the most widely used database model today. The main feature of this model is that the data is stored in tables (relations), in which the table is a matrix made up of M number of columns (attributes) and N number of rows (records). The values that can be assigned to an attribute (column) must be selected from a set or range of values that the column can take. This set of values is known as a domain. For example, a test score has a domain of 0 to 100.

Data tables are independent of each other. However, a relationship can be established between the tables through the use of PKs and FKs. A PK in one table creates a 1:M (one-to-many) relationship with a FK in another table.

All relations (tables) in a relational database must meet the following requirements:

- Each table must have a unique name.
- The ordering of columns and rows in a table is not important.
- Each row in a table must be distinct. Each attribute in a row must have a single value.
- A relationship (1:1, 1:M, or M:N type) between the two tables must be established.

A structured query language (SQL), the standard query language for relational databases, is used to create a database structure; to insert, update, delete, and organize data in relations; and to provide data security by giving access rights to insert, view, and manipulate data in a database. For example, a payroll employee can only insert or view data that is concerned with generating a paycheck of an employee, but cannot view the job performance of another employee.

Object-Oriented Database Model System (OODBMS)

In an object-oriented database model, the data is stored in the form of objects and uses OOP logic, where each object contains data about objects in the form of attributes (fields). Objects that have the same attributes are grouped together and stored as classes containing the attributes of objects and methods to perform operations on those objects. To organize classes, a hierarchy of classes is formed, where there is a parent-child relationship between classes at different levels and where a child class can have only one parent. As in OOP, in an OODBM one object of a class can inherit the method and the attributes of the parent class. OODB models are described using Unified Model Language (UML) to show attributes and the relationships among different objects.

Multimedia Database

Multimedia databases can store text, numbers, pictures, sound (audio), movies, and hyperlinked data fields. For example, in federal security offices, the employee's voice and picture data is stored to establish the identity of the person accessing secured areas.

Hybrid Database

A hybrid database uses a combination of the database models listed above. The most powerful hybrid model uses a combination of relational and object-oriented databases.

Entity Relationship Model (ERM)

An *entity relationship model* (ERM) is described through entities having relationships between them. An ERM model uses "connectivity" to describe the type (1:1, 1:M, M:N) of relationship, and "cardinalities" to show lower and upper limits of the type of relationship as shown below in the entity relationship diagram (ERD) in Figure 5.21.

Figure 5.21   Entity Relationship Diagram (ERD)

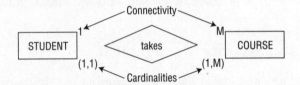

- Connectivity indicates that there is a 1:M type of relationship between STUDENT and COURSE entities. It means that one student can take many courses and many courses can be taken by one student.
- Cardinalities (1:M) written on the bottom left corner of the COURSE entity indicates that the student can take a minimum of 1 course and a maximum of M courses.
- Cardinalities (1:1) written on the bottom right corner of STUDENT entity indicates that a particular course can be taken by one and only one student.

5.12   FUNCTIONS OF DBMS

A DBMS has to perform many functions when creating a database (creating table structures): inserting data into tables, manipulating (editing, deleting, etc.) data stored in tables, retrieving data from tables, and so on. The DBMS functions are described below.

Data Integrity and Data Consistency Management

A DBMS has to maintain data integrity and data consistency of the data stored inside databases. This is done by creating relationships among entities, by enforcing data integrity rules and using SQL.

Data Redundancy Minimization

Data redundancy means the storing of the same data in different locations of a database, which can lead to data inconsistency. When updating redundant data, it is possible to miss updating some of the locations. A DBMS must ensure that data redundancy is minimal.

Data Processing Management

The DBMS processes the entered data into information and makes sure that the information stored conforms to a set format. For example, the date of birth of a child is entered as month, day, and year. The DBMS should ensure that after data entry, the date of birth is stored in one standardized format: mm/dd/yyyy.

Data Privacy and Security Management

All databases store confidential data that is used in the day-to-day operations of an organization. A DBMS must ensure that only authorized people can access, manipulate, and perform data operations to the data stored inside the database. A DBMS should have logical and physical security of all the data stored in a database. Logical security is implemented in the form of a user ID and password, as well as biometric authentication when a user is trying to access data. Physical security is implemented by physically securing the locations where the data is stored in computers, locking buildings, and installing alarm systems. The database administrator (DBA) decides who can have access to data and who performs database operations such as reading, writing, updating, and deleting data in a database.

Backup of Data and Recovery Management

A DBMS should ensure that backup and recovery procedures are in place to recover lost data in emergency situations, such as a power failure, damaged storage (hard disk) devices, equipment failure, and data corruption. Usually, back-up data is stored in separate locations from the original data.

Data Storage and Access Management

A DBMS has to provide storage for the created database structure, the data inserted into tables, the created forms and reports, the manipulated data, the structures that handle multimedia data, etc. A DBMS must provide procedures that enable the user to access and store data efficiently. The data may be stored in different locations in different files and in different storage media. A DBMS must be able to handle storage and access management in these types of situations.

Use of SQL to Access Data

A DBMS provides access to data by using a query language such as SQL (standard query language for relational databases). SQL is a simple query language that allows the user to specify what to do in a database without knowing how it is done internally.

5.13   DATA PROCESSING

Data stored inside a database can be processed using batch or transactional processing techniques.

Batch Processing

In batch processing, data processing is done on the bulk of the data at the end of a certain time period, depending on the usage requirement of the data stored inside the database. The processing of data may take place at the end of the day, at the end of the week, at the end of the month, etc. In the banking industry, deposited checks are collected and then processed at the end of the day. In the case of hourly employees, their daily working hours are totaled and processed at the end of the week to generate their paychecks. Batch processing is usually done after business hours.

Transactional Processing

A database transaction is a logical unit of work within a DBMS, comprising a sequence of database operations required to insert, view, or manipulate data stored in a database. A logical unit of work means that the transaction must be completed or aborted. A transaction is like a light switch that can be turned on or turned off.

All DBMS systems keep records of all the transactions and changes in the database. In the case of a system failure, the transaction log and a rollback statement is used to rollback uncommitted transactions. Every transaction must fulfill the following requirements:

- Be automatic, that is, all operations required to complete a transaction must be completed; otherwise, the transaction will be aborted.

- Be completed in isolation, that is, while the first transaction is working on one piece of data, another transaction cannot operate upon the same piece of data. The second transaction can only operate on the piece of data when the first transaction has completed all of its operations on that data, or has aborted the operation.

- Have consistency, which means that once the transaction is complete, the database reaches a consistent state (when all the data integrity rules are fulfilled).

- Be durable, that is, once the transaction is completed, the changes made to the data cannot be reversed or lost.

- Completed transactions must be written to data storage.

Online Transaction Processing (OLTP)

When a customer buys merchandise online, it is known as e-commerce, and the transaction is known as Online Transaction Processing (OLTP). Most of OLTPs can take place seven days a week/24 hours a day. The customer makes payment using a credit card to complete the transaction and knows immediately whether the transaction was completed or not.

Mixed (Batch and Transaction) Processing

Some computer systems may use both batch processing and transaction processing in one unit. For example, when renewing a car registration online, the registration fee is paid by credit card and is handled as a transaction processing, and the mailing of the renewed registration card is handled as a batch processing.

5.14 DATABASE HIERARCHY—ORGANIZING DATA AND INFORMATION IN DATABASES

Before we discuss database hierarchies, we need to discuss terms that are involved in usage of databases.

In Chapter 2, terms such as "data," "information," and "data vs. information" were discussed. *Data* is a collection of text, numbers, images, audio, and video that has not yet been processed. *Information* is processed data that helps with decision making or means something to you. The terms *data* and *information* are used interchangeably depending upon the stage of processing and are important terms in understanding the use of computerized databases.

A traditional database is organized in a hierarchical relationship in this order: bit, character, entities, field, record, file, and database.

A *bit* is the smallest unit of data that a computer can perform an operation on. A computer only understands machine language or binary language that is made up of two bits (short for binary digits), or the numbers 0 and 1. All the operations done inside a computer are done using the digits 0 and 1 only. Any character (alphabet letter, numerical digit, or special character (such as % or #) is converted to a unique combination of 8 bits (8 bits = 1 byte) of 0s and 1s. For example, the number 6 in binary language is equivalent to 00000110 in binary code.

A *character* is the smallest unit of meaningful information. For example, when filling out an employment application form, the character "S" in the "Marital Status" field indicates a person is single. Every character occupies 1 byte of space in the computer's memory.

An *entity* is a noun, and a noun is a place, person, thing, or any other item about which we can collect data or information. For example, we can collect data about a student or an employee of a company, an automobile, a city, and so on. Databases store and organize data about entities in terms of fields, records, and files (table or relation). For example, in order to collect data for an automobile, the data fields could include information regarding the make, model, manufacturer, year, number of cylinders, number of doors, color, etc.

A *field* is the smallest piece of data that a database user can read from a database table. For example, "Full Name," "Street Address," "City," "State," and "Zip Code" are the fields used to create an entity "Address Label." In order to describe a field, four attributes need to be specified:

- Name of the field; for example, Name, Date of Birth, Time of Birth, Height, Weight and Gender are field names used to describe a newborn in a hospital.

- Data types of the field, such as number, date/time, text, currency, memo, object, and hyperlink. In our example of a child, the height and weight fields store values of number data type, the name field stores values of text (character) data type, and the date of birth field stores values of date data type. A value such as "2500 Park Ave." in an address field is an alphanumeric data type since it is a mixture of alphabet letters and numerical digits.

- Length (size) of the field, which specifies the maximum number of characters that can be used to store values in the field. For example, to store values for a field that stores social security numbers, the size of the field will be nine characters. To store values for a field "Name," the size of the field is based on the longest name to be stored in the database.

- Format of the values, which specifies the way a value is stored in a field. For example, the Date of Birth field may store the date in the form mm/dd/yyyy and the Social Security Number field stores the number in xxx-xx-xxxx format.

Records in a Database

A record is a group of related fields used to completely describe one instance of an entity. For example, to describe the entity "child born in a hospital," fields such as the name, gender, date of birth, time of birth, name of hospital, city, state, zip, country, height, and weight are used. Each record uses the same set of fields, and the fields are listed in the same order. In databases, a record is also known as rows or a tuple.

Database File

A file is a collection of identical types of records. In database terms, a *file* is also known as *relation* or *table*, where the data is stored in a rows and columns format. In a table, the column represents data fields and the rows represent records by providing data for each of the fields in a table.

Database

A relational database (RDB) is a collection of relations (tables) where data in different tables is linked through a common field or attribute, and where data or information stored in one relation (file) can be cross checked for the same data or information stored in another relation (file).

5.15 DATABASE STRUCTURES—IMPORTANT TERMS IN DATABASES

A database structure is a scheme to structure (arrange or organize) database tables so that data can be entered, stored, retrieved, and manipulated efficiently in tables by a computer program. Oracle SQL is a computer program that structures data.

In order to understand the concept of database, the following terms need to be understood: relation, relational database, primary key (PK), foreign key (FK), domain, data definition language (DDL), data manipulation languages (DML), entity integrity rule, and referential integrity rule. All of these terms are discussed below.

Relation (Table)

A *table* or a *relation* in a database is considered to be an entity (noun) and is created by organizing data in M number of columns and N number of rows. Some important facts about an entity are outlined below.

- Data is collected about an entity by using column names (field names), where each column describes a particular attribute about the entity.

- Each column in a table must have a distinct name, and the value stored in that column must be an allowed value for that column.

- Each row (record) in a table stores the data for all the columns (attributes) in that table.

Primary Key (PK) and Composite Primary Key in a Table

As defined previously, a *primary key* (PK) is a column name that uniquely identifies a row or a record in a table. In business, a social security number (SSN), a patient identification number, a vehicle identification number (VIN), and an employee identification number are common column names that are used as PKs. There cannot be two people with the same SSN, and there cannot be two cars with the same VIN. A PK and a foreign key (FK) are used to establish relationships between tables of a database and to access a particular record in those tables.

If two columns together uniquely identify a record in a table, the columns are then called *composite primary keys*. For example, a student may be registered in any number of courses at a college. In such cases, for each course registered, the "StudentID" remains the same but the "CourseID" changes. The example from Table 5.4 below shows "StudentID" and "CourseID" as composite PKs. To determine a letter grade in a particular course for the same student, both "StudentID" and "CourseID" values must be entered into the computer system. For example, for "StudentID" 345678 and "CourseID" CSC110, the letter grade is A.

Table 5.4 Letter Grade Table

Field names	StudentID	CourseID	LetterGrade
Record (Row) 1	1234	CSC110	A
Record (Row) 2	1345	CSC121	B−
Record (Row) 3	1234	CSC121	B+
Record (Row) 4	1234	CSC122	C+

Foreign Key (FK) in a Table

A foreign key is a column in one relation P that is also a primary key in another relation Q, thus setting a stage to establish a relationship between two relations P and Q.

One relation can have both a primary key and a foreign key. Foreign key values can repeat in a table. For example, in Table 5.4 above the column "StudentID" is a foreign key, and is a primary key in Table 5.5, since it repeats three times for "StudentID" 1234.

A table that contains a PK is called a "PK table," and a table that contains a FK is called a "FK table." There is a 1:M (1 to many) type of relationship between a PK and a FK, indicating that for every one row in a PK table, there can be more than one row in a FK table.

Domain of a Column

A *domain* is a collection of values of the same data type that are allowed for a particular column in a table. For example, the domain for a letter grade a student can get in a course is A, A−, B+, B, B−, C+, C, D, or F. Similarly, the domain for a student's test score is 0 to 100.

Relational Database

In a relational database, data is stored in tables and each table consists of M number of rows and N number of columns. Each row in a table may have a PK or a FK to identify a unique row in a table.

In databases, a table structure describes the name of the table, the data fields and their data types, the selection of PKs/FKs/composite PKs, and the relationships with other tables. Figure 5.22 uses a short form of table structure to describe the relationship between tables in a relational database. The boldfaced and underlined field inside ( ) means that the field is a PK or a composite PK. The relational diagram shows entities, attributes in each of those entities, and the relationship between entities using PKs and FKs.

Student (StudentID, Name, Street, City, State, Zip)

Course (CourseID, Description, CreditHours)

Schedule (StudentID, CourseID, Day, Bldg, RoomNo, Time)

Figure 5.22   Diagram of Relationship Between Database Tables

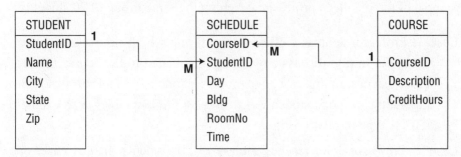

- **StudentID** in "Student" table is a PK, and in "Schedule" table is a FK
- **CourseID** in "Course" table is a PK, and in "Schedule" table is a FK
- **StudentID**, and **CourseID** collectively are composite PK
- Tables "Student" and 'Schedule" have 1:M relationship through common field StudentID.
- Tables "Course" and "Schedule" have 1:M relationship through common field CourseID.

Types of Relationships Between Entities

A relationship between entities is the connection between two entities through the use of common fields that act as PKs and FKs in tables to access data stored. For example, in Figure 5.22, the entity "Student" has a relationship with the entity "Schedule" through the common data field "StudentID", where "StudentID" is a PK in the "Student" table and an FK in the "Schedule" table. Similarly, the table "Course" (PK—"CourseID") has a relationship with the table "Schedule" (FK—"CourseID") through the common field "CourseID."

There are three ways to describe relationships between two tables: a one-to-one (1:1) relationship, a one-to-many (1:M) relationship, and a many-to-many (M:N) relationship.

- A 1:1 relationship exists between tables A and B, if exactly one row in table A matches one and only one row in table B and vice versa.

- A 1:M relationship exists between tables A and B, if one row in table A matches more than one row in table B, and only one row from table B matches at the most one row in table A.

- A M:N relationship exists between tables A and B, if more than one row in table A matches more than one row in table B, and vice versa. Since databases don't like M:N types of relationships, each M:N type is broken into a number of 1:M types of relationships.

In order to describe the three types of relationships in more detail, let us take an example of three college professors teaching the same group of 20 students.

Case 1: Professor John has office hours during which time a student can meet with him to discuss any difficulties related to the course the professor teaches. In this case, one professor (one row in a Professor table) interacting with one student (one row in a Student table) is an example of a 1:1 type of relationship.

Case 2: Professor John teaches a class of 20 students. In this case, one professor (one row in a Professor table) interacting with 20 students (many rows in a Student table) is an example of a 1:M type of relationship.

Case 3: Three professors meet the same group of 20 students in one classroom. In this case, three professors (many rows in a Professor table) interacting with 20 students (many rows in a Student table) is an example of a M:N type of relationship. Three professors teaching different subjects will never teach the same group of students at the same time in the same classroom.

Data Definition Language (DDL)

Before values are stored in a table, a table structure must be created using a data definition language. As described earlier, a structure query language (SQL) is a common language used to define and manipulate databases. When defining a database for each table in a database, the following requirements are needed:

- Select the name of the table.
- Select the names of all the columns in the table.
- Select the data type associated with each column in the table.
- Decide whether a column can be either a primary key, a foreign key, or part of a composite primary key.
- Establish the relationship between two or more tables using primary keys and foreign keys.

Creating a Table Structure

Oracle SQL uses the CREATE command to create a table in a database. For example, the following SQL CREATE command creates a "Student" table in a database as follows:

```
CREATE TABLE STUDENT
    (StudentID CHAR(8),
        StdName VARCHAR2(20),
        Address VARCHAR2(20),
        City VARCHAR2(20),
        State CHAR(2),
        ZIP CHAR(5),
        PRIMARY KEY (StudentID)
    );
```

Entity Integrity Rule in DBMS

An entity integrity rule ensures that when inserting data in a table, the value of the PK field in a particular row must be unique and must not be null (blank). Using constraints during the database design of the table(s) enforces this rule. For example, in the previous example, when a "Student" database table was created, the last statement "PRIMARY KEY (StudentID)" enforced the entity integrity rule for the PK field "StudentID."

Referential Entity Integrity Rule in DBMS

A referential entity integrity rule enforces that when two tables are related through a PK and a FK, then in the FK table, the FK contains either matching values in the PK table or be left null (blank).

Constraints in Databases

Constraints in databases are restrictions placed on the data stored in the tables of a database. These constraints are enforced using the entity integrity rule, the referential integrity rule, and some other rules. Examples of constraints are:

- A student's test score must be between 0 and 100.

- A student's GPA must be between 0.00 and 4.00.

- A student can register for a maximum of 15 credits per semester.

- Each class can be taught by one and only one teacher at a particular time.

5.16   STRUCTURED QUERY LANGUAGE (SQL) AND DATABASE MANAGEMENT

As defined earlier in the chapter, structured query language (SQL) is a database computer language designed to manage data in relational database management systems (RDBMS) as follows:

- Perform data administration functions by creating databases, database table structures, indexes, and views using data definition language (DDL).

- Manipulate data stored in tables using data manipulation language (DML).

- Allow the writing of queries to process data stored in tables and retrieve information stored in various tables.

Major Functions of SQL

1. Creating Objects in a Database
   SQL performs data administration functions by creating database, database table structures, indexes, and views, by using data definition language (DDL). SQL uses the CREATE command to create database objects.

2. Performing Data Manipulation Operations
   By using data manipulation language (DML) and commands such as INSERT, SELECT, UPDATE, and DELETE, SQL performs data manipulation operations on data inside a database.

Data Manipulation Language (DML)

SQL uses data manipulation language (DML) commands to query and manipulate (maintain) data inside a database by performing the following operations in a database:

- Insert records in table(s) of a database.
- Query (retrieve information) table(s) in a database.
- Delete records from table(s) of a database.
- Update (edit) records in table(s) of a database.

Query in Databases

A query (simply known as a question) is a technique using statements that are written in a standardized format to retrieve information from a database and manipulate (insert, update, delete) the data stored in a database. Many database management systems use the structured query language (SQL) standard query format.

In the following sections, we will be writing basic SQL queries to create database tables and to get information from those database tables.

Data Manipulation Operations Using SQL

INSERT, UPDATE, DELETE, SELECT, COMMIT, and ROLLBACK are all SQL data manipulation commands.

INSERT Command

SQL uses the INSERT command to insert data one record (row) at a time in a database table. Columns in a table are data fields, and records are a collection of related fields. The general syntax to insert a record in a table is shown below.

INSERT INTO TableName VALUES (Field1 Value, Field2 Value, . . . , FieldValueN);

To add a record to the "STUDENT" table created earlier, follow the same syntax, remembering that character data type fields are written within a pair of single quotes and numerical values are written without any quotes.

INSERT INTO STUDENT VALUES
('1234', 'Jack Smith', '123 Park Ave', 'Nutley', 'NJ', '07765', 23);

For example, the rows (records) added to the STUDENT table are shown below in Table 5.5. Table 5.5 will be used to run the SQL queries shown in this section.

Table 5.5   Records in the Student Table

StudentID	Name	Address	City	State	Zip	Age
1234	Jack Smith	123 Park Ave	Nutley	NJ	07765	23
1345	John Moore		Cherry Hill	NJ	07865	15
1125	Alice Jones	1 College Hill	Springfield	NJ	05432	25
1167	Robert Watson	345 Park Ave	Spotswood	NJ	08871	17
1567	Josh Becket	67 Gill Lane	Iselin	NJ	07765	34
3421	Nancy Bell	45 Arnold Dr	Union	NJ	07654	19
4512	Mary Allen	23 Plainfield Ave	Cranford	NJ	08213	26
5123	Martha Jones	123 Grove Ave	Newton	NJ	07765	21
1378	Victor Kennedy	432 Main St	Nutley	NJ	05678	45
5612	Frank Bailey	34 Kennedy Ln	Elizabeth	NJ	07612	28
2315	Farida Mathew	45 Micco Dr	Woodbridge	NJ	08871	35

SELECT Command

SQL uses the SELECT command to retrieve information from the database tables. A wild card (*) in the SELECT command means to display information for all the fields in a table, and the SQL statement ends with a semicolon (;). Table 5.6 shows the use of the SELECT command with examples.

Table 5.6   SELECT Command in SQL

Operation	Syntax	Example
Display all the fields in a table	SELECT * FROM TableName;	SELECT * FROM STUDENT;
Display selected fields from a table	SELECT Field1, Field2, FROM TableName;	SELECT StudendID, Name, Age FROM STUDENT;

The SQL command: **SELECT * FROM STUDENT** will display all the rows from Table 5.5.

The SQL command: **SELECT StudentID, Name, Age FROM STUDENT** will display only the StudentID, Name, and Age columns from Table 5.5

WHERE Command

SQL uses the WHERE command to display information with values in selected field(s) of table(s). The syntax, query, as well as an example of the SQL query using the SELECT and the WHERE commands are shown below. When using the WHERE command, the character values written inside parentheses are case sensitive. For example, "John" and "JOHN" are two different values.

SQL Syntax: **SELECT * FROM TableName**
WHERE condition;

Query: In the STUDENT table, display all the fields for students living in the city of Nutley

SQL Query: **SELECT * FROM STUDENT**
WHERE CITY = 'Nutley';

This SQL query displays the rows shown below in Figure 5.23.

Figure 5.23   Select * From Student Where City = 'Nutley';

StudentID	Name	Address	City	State	Zip	Age
1234	Jack Smith	123 Park Ave	Nutley	NJ	07765	23
1378	Victor Kennedy	432 Main St	Nutley	NJ	05678	45

WHERE command and SQL Logical Operators

Along with the WHERE command, SQL uses the logical operators AND, OR, and NOT in searches to have multiple conditions in a query.

SQL Example, WHERE command and "AND" logical operator

The AND logical operator acts just like the English word "and" used in sentences, and find the rows in a table that matches the conditions separated by the AND operator. For example, Jack AND Jill are eating lunch.

SQL Syntax: **SELECT * FROM TableName**
              WHERE condition1 AND condition2;

Query: In the STUDENT table, display all the students living in city of Nutley who are 21 years of age, by using the AND logical operator.

SQL Query: **SELECT * FROM STUDENT**
              WHERE CITY = 'Nutley' AND AGE = 21;

This query displays no rows (empty table) as there are no records to match both the conditions in Table 5.5.

SQL Example, WHERE command and "OR" logical operator

The OR logical operator acts just like the English word 'or' used in sentences, and finds the rows in a table that matchconditions separated by the OR operator. For example, Jack OR Jill will attend the meeting.

SQL Syntax: **SELECT * FROM TableName**
WHERE condition1 OR condition2;

Query: In the STUDENT table, display students living in the city of Nutley or who are 21 years of age, by using the SQL logical operator OR.

SQL Query: **SELECT * FROM STUDENT**
WHERE CITY = 'Nutley' OR AGE = 21;

This SQL query displays the rows from Table 5.5 above.

Figure 5.24   Select * From Student Where City = 'Nutley' OR AGE < 21;

StudentID	Name	Address	City	State	Zip	Age
1234	Jack Smith	123 Park Ave	Nutley	NJ	07765	23
1345	John Moore	15 Watson Dr	Cherry Hill	NJ	07865	15
1167	Robert Watson	345 Park Ave	Spotswood	NJ	08871	17
3421	Nancy Bell	45 Arnold Dr	Union	NJ	07654	19
1378	Victor Kennedy	432 Main St	Nutley	NJ	05678	45

SQL Example, WHERE command and "NOT" logical operator

The OR logical operator acts just like the English word "not" used in sentences, and finds the rows in a table that do not match a specified condition by using the NOT operator. For example Jack will NOT attend the meeting. For example, NOT(4) means all values but not 4.

SQL Syntax: **SELECT * FROM TableName**
WHERE NOT (condition);

Query: In the STUDENT table, display all the students who are not 21 years of age, by using the SQL logical operator NOT.

SQL Query: **SELECT * FROM STUDENT**
WHERE NOT (AGE = 21);

Figure 5.25 below shows extracted rows from Table 5.5 by using this SQL query.

Figure 5.25   Select * From Student Where Not (Age = 21);

StudentID	Name	Address	City	State	Zip	Age
1234	Jack Smith	123 Park Ave	Nutley	NJ	07765	23
1345	John Moore	15 Watson Dr	Cherry Hill	NJ	07865	15
1125	Alice Jones	1 College Hill	Springfield	NJ	05432	25
1167	Robert Watson	345 Park Ave	Spotswood	NJ	08871	17
1567	Josh Becket	67 Gill Lane	Iselin	NJ	07765	34
3421	Nancy Bell	45 Arnold Dr	Union	NJ	07654	19
4512	Mary Allen	23 Plainfield Ave	Cranford	NJ	08213	26
1378	Victor Kennedy	432 Main St	Nutley	NJ	05678	45
5612	Frank Bailey	34 Kennedy Ln	Elizabeth	NJ	07612	28
2315	Farida Mathew	45 Micco Dr	Woodbridge	NJ	08871	35

SQL's DISTINCT clause

The SQL's DISTINCT clause displays rows of only those values that are distinct (different) from another. For example, the following SQL query displays rows only with distinct StudentIDs from Table 5.5, as each StudentID appears only once in the table.

SELECT DISTINCT StudentID
FROM STUDENT;

SQL's ORDER BY clause

SQL's ORDER BY clause is used to list rows in ascending or descending order based on a selected column. The SQL syntax and the SQL query example of the ORDER BY clause is shown below.

SQL Syntax: **SELECT   Field1, Field2**
FROM   TableName
WHERE   condition
ORDER BY   FieldName;

Query: Display all the rows from the STUDENT table, for students who live in the city of "Nutley," listed by age in ascending order.

SQL Query: **SELECT Name, City, Age**
FROM STUDENT
WHERE CITY = 'Nutley'
ORDER BY AGE;

This SQL query displays rows from Table 5.5 in Figure 5.26.

Figure 5.26   SELECT * FROM STUDENT WHERE CITY = 'Nutley' ORDER BY AGE;

Name	City	Age
Jack Smith	Nutley	23
Victor Kennedy	Nutley	45

SQL's UPDATE command

The SQL's UPDATE command is used to update data in existing rows in a table based on the value of a primary key column. The SQL syntax and the SQL query example of the UPDATE command is shown below.

SQL Syntax: **UPDATE TableName**
SET Field = Value
WHERE PK Field = Value;

Query: Update address of Student ID "1234" to "56 Holland Ave" in Table 5.5.

SQL Query: **UPDATE   STUDENT**
SET Address =   '56 Holland Ave'
WHERE StudentID =   '1234';

As shown in Figure 5.27, this SQL query will update the Address field of the first row in Table 5.5 for StudentID "1234."

Figure 5.27 UPDATE STUDENT SET Address = '56 Holland Ave' WHERE StudentID = '1234';

StudentID	Name	Address	City	State	Zip	Age
1234	Jack Smith	56 Holland Ave	Nutley	NJ	07765	23
...	...	...	...	...	...	...

SQL's DELETE command

The SQL's DELETE command is used to delete rows from rows in an existing table, usually based on the value of a primary key column. The SQL syntax and the SQL query example of the DELETE command is shown below.

SQL Syntax: **DELETE FROM TableName**
              WHERE Condition;

Query: Delete row of student ID "1234" in STUDENT table.

SQL Query: **DELETE FROM STUDENT**
              WHERE StudentID = '1234';

This SQL query will delete a row in Table 5.5 for StudentID "1234," leaving other rows intact in the table.

Joining Two or More Database Tables

Two or more database tables can be joined using common data field in a SQL query to retrieve information from one table at a time.

Let's imagine that we have the following two tables with their fields listed in a pair of parentheses ( ), and that the underlined fields are PKs in the respective tables. Field F11 is a PK in table T1, a FK in table T2, and a common field in the two tables used to join them.

T1 (**F11**, F12, F13)

T2 (**F21**, F22, F23, F11)

The SQL syntax to retrieve information for fields F11, F12, and F21 by joining the two tables is shown below. Two tables are joined using a common field from both the tables, where the common field is PK in one table and FK in the second joining table. Additionally, in the SELECT command, the common field must be preceded by one of the table's name and a period. For example, in a general syntax and SELECT statement, common field F11 is preceded by the table name T1 followed by a period (.) (as shown below by boldfaced and underlined text).

SELECT **T1.F11**, F12, F21

FROM T1, T2

WHERE T1.F11 = T2.F11;

In Table 5.7 and Table 5.8 below, let's imagine that we want to display StudentID, CourseID, and CourseDescription by joining the Schedule (FK—CourseID) and the Courses (PK—CourseID) tables, using the common field CourseID in the WHERE clause.

Table 5.7 "Schedule" Table

Field names	StudentID	CourseID	Day	RoomNo	Bldg.	Time
Record 1	345678	CSC110	Mondays	121	JLC	9 A.M.
Record 2	321456	CSC121	Tuesdays	134	EH	11 A.M.

Table 5.8 "Courses" Table

Field names	CourseID	CourseDescription	CreditHours
Record 1	CSC110	. . . .	3
Record 2	CSC121	. . . .	4

Query:
Get Course Description for each course along with the StudentID and the CourseID by joining the Schedule and the Courses tables. (Please note that the two tables will be joined by the common field CourseID in WHERE class) for the CourseID "CSC110.")

SQL Query:

SELECT StudentID, Courses.CourseID, CourseDescription
FROM SCHEDULE, COURSES
WHERE Schedule.CourseID = Courses.CourseID;
AND CourseID = 'CSC110';

Effect of Query: The above SQL query will display the course description of the CSC110 Course along with the StudentID and the CourseID.

CHAPTER 6

Business, Social, and Ethical Implications and Issues

Business, Social, and Ethical Implications and Issues

6.1 THE ECONOMIC EFFECTS OF INFORMATION TECHNOLOGY

Economics is a social science that deals with the production, distribution, and consumption of goods and services by individuals, businesses, and governments. Individuals make economic decisions based on their available resources and their life goals.

Economics impacts individuals, companies, governments, and countries. It can have a domino effect. For instance, when an oil-producing country raises the price of its crude oil, an oil-consuming country will feel the effect of the price increase of some commodities such as gasoline and food.

E-Business

Created by IT, e-business (electronic business) allows the processing, transmission, storage, and viewing of data in a digital (computer readable) form by using the Internet or a computer network. For its operations, e-business involves the use of hardware, software, people, and other systems. E-business activities include all types of buying and selling of merchandise, customer service, and management functions. E-business is conducted by private, for-profit, non-profit, government, and other types of organizations, offices, and agencies.

Impact of e-Business

E-business has automated many functions and replaced them with self-service operations. This has caused the elimination of jobs in some sectors, while causing an increase in output. For example, some parking garages have eliminated garage attendants and replaced them with self-service vending machines to pay for parking. At train stations, passengers can buy train tickets using vending machines. Some businesses have closed their storefronts and have opted to sell their merchandise only on the Internet.

Even though e-business has eliminated some jobs, it has created others, especially where IT is involved. For example, many jobs have been created to manufacture hardware as well as to write software for e-business companies.

Effect of IT in Manufacturing and Production

IT has impacted manufacturing in many areas. Manufacturing schedules have been computerized so that products are ready to ship on time. IT provides quality control processes and tests to ensure the production of products at reduced costs. IT has also impacted manufacturing by managing the constant need for raw material, equipment, manpower, and real estate. For example, computers can automatically reorder raw materials when the stock on hand falls below a minimum level.

Furthermore, there are software programs available that can automate and streamline many processes in manufacturing and produce better quality products at prices customers can afford. These programs also improve customer relationships, supply chain management, and many other aspects of businesses.

In the entertainment industry, while the prices of high definition televisions have dropped, the image quality has improved dramatically. In the car industry, the quality, performance, and features in modern cars have vastly improved.

Effect of IT in Manufacturing and Employment

Although the IT industry has automated some functions or processes in manufacturing, thus eliminating some jobs, it has also created jobs involved in manufacturing and assembling equipment that uses computer hardware and software.

Effect of IT in the Healthcare Industry

In the healthcare industry, recent advances in IT have provided new tools and better information systems to healthcare providers which, in turn, have improved the quality of patient care. New software has provided support for medical processes, and new hardware has allowed for easier access of information at the point of care. The diagnosis of patients is done by using improved computerized medical equipment. In addition, IT has been involved in direct patient care and has been able to perform functions such as diagnosing, treating, and monitoring patients.

Telemedicine, through the use of computer hardware, software, and telephone lines, provides health care to patients whose doctors could be thousands of miles away. It involves specialties such as tele-cardiology, tele-pathology, tele-dermatology, tele-radiology, tele-pharmacy and tele-psychiatry. For example, tele-radiology allows radiological images (MRIs) to be sent to specialists to help them diagnose patients. All of this happens using computers and telephone lines.

6.2 PRIVACY CONCERNS IN THE AGE OF INFORMATION TECHNOLOGY

Privacy is defined as the right of a person or an organization to decide where, when, how much, and what portion of their personal information can be collected in computers, shared, and used by others. Examples of personal information include social security number, date of birth, mother's maiden name, yearly income, health issues, bank statements, credit card account details, etc.

Once an individual's personal information is available to others, it becomes possible for others to use it for personal gain. For example, many people have been arrested for assuming the identity of a deceased person in order to receive social security benefits.

Fairness in privacy means that if an individual reveals his personal information to others, it should be used only for its intended purpose. For example, when a customer makes an online purchase he gives his credit card details to the online salesperson. The salesperson should use the customer's credit card details only for the payment of merchandise and never for the purchasing of goods for himself.

Because of stolen identities, privacy is becoming more and more a matter of great concern in today's age of information technology.

Categories of Privacy

Privacy can be categorized according to its contextual use as follows:

Occupational Privacy

Occupational privacy relates to information stored in a computer system, about an individual's activities performed during the course of their profession. For example, an FBI agent would not want to reveal his activities during an investigation of a case to non-intended entities or persons.

Informational Privacy

Informational privacy relates to an individual's personal information that is collected and stored in a computer system. An individual can choose to reveal personal information as a part of a transaction; however, the individual must have full control over the use of that personal information.

Financial Privacy

Financial privacy relates to an individual's financial data that is stored in the computer systems of financial institutions. Each institution has the obligation to protect each individual's information from any non-intended entity or person.

Organizational Privacy

Organizational privacy refers to organizations or governmental agencies that do not want to reveal their trade secrets or any other activities to non-intended entities or persons, especially to competitors of their products or services. For example, if a drug company is researching a new treatment for a specific disease, they would want to protect all the information related to their research.

Physical Privacy

Physical privacy relates to an intrusion into someone's physical body or medical information. For example, when a health-care professional reveals medical information stored in a computer system to a non-intended entity or person is an invasion of physical privacy.

Vulnerability of Privacy/Threats to Privacy

Many everyday activities can cause a person's private information to be compromised. For example, during the course of a visit to the doctor, a patient talks with the receptionist, the nurse, and the doctor. If the patient receives a prescription, then he talks to the pharmacist and his information is sent to the insurance company for reimbursement. In short, quite a few people get to know about this individual's personal health information and depending on these people, his personal information could be compromised. Examples of threats to privacy are described below.

- **Filling out forms and buying merchandise over the Internet**
  When a person buys a product or requests information about a product using the company's website, the company gathers information about the interests of that person. This information is not protected and is not private. The company can then start e-mailing this person to promote their products.

- **Electronic commerce**
  An enormous amount of information travels over the Internet every day, and there is a chance that some of this information can be stolen and misused, posing a threat to the privacy of individuals. For example, in e-commerce, people make purchases and use their credit cards. There may be hackers using spyware who steal the credit card numbers and use them for their own advantage.

- **Electronic monitoring of people in their workplace**
  Employers use "electronic eyes," by monitoring e-mails sent by their employees, in order to ensure that they are not using company time for personal business. This may be considered a threat to privacy.

- **Internet identity theft**
  Internet identity theft occurs when someone steals someone's personal information without the person's knowledge. This is done by going through the information that is traveling over the Internet in the form of e-mails, online bank statements, and personal information sent to unsecured websites.

Protecting the Privacy of Individuals

Privacy of individuals is protected in a number of ways through government regulations; companies using software to protect private information; and customers taking their own protective measures.

Government Regulations to Protect Privacy

Governments have regulations in place to protect the private information of people wherever IT is involved. Some of them are defined below.

- The **Gramm-Leach-Bliley Act**, which requires that financial as well as non-banking institutions ensure the confidentiality and security of their customers' records and information. Before disclosing nonpublic customer information to affiliates and non-affiliates, these institutions must disclose their policies and practices to their customers and give them an opportunity to opt out. They must also provide appropriate safeguards to protect their customers' personal information.

- The **Health Insurance Portability and Accountability Act of 1996** (HIPAA), which applies to all individuals whose health information is created by health care providers, health plans, and health care clearinghouses, whether on paper, in electronic form, or orally communicated. Consumers have the right to see a copy of their medical records, to request a correction to those records, and to get a notice of a covered entity's privacy policies.

- Under federal law, telecommunications carriers have a duty to protect the confidentiality of Customer Proprietary Network Information, or CPNI.

- The **Children's Online Privacy Protection Act (COPPA) of 1998**, which took effect on April 21, 2000, requires commercial websites that are geared towards children, or that have actual knowledge that children under the age of 13 are using those sites, to obtain "verifiable parental consent" before collecting personal information from children online.

- The **USA PATRIOT Act** enables FBI investigators to track emails and website visits by individuals without obtaining a wiretap order or subpoena. Investigators need to inform only a judge that the investigation is relevant to an ongoing criminal investigation.

Companies Using Software to Protect Private Information

In today's age of Information Technology, financial institutions and other organizations are providing online access to their customers. For example, many banks allow their customers to create online transaction accounts for free. Customers can pay their monthly bills online on a regularly scheduled basis by directly transferring funds from their bank account to the company's bank account. In such cases, institutions use *Secure Socket Layer* (SSL) protocol for transmitting private information over the Internet.

SSL uses encryption technology, known as a cryptographic system, in which the personal information of a customer is encrypted or scrambled, through the use of a public key, before it is transmitted over the Internet and then deciphered or de-scrambled, through the use of a private key, after it reaches its destination. In short, SSL creates a secure connection between a client computer and a server computer so that the information transmitted online is only readable and understood by the recipient of the information. Figure 6.1 below shows an example of a simple encryption scheme.

Figure 6.1   Example of the Encryption of Data

Original data:	Word
Encrypted data:	Yqtf
Where:	W = Y, o = q, r = t, d = f
Replacing each letter in a document with a third letter in alphabet scheme.	

Another protocol used for secure data transmission is S-HTTP, which is used to send personal messages securely. HTTP is the protocol used when you visit a website on which data is not secure.

Customers Taking Their Own Privacy Protection Measures

Computers track all online activities from Internet searching and browsing, to e-mails sent and received, and programs and files accessed and modified. All this information may be collected by an Internet Service Provider (ISP), hackers, spyware, and other programs. Additionally, a computer may be prone to attack by software such as malware, spyware, phishing, and others. Therefore, many computer users use combinations of software to protect their computers from harm and threats to privacy. Some of the most popular software would be.

- *Clear history*, which clears a computer's search history over the Internet
- *Proxy software*, which makes a computer's Internet surfing anonymous
- *Anti-virus software*, which provides:
    - security and protection against viruses
    - protection against Web attacks

- identity protection, by inspecting websites to make sure they are not fakes

- protection against online identity thefts

- help in securing and monitoring a computer's home network

- *Anti-phishing Software,* which verifies the authenticity of websites that hide their true URL address. A computer user should always use software that hides his IP address when he visits a website.

File Shredding and Privacy

File shredding should be done for the sake of privacy. File shredding means to delete a file from the computer system in such a way that it cannot be restored by any means. File shredding is done with the help of software, as operating systems may not be able to delete a file completely. File shredding should include shredding files from all types of media, including CD shredding and video shredding.

6.3   INTELLECTUAL PROPERTY RIGHTS AND LEGAL ISSUES/OPEN SOURCE INITIATIVES

Intellectual property is the term used to describe a human creation or invention, which can be new artwork, new inventions of equipment or drugs, new literature, new clothing designs, etc. Most are used for commercial purposes.

Intellectual property rights refer to the rights a creator has for his work, in such a way that he is recognized as its rightful owner. There are two categories of intellectual property:

- Copyright, which includes books, actor performances, artwork, music composition, etc.

- Industrial property, which includes processes, industrial designs, patents, trademarks, etc.

Purposes of Intellectual Property

The main purposes of intellectual property are as follows:

- *Monetary incentives*, in which the creator of the intellectual property is given exclusive rights to use it and receive monetary gains for its use.

- *Exclusive rights*, which include copyrights, patents, names, etc., and which, in terms of the law, gives exclusive rights to the owner of the intellectual property for its use.

- *Economic Growth*, when intellectual property is protected by the exclusive rights law and promotes economic growth as far as creating new products, creating more jobs, etc.

- *Progress of human beings*, in terms of saving time, money, and natural resources; having a better living style; and promoting better health.

For example, the use of cabin filters in cars helps passengers breathe cleaner air. Also, solar panels convert sunlight into electricity to heat homes or offices, thus saving other natural resources used to generate electricity.

Types of Intellectual Property

Trademarks, industrial design rights, trade secrets, copyright, symbols, names, and patents are all forms of intellectual property.

Trademark

A trademark is a unique symbol or sign used by individuals or organizations to identify their products. Trademarks are used to indicate the quality and standard of a company's products sold in the market; identify an organization; and identify the image of an organization in the business world.

A trademark can be created from a combination of numbers, alphabet letters, pictures, sounds and so forth. The trademark provides the owner of the intellectual property with the exclusive rights to his work. However, the owner can let someone use it for a fee. There is no time limit on a trademark and it can be renewed by paying a fee. In their advertisements, a company might include the following wording: "[blank] is a Trademark of XYZ Co.," [blank] being where they display the trademark. Trademarks are protected by the Lanham Act.

Industrial Designs

An industrial design provides the internal details and functions, form, shape, or color of an object that will be manufactured and used for a specific purpose in an organization or business. The industrial design may be a two- or three-dimensional pattern used to manufacture an object. An industrial design right is an intellectual property right that protects the visual design of the object. To protect the industrial design, the owner must register the product. Usually, organizations continually try to improve the design of an object to keep their market share of the product.

Trade Secrets

A trade secret can be a process, the design of a machine or equipment, a chemical formula, or an instrument whose details are known only to its owner and are used for commercial purposes and economic gains, and whose details are kept secret from the public. In the United States, trade secrets are not protected in the same fashion as trademarks and patents. A trade secret is only protected until someone else knows it. The owner of a trade secret may try to protect it with a nondisclosure clause agreement in an employee's contract, which states that the employee will not reveal the trade secrets of his/her employer.

Patents

When a patent is issued for a product or intellectual property, the patent owner receives exclusive rights for his work and any financial gains that result from it. The patent may last for 20 years. Once patented, the work of the owner cannot be manufactured, used, or sold without the owner's express permission. Patents give recognition to the owner of the intellectual property.

Copyright

A copyright protects the owner of intellectual property. This owner can be a software writer, an author, an artist, a machine designer, or other similar owners. No one can use, copy, or adapt their work in any form without the owner's consent. Software companies, TV and radio broadcasting stations, authors of books and publications, music recording studios, databases, and other similar owners of intellectual property are protected under copyright laws.

Software companies sometimes require that a computer user has a proof of purchase and install the program only on the number of computers specified on the package.

Threats to Intellectual Property Rights: Counterfeiting, Piracy, and Poor Quality of Products

Many individuals and organizations are victims of counterfeiting, piracy, and products made of poor quality. Counterfeiting has, at times, made the software industry its victim. Counterfeiting software, also known as software piracy, means that someone makes imitation copies of software sold on CDs/DVDs. While it appears to be original, it is not, and it is usually sold at a lower price than the original software.

Currently, it appears that much of the pirated software is coming from overseas thus making it difficult to enforce intellectual property rights. Protecting intellectual property is essential to technological and industrial innovation and is fundamental to economic growth.

Open Source and Open Source Initiatives

An open source is software whose source code, written by a programmer, is made available to the public. Anyone may copy the code and make changes in it and redistribute the modified source code without paying royalties or fees. The open source concept involves the public and does not have any licensing restrictions. The main purpose of open source is to make the source code more reliable and flexible, and to lower operational costs. Linux is an example of open source technology.

The Open Source Initiative (OSI) is a nonprofit corporation formed to educate people about the concept and benefits of open source technology and to form a community of people involved in open source projects. The user and/or modifier of open source software has to comply with the following requirements:

- No fee may be charged when redistributing it to others;

- The open source must include the source code and its compiler form;

- The modified open source may not discriminate against any person, group, or business.

- There may not be any restriction against other software installed on the computer.

6.4 TELECOMMUTING AND VIRTUAL TEAMS

Telecommuting happens when an employee of a company works from home using a company-provided computer, telephone lines, and Internet connections. Telecommuting sometimes involves working with a group of other employees. This is known as "working in a virtual team." A virtual team is a group of people who communicate electronically with each other while performing their jobs. A virtual team usually has members with a variety of skills and talents.

Benefits of Virtual Teams

Virtual teams operate in all types of organizations. Virtual teams can "meet" and make important decisions related to the project they are working on, even though they are separated geographically. Global companies can have "meetings" without the added expenses of gathering the employees in one area, saving on time, traveling, lodging, and food costs. In addition, by supporting a virtual team, employers have the advantage of hiring an employee based solely on her skills rather than her geographic location.

Types of Virtual Groups in Virtual Teams

Friendship group

A friendship group is formed when a number of individual virtual teams communicate with each other.

Task group

A task group is formed when a number of individuals are working on a common task. For example, reporters stationed throughout the world reporting on an important global occurrence.

Interest group

An interest group is formed when individuals share a common interest and come together online to discuss that interest.

Command group

A command group is formed when a number of individuals work for the same department.

Global group

When members of a team are from different parts of the world, they form a global virtual team. Because of globalization, networking, and the Internet, more and more global virtual teams are being formed.

6.5 ERGONOMICS AND INFORMATION TECHNOLOGY

Ergonomics addresses the positioning of an individual's computer monitor, keyboard, and chair, as well as other accessories involved in operating a computer. The purpose of ergonomics is to safeguard the computer user's health, safety, and comfort (e.g., reducing eye and neck strain) in order to maximize productivity and efficiency, and reduce the chances of bodily injury. Poorly positioned computer equipment can cause the user to have physical problems with joints, muscles, nerves, tendons, eyes, neck, and back. These physical stresses can also affect efficiency and productivity.

The Importance of Ergonomics

Working at a computer for prolonged periods of time can actually be harmful to one's overall health. The Occupational Safety and Health Administration (OSHA) has identified that Work-Related Musculoskeletal Disorders (WMSDs) are the single largest job-related injury and illness problems in the United States. The cost of WMSDs to businesses is measured in terms of job turnover, product quality and customer satisfaction and efficiency, and lost productivity from absences due to work-related injuries. These factors may affect a company's performance in the market, its market share, and profitability.

Guidelines in Ergonomics

To increase bodily comfort and reduce bodily injuries follow these guidelines:

- Set your keyboard at a comfortable height and angle.

- Use mouse and wrist pads to support your wrists while typing. This can prevent carpal tunnel syndrome (the pinching of the nerve that runs from the hand to the forearm and results in pain and numbness in the wrist and arm).

- Set the placement and angle of your computer monitor to eye level or below to avoid neck strain.

- Obtain and place ample lighting assuring that there is no glare on your monitor screen (to avoid blurred vision and headaches).

- Use a computer chair with back support to help avoid neck and back strain.

- Verify that the height of your computer desk is adjusted for comfort and that you have enough space to comfortably move your legs and feet.

- Take breaks. Avoid sitting at your desk for prolonged periods of time. Schedule short breaks of 5 minutes now and then to relax your body and avoid straining specific areas. Be sure to flex your fingers and hands to avoid stiffness and reduce the chances of developing carpal tunnel syndrome.

Job Design

Job design is a procedure that lists all of the assigned tasks, including sub-tasks and duties, a person has to perform to do his/her job. The job design keeps the organizational objectives and the individual worker's requirements in mind, along with the environment (health and safety aspects) in which the person has to perform required tasks. In the case of IT workers, ergonomics is an important aspect of job design. Job design includes working hours, work breaks, the criteria for future raises and promotions, training period, retirement and pension plans, and health related benefits.

The main objectives of job design are to provide employee job satisfaction and to help the employee feel a sense of achievement and increased self-esteem.

A good job design should provide the following:

- Job satisfaction.

- A job evaluation process. Explains how the employee's job performance will be evaluated and at what time intervals.

- Criteria that will be used for raises and promotions.

- Details about the employee's breaks and defined working hours.

- How job training is addressed, including funding, when a new function is added to an employee's job.

- The title and name of the employee's supervisor.

- A complete list of job-related benefits, such as health and pension benefits.

The methods used in job design include:

- Job enlargement which means to give different tasks to an employee in order to reduce boredom, motivate the employee to learn more, and increase job specialization. Helps increase job satisfaction.

- Job rotation allows an employee to work in different departments in order to give him a better understanding of, and the skills and knowledge needed for, various positions in the company.

- Job enrichment is used to motivate employees to assume additional job responsibilities to allow transitioning into a management position.

- Work restructuring, usually done by a job analyst, studies current procedures and techniques used to complete a job and explores how to simplify and make the procedures more efficient. The job is sometimes re-defined.

6.6   THE IMPACT OF INFORMATION TECHNOLOGY ON GLOBALIZATION

Globalization is the process by which employees of companies and governments of different countries cooperate with each other to do business. They exchange goods and services using information technology. This includes a company in one country investing money in its operations in another country. In short, globalization can be defined as international trading and investment between different nations to conduct business, made possible by using information technology.

Factors that Lead to Globalization

The Emergence of Multinational Companies

In the past, a company's business operations were limited to one country. In recent years, however, many organizations have expanded their business operations into many different countries.

Political Reasons

At one time, countries such as China and India did not allow foreign companies to invest in their countries. Due to changes in government policies, liberal rules and trade liberalization, those governments now allow free trade and investment in their countries.

Easier Flow of Information

The expansion of networking and the Internet has made data communication easier and faster, thus leading to globalization. The emergence of fiber optics communication with satellite and other fast communication technologies has helped to expand globalization.

IT Outsourcing

Companies have outsourced at least some of their operations overseas. Much of the development of accounting software has been outsourced to India.

Interdependence Among Nations

Due to environmental, social, economical, political, and other factors, the nations of the world have become interdependent, thus leading to globalization.

Effects of Globalization

Globalization has interconnected the economies of different countries and people from different parts of the world. The increased use of computer networks and the Internet has improved worldwide communications like never before. Globalization has had a profound effect on businesses and people. Some of the most important effects are noted below.

Living Standards

Due to international agreements and to some governments placing low tariffs on manufactured goods for exporting purposes, some poor nations have benefited and raised their standard of living by exporting goods to rich nations.

Manufacturing and Services

The IT growth has led some companies to globalize their manufacturing and service operations.

Finance and Economics

Worldwide production industries are coming into existence and goods are flowing more freely between nations allowing the emergence of a global common market.

Increased Competition

Because of the global trade market, companies are facing stiff competition to sell their products. Therefore, these companies are trying to efficiently produce quality products at reduced prices.

The Environment

Companies are opening their operations overseas in third-world countries. If those countries don't follow the same environmental rules as first-world countries, pollution will increase.

On Technology

High technology systems have emerged such as the global positioning system (GPS), communication satellite systems, networking, higher speed Internet, and wireless phones.

Outsourcing

Outsourcing takes place when a local company contracts with an outside company (usually overseas) to provide services and manufactured goods, which otherwise would have done by an employee of the local company itself. When outsourcing, the company may form a partnership with a local company in the outsourced country.

Outsourcing started in the 1990s as a way for companies to compete in the world market. Some of the main objectives of outsourcing are outlined below.

- Reducing operation costs by hiring cheap labor and lowering transportation costs. This enables companies to be more competitive and increase their business edge;

- Possibility of getting cheaper raw materials;

- No need to pay taxes for their employees since the outsourcing provider is responsible for these taxes.

Advantages of Outsourcing

Some of the advantages of outsourcing are listed below.

- *More choices of services*
  Countries to where the jobs are outsourced may provide a variety of services to choose from, thus allowing the company to select a specific service.

- *Stay competitive*
  By lowering their operation costs, companies can have a competitive edge in the business world.

- *Expansion and growth*
  Outsourcing allows companies to grow and expand as the demand for their services increases. After the initial entry into a country, the company can make strong roots there and expand by employing other services.

- *Time zone advantages*
  A big advantage of outsourcing is utilizing the differences in time zones between countries. For example, it is possible for a company located in the United States to send something for processing to India. With the differences in time zones, India could process the work and send it back to the company in the U.S. overnight.

- *Search for new technology*
  Some portion of the money saved by outsourcing can be utilized in research and development of new technology to make IT more efficient. Due to the increase of commerce and data communications over the Internet, increases in bandwidth to handle traffic on the Internet is needed.

- *Increased productivity*
  Proper usage of advanced technology as well as of a multi-talented workforce in outsourced countries, will result in an increase in productivity.

Disadvantages of Outsourcing

Although outsourcing provides considerable benefits, it also has a number of drawbacks, which are listed below.

- *Lag time in setting up a business*
  Any time a new business is opened, it takes some time to set it up and build customers. Similarly, it may take some time to set up an outsourced business. Therefore, the time required to setup an outsourced business must be kept in mind. In some cases, gradual outsourcing is a better option.

- *Language barriers*
  Language barriers may pose communication problems and lead to mis-understandings on the business operations.

- *Loss of jobs in the domestic market*
  Outsourcing can lead to the elimination of jobs in the domestic market, which can cause a strain on the domestic economy.

- *Trade secrets*
  Outsourcing can cause a company to share trade secrets with the out-sourced vendor, who might use the system for personal gain and un-dermine the company's operations.

- *Failure to train staff*
  In the event that outsourced vendors do not train their staff according to the hiring company's requirements, production or service output may be lowered. This can lead to lower profits.

Insourcing

Insourcing is the opposite of outsourcing. Insourcing occurs when services or operations are contracted to an outside company but are performed locally. The main objective of insourcing is to reduce operation costs by lowering labor, raw material, taxes, and transportation costs, which might enable the company to be more competitive.

Advantages of Insourcing

- *Creates jobs for the domestic market*
  Insourcing allows a company to create jobs for other industries whose operations are tied to their operations.

- *Helps domestic economy*
  The creation of more jobs in the domestic market helps the domestic economy.

- *Better quality of service*
  An outsourced vendor may not provide the same quality of service that a local company can provide. When outsourcing, companies have to sign Service Level Agreements (SLA) that deal with contract and warranties of services provided to customers.

- *In-house management and control*
  Outsourcing leads to the control of the operations by the outsourced vendor. By insourcing, local management has control over the operations.

6.7   CAREERS IN INFORMATION SYSTEMS AND INFORMATION TECHNOLOGY

Information technology (IT) no longer deals with only computer or computer engineering. IT is used in all areas of business and industry. New applications using IT in every field imaginable are being invented daily, since IT has become part of our daily lives.

Following is a partial list of jobs available in the IT industry today, along with the job description and the basic qualifications required.

- *Applications Architect*
  An applications architect designs components of applications, including interfaces, middleware and infrastructure, and complies with employer's design standards. A bachelor's or master's degree in computer science or information systems is required.

- *Business Systems Analyst (BSA)*
  A BSA is responsible for guiding, aligning, and accurately communicating business needs and processes with IT solutions for various types of customers. A bachelor's or master's degree in computer science or information systems is required.

- *Chief Technology Officer (CTO)*
  A CTO is responsible for setting the firm's overall technology standards and practices; making recommendations and explaining technology solutions to senior management through presentations and advocacy; managing the implementation of data systems and monitoring their effectiveness in meeting business unit needs; providing leadership and managing staff; creating reports in functional areas such

as systems operations, LAN/WAN architecture, and hardware and software support. A degree in computer science or a related field and experience in IT management is required.

- *Computer Security Specialist*
  A computer security specialist is responsible for assisting with the administration of the information system's security. A bachelor's degree in computer science, information systems, or mathematics is required.

- *Computer Programmer*
  Computer programmers write programs. After the computer software engineers and systems analysts design the software programs, the programmer converts that design into a logical series of instructions that the computer can follow. The programmer codes these instructions into programming languages, depending on the need. The most common languages are C++, Java, Visual Basic.net, and Python. Computer programmers also update, repair, modify, and expand existing programs; those working on large projects that involve many programmers use computer-assisted software engineering (CASE) tools to automate much of the coding process. These tools enable a programmer to concentrate on writing the unique parts of a program. Many programmers need a bachelor's degree, but a two-year degree or certificate may be adequate for some positions. Some computer programmers hold a college degree in computer science, mathematics, or information systems, whereas others have taken special courses in computer programming to supplement their degree in a field such as accounting, finance, or other areas of business.

- *Computer Scientist*
  A computer scientist is a scientist who studies and uses the theoretical foundations of information and computation and their application in various computer systems. A bachelor's degree is a pre-requisite for most employers. Relevant work experience is also very important. For some of the more complex jobs, persons with graduate degrees are preferred.

- *Computer Hardware Engineer*
  Computer hardware engineers generally design, develop, test, and supervise the manufacture of computer hardware—for example, chips or device controllers. Computer hardware engineers generally require a bachelor's degree in computer engineering or electrical engineering.

- *Computer Software Engineer*
  Computer software engineers design and develop various types of software, including computer games, business applications, operating systems, network control systems, and middleware; they apply the theories and principles of computer science and mathematical analysis to create, test, and evaluate the software applications and systems

that make computers work. For software engineering positions, most employers prefer applicants who have at least a bachelor's degree as well as a broad knowledge and experience with a variety of computer systems and technologies. The usual college majors for applications software engineers are computer science, software engineering, or mathematics. Graduate degrees are preferred for some of the most complex jobs.

- *Computer Database Administrator*
  Computer database administrators design, write, and take care of computer database systems so that the right person can get the right information at the right time. They also write programs to perform queries to extract useful information and to produce reports as necessary; and they watch over the system to ensure that users do not tamper with the information or the structure of the database. A bachelor's degree in computer science, systems science, telecommunications, or a related field of study is usually required.

- *Digital Media Specialist*
  Digital media specialists or digital public relations specialists work with computer technology to promote a company, cause, or idea. Digital media specialist jobs are found in both the private and public sectors where a message or idea needs to be conveyed to the public quickly. A bachelor's degree in a digital media related discipline or equivalent combination of education and work experience is usually required.

- *Helpdesk Support Specialist*
  Helpdesk support handles software and hardware issues. Helpdesk support staff resolve issues and decide when to create work tickets for issues that can't be solved by phone or e-mail and that require a visit to the user's workspace. Besides patience and a positive attitude, some work experience, a bachelor's degree, or a two-year degree is required.

- *Information Systems Manager*
  Computer and information systems managers plan, coordinate, and direct research and design for the computer-related activities of firms. A bachelor's or master's degree in computer science or information systems or a master's degree in business administration (MBA) is required.

- *Lead Applications Developer*
  A lead applications developer manages software development teams on the designing, developing, coding, testing, and debugging of applications. A bachelor's degree in computer science or a related field and three to five years experience are required.

- *Manager of Technical Services*
  A manager of technical services manages help desk operations and support service; manages staff with regards to hiring, training, scheduling work assignments, and conducting evaluations; monitors response times, evaluates user satisfaction levels and makes recommendations for improvement in services; evaluates and manages technical support systems hardware and software and makes recommendations regarding upgrades or changes; and negotiates, writes, and reports on internal and external service level agreements (SLA). A bachelor's degree in information systems or a related discipline is required along with several years of managerial experience in operations and support. Additional professional certifications such as the Microsoft Certified Systems Engineer (MCSE) as well as the Help Desk Institute's Help Desk Manager (HDM) certification are a plus.

- *Messaging Administrator*
  A messaging administrator controls e-mail and groupware systems, including associated servers, operating systems, and backup and recovery programs; he fixes system problems and attends to service requests. A bachelor's degree in computer science, computer information systems or a related field, plus two to three years or more of experience working with messaging systems is required.

- *Network Architect or Network Engineer*
  Network architects or network engineers are the designers of computer networks. They set up, test, and evaluate systems such as local area networks (LANs), wide area networks (WANs), the Internet, intranets, and other data communications systems. They need to have a bachelor's degree in engineering, computer science, information system, or closely related discipline.

- *Network Manager*
  A network manager performs direct day-to-day operations and maintenance of the firm's networking technology; collaborates with network engineers, architects, and other team members on the implementation, testing, deployment, and integration of network systems. Several years of experience in a networking environment and managing technical personnel is required.

- *Network and Computer Systems Administrator*
  A Network and Computer Systems Administrator designs, installs, and supports an organization's computer systems. This person is responsible for LANs, WANs, network segments, Internet and intranet systems. A bachelor's degree is usually required, although an associate's degree or professional certification, along with work related experience, may be adequate for some positions.

- *Systems Administrator*
  A systems administrator should have in-depth technical knowledge of systems hardware and software as well as of operating systems. He should have experience with installing operating system software, patches, and upgrades; analyzing, troubleshooting, and resolving system hardware, software, and networking issues; configuring, optimizing, fine-tuning, and monitoring operating system software and servers; and performing system backups and recovery. Some employers may require a bachelor's degree in computer science or a related field, while others may accept an associate's degree or technical training certificate. Three to five years of experience working with the specific types of hardware and software systems used by the company are generally required.

- *Systems Programmer*
  A systems programmer is responsible for the installation, maintenance, implementation, and tuning of UNIX and other operating systems' hardware and software along with other associated components. She supports various Web servers, and performs troubleshooting, performance, and capacity tuning. A bachelor's degree in computer science or the equivalent in education and/or experience is required as well as an overall knowledge of the hardware and software components of operating systems.

- *Technical Writer*
  A technical writer writes technical materials such as equipment or product manuals, appendices, and operating and maintenance instructions. A technical writer knows how to use software such as Author IT, Photoshop, and Frame maker. A bachelor's degree from a four-year college or university preferably in technical/business communications, engineering, computer science, or information technology is required.

- *Web Developer*
  A Web developer plans and implements Web-based applications; and coordinates with the product development, marketing, product management and other teams to bring new applications online. A bachelor's degree in computer science, electrical engineering, or a related field is required.

- *Web Programmer*
  A Web programmer provides technical guidance to the program manager and team members on the implementation and maintenance of a project's website; translates detailed website design into code, and programs, tests, debugs, and updates the website as required. Proficiency in HTML and Java is required as well as a bachelor's degree in computer science, electrical engineering or a related field.

Factors to consider when choosing an IT career

The Changing Nature of IT

The IT field is constantly changing. With upgrades in hardware and software in IT technology, operations performed may change. Therefore, in an IT career, one should be willing to adjust with those changes.

Certifications in IT

IT professionals can choose from a wide variety of information-technology certifications. Certifications provide increased job security, additional career opportunities, and increased credibility in the workplace. Achieving certification shows an employer that a job candidate possesses the right skills, dedication, and commitment to an IT career. Certifications are available in different areas of IT such as networking, database, security, software development and so on.

Some of the IT certifications are listed below.

- **CompTIA (The Computer Information Technology Industry Association)**, which is primarily recognized for the A+ certification for an IT professional's ability to work on hardware and software. Some advanced certifications from CompTIA include Network+, Linux+, Security+ and Server+. CompTIA certifications are awarded through testing in a particular area of IT. CompTIA certifications are used when evaluating candidates for job interviews and promoting employees.

- **Microsoft IT Certification** is awarded after candidates pass a Microsoft exam. They become Microsoft Certified Professionals. Microsoft's certifications are desired certifications when an IT professional is working with Microsoft products. Microsoft certifications can be awarded for different areas of IT such as database, desktop support, internet, security, and systems administration.

Other certifications awarded are:

- Apple Certified System Administrator (ACSA)
- A+ Certification PC Repair Technician Program
- Cisco Certified Network Professional (CCNP)

- HP Certified IT Professional

- IBM Certified Enterprise Developer

- Certified Information Systems Auditor

- Certified Wireless Network Professional (CWNP)

- CISCO certifications in wireless technology that cover the installation, security and troubleshooting of products.

- ECouncil offers certifications that focus on security and hacking.

- Microsoft Certified Database Administrator

- Microsoft Certified Systems Administrator

- Nortel Networks Certified Network Architect

- Oracle Certified Professional Java Developer

- Sun Certified Java Programmer

- Symantec Certified Security Engineer

6.8 KNOWLEDGE MANAGEMENT (KM)

Knowledge can be defined as information about some object (person, place, or thing) that is collected and analyzed to learn more about its characteristics. After acquiring information about an object, this information is processed in order to generate other types of information which, if needed in the future, will be stored in memory.

Through various means, organizations collect knowledge about its resources, processes, and other things that are involved in its operations in order to accomplish organizational objectives. Therefore, knowledge management is necessary to help organizations make important decisions on how to increase company profits and retain a competitive edge in the market.

Types of Knowledge

Implicit knowledge (tacit) is acquired through experience and observation. People usually pass this knowledge onto others through word of mouth (i.e., discussion groups, seminars, meetings, etc.). Implicit knowledge is not written or stored in computers.

Explicit knowledge (formal) is communicated in a systematic way using methods such as collecting data, writing formulas, designing operational manuals, etc. It is stored in computers and it is easily shared.

Knowledge Management (KM) is defined as a variety of techniques, strategies, or practices that identifies, collects, and organizes knowledge to meet a company's objectives by increasing the competitive edge of the company, its profits, productivity, and market shares.

To be effective, Knowledge Management should use the 4 W's principle:

- "Where" (location) the information should come from
- "Who" can provide the information
- "When" the information should be collected
- "What type" of information should be collected

Objectives of Knowledge Management

- To create a database and a data warehouse
- To make decisions based on acquired knowledge to compete in the business market
- To replace knowledge when experienced people leave
- To increase performance of employees in the workplace
- To use time efficiently, by implementing strategies that use time efficiently for knowledge management

Strategies in KM

Listed below are some of the strategies used in knowledge management.

- *Push technology*
  Push technology uses products and services, such as PointCast and BackWeb, that pushes information into a computer based on the selection criteria. For example, collecting information from employees on a constant basis and storing it in a database.

- *Pull technology*
  In pull technology, the information is collected from outside sources or experts when the company realizes that there is a need for improvement in the company's operations.

- *Databases*
  Databases are used in knowledge management to store large amounts of information. The stored information can be organized according to the specific requirements of an organization in making decisions to improve a company's operations.

- *Software tools*
  Software, such as groupware (used in collaborative technologies), social software (such as wikis) and databases can be used collectively to help KM.

- *Network community*
  In order to support management of implicit knowledge, the use of e-mail and Web logs in computer networks will encourage people to communicate their implicit knowledge through those and store it in databases.

- *Data mining techniques*
  Data mining was discussed earlier in the book.

Knowledge Management is a part of other software called *Enterprise Content Management* (ECM), which refers to the techniques and strategies used to acquire, organize, manage, warehouse, and deliver content and documents related to an organization and its processes.

6.9   SYSTEM, APPLICATION, AND PC SECURITY AND CONTROLS

In the same way that thieves steal items from homes and businesses, "hackers" steal the data stored in computers. Therefore, in the same way homes and businesses are protected by alarm systems, computer data and information must also be protected.

Computer Security

Computer security, also known as information security, is a collection of techniques, processes, and protocols that secure all types of information and services provided by computer networks and the Internet from harm, misuse, theft, tampering, natural disasters, unauthorized publication, and stealing by hackers or unauthorized people for personal gain. Computer security should protect all the computers and networks at all times, including when the computer systems are in use to access and process information.

Security Architecture is the designing of computer security in such a way that decides how, where, and why security should be placed to protect computers and computer networks on which data is stored and transported. The integrity (truthfulness) and the confidentiality of data should be protected as well as its quality and should not be vulnerable to attacks by viruses, hackers, or spyware. The data, however, should be accessible whenever required.

In short, all computer hardware and software, data stored on computers, and data that travels on computer networks and the Internet should be protected.

Computer Security Measures

Various measures that can be taken for computer security are listed below.

- *Use of Computer Access Controls (Physical Security)*
  Computer access controls deal with the physical security of buildings and rooms where computers storing data and computer networks are located. All should be protected by installing security alarm systems. The buildings should be locked and entry should be restricted to authorized personnel only and protected by personal biometric devices—authentication techniques.

- *Hardware Security*
  Hardware security uses logins and passwords to access computers and data stored on those computers. It also uses a logout feature for computer users to logout. The database administrator sets access privileges for accessing and processing of data stored in computers, and manages logins/logouts. Hardware devices, such as biometric keyboards, can be used to stop illegal access to data stored in computers. The use of these devices is controlled by peripheral device controllers that control access to hard disks by hackers or other people who want to steal data and cause damage to computer systems.

- *Cryptographic Technique*
  Cryptographic technique, described earlier in this chapter, is used to protect data being transported between computers so that it cannot be intercepted, altered, or stolen by hackers.

- *Authentication Techniques/ Biometric Devices*
  Authentication techniques are used to control access to data stored in computers. Biometric devices use human body parts, such as fingerprints, palm prints, and facial recognition systems, to identify the authorized users of the computer systems.

- *Chain of Trust Techniques*
  Chain of trust techniques are used to ensure that all software installed on computers is authentic software carrying a seal of authenticity and purchased from authorized distributors or sellers of software.

- *Firewall Hardware Devices (Internet Security)*
  Firewall hardware devices are devices, such as routers, that when attached to computers are configured to act as firewalls by keeping unused logical ports closed.

- *Software Firewall (Internet Security)*
  A software firewall is installed to protect attacks on computer networks or computers that are using networks or the Internet. Personal firewalls close all open logical ports on computers to protect computers from attackers when using the Internet.

- *Anti-Virus Software*
  Anti-virus programs are installed to protect computers from attacks by viruses such as Trojan horses, encryption viruses, worms, boot-sector viruses, script and macro-viruses, and logical bombs. Viruses will be discussed later in this chapter.

- *Anti-Spam Software*
  Anti-spam software protects computers from unwanted (junk) email.

- *Anti-Spyware*
  Anti-Spyware protects computers from spyware programs that collect information from computers without the user's knowledge. It can steal the personal information stored on a computer system, such as a Social Security Number or a credit card number.

- *Internet Security Suites*
  Whenever the Internet is in use, computers are vulnerable to attacks from viruses, malware, spyware, and more. Internet security suites have a number of programs built into one suite such as anti-virus, anti-spyware, and firewall programs to keep information and systems safe.

- *Other Security Software*
  Anti-phishing and e-mail scanner programs are also available for security purposes. Endpoint security software is used to secure data from theft and virus infection on portable storage devices, such as USB drives, when they are used on a network.

- *Computer Audits*
  Computer-Assisted Audit Tools and Techniques (CAATTs) use computers to automate or simplify the audit process in the financial sector. They are also used for fraud detection and continuous monitoring to acquire and analyze business data.

- *Computer Intrusion Detection*
  A computer intrusion detection system is a system used to monitor all activities taking place in a computer system or network. The system checks for possible violations or imminent threats of violation of computer security policies, known as incidents. There are two types of intrusion detection systems: a Network Intrusion Detection System that detects intrusions on networks, and a Host Intrusion Detection System that detect intrusions on the Host computer.

- *Incident reporting*
  Incident reporting is used to check for signs of possible violations or imminent threats of violations to computer security policies.

- *Security Provided by the Operating System*
  The operating system may provide security of its own to identify requests that allow processing and requests that should not allow processing on the computers. In such cases, the OS uses some form of user identification, such as a user name and a password. This process to establish identity is known as authentication.

- *Perform Backups*
  In order to secure a computer system's data and programs, they can be backed up on a hard disk or other devices such as CDs or DVDs. For additional security reasons, the backup data can be on a system that is at a different location. Backups are also used to avoid data loss due to natural disasters, such as volcano eruptions, hurricanes, earthquakes, tornadoes, fires, or lightning strikes where the computers are located.

6.10 BUSINESS STRATEGIES—COMPETITION, REENGINEERING, PROCESS MODELING E-COMMERCE, TQM

An organization should develop short-term and long-term goals, known as a business strategy. Using all of its resources, the company should decide which markets the company should enter or exit, as well as what types of products or services to provide. There are three levels of business strategies: organizational, business, and departmental.

Figure 6.2   Three Levels of Business Strategy

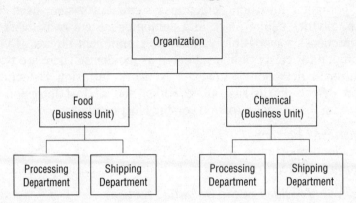

- *Organizational level strategy*
  All actions for a company's operations are the company's responsibilities. These actions include the company's long- and short-term goals—which markets the company should stay in or enter into, as well as what types of products or services the company will provide. The company must decide how to manage all the activities of its individual units. Will each business unit have local (decentralized) power for its operations or will the business be controlled centrally?

- *Business unit level strategy*
  An organization can be made up of individually existing business units in different locations. Each business unit can be one division or a wing of the company. Each unit is responsible for its assembly or manufacturing of products or services provided to the market. Each unit has to create its own business strategy to maintain its competitive edge in the market. The business strategy at this level deals with the unit's performance against its competitors in the market. In its strategy, it should develop actions that will exert influence on the market and it should be able to adjust according to the changing demands of products or services.

- *Departmental unit level strategy*
  Each business unit is made up of a number of departments. Each department provides information about its local resources, processes, and manpower. Once the higher organization level strategy is developed, then each business unit develops its own tasks to be completed to attain the objectives, which leads to the achievement of each business unit's strategies.

Competition in Business Strategy

A competition is a contest between two or more entities or objects on a selected act, where one entity tries to prove that it can perform better than the other. The entity can be a person, a student, or a business. The act can be singing a song, car racing, playing tennis, or a business making a larger profit than its competitor.

Competitive edge means that a business provides a better product or service compared to its competitor. Competitive edge may involve a plan to develop a new product through research and development, and bring it to the market before the competitor does. Gaining a competitive edge also means that, when compared to its competitor, the company provides better customer service, has a better return policy, a lower price, a better quality product, a longer warranty period, better technology in producing the product, etc.

Levels of Economic Competition

There are three levels of economic competition: direct competition, indirect competition, and budget competition.

Direct competition (category or brand competition)

Direct competition is a competition between two products or two services, in which each of them performs the same function (e.g., when automobile manufacturers compete for their share of the SUV market).

Indirect competition (substitute competition)

In indirect competition, two products or two services perform similarly and one product or service can easily be substituted by another (e.g., although different companies produce laser printers, they perform similar functions, but may differ in pages printed per minute).

Budget competition

In budget competition, a customer will spend whatever money he has available on products or services (e.g., a married couple has budgeted two thousand dollars to spend on vacation).

Other Types of Competition

Perfect or pure competition

In perfect or pure competition, there are a large number of manufacturers of products or service providers who sell identical products or provide similar services. Since no one company manufactures the product, the market sets the price of the product.

Monopoly competition

Monopoly competition means that there is one and only one manufacturer of a particular product or one and only one service provider, and other companies are not allowed to enter the market for that product. In monopoly competition, the single manufacturer of the product sets its price.

Factors that Affect Competition

Factors that affect competition include the technology used in production, production costs, and the unit selling price.

Technology in production

A company having better production technology will have a competitive edge over its competitor. Better technology results in cutting production costs. By using mechanical devices (such as robots in production), faster network technology to send data faster, and skilled employees to handle production processes, a company can build and maintain a competitive edge.

Production costs

Production cost is the total cost the company pays for producing an item. For example, to produce one item, the raw material cost is $2.35, the manual labor cost is $12.99, and the machine operation cost is $3.99. The total cost to produce that item is $19.33 ($2.35 + $12.99 + $3.99).

Unit selling price

The unit selling price of an item determines how much profit a company makes, when the item is sold and the production cost is known. For example, if the product whose production cost is $19.33 is sold for $31.49, then the company will make a profit of $12.16 ($31.49 – $19.33) per unit.

6.11   BUSINESS STRATEGIES AND BUSINESS PROCESS REENGINEERING (BPR)

Business Process Reengineering (BPR) is the study and modification of existing business strategies, existing business processes, existing technology, existing hierarchical organizational structure, and existing computer information systems in order to improve business performance and increase market share, profit, and competitive edge in the market. Performance in businesses is judged on cost, quality, speed, and service.

Role of IT in Business Process Reengineering (RPR)

Information technology (IT) plays an important role in the reengineering concept. IT uses a variety of software to aid BPR, including databases, wireless communication devices, decision support systems, customer resource management, supply chain management, amongst others described below.

Databases

Databases provide information wherever or whenever it is required.

Wireless communication devices

Wireless communication devices, such as cell phones, make it easy to communicate with anyone in a company at any time or at any place including remote sites.

Mobile computers

Mobile computers help employees collaborate through e-mail and multimedia communication systems by sending any type of data (including audio and video data) through e-mail and video conferencing and then using the date to make decisions.

AutoCAD and AutoCAM software

AutoCAD software can help redesign products and AutoCAM software can help improve the manufacturing process of products.

Expert systems

Expert systems allow employees to perform specialized tasks.

Decision Support Systems (DSS)

DSS provide support to arrive at decisions fast.

Electronic Data Interchange (EDI) Software

EDI helps to monitor the flow of electronic data over networks in required data formats. EDI reduces transaction costs.

Enterprise Resource Planning (ERP)

ERP helps employees share the same information in a centralized location.

Customer Resource Management (CRM)

CRM helps manage customer information. It also helps customer satisfaction.

Supply Chain Management (SCM)

SCM helps to manage the supply of raw materials and finished products.

Total Quality Management (TQM) Software

TQM makes the process of redesigning products easier.

Automatic identification and tracking

Helps track items or products rather than having an employee locate the product.

6.12 BUSINESS STRATEGIES AND BUSINESS PROCESS MODELING (BPM)

A business process is a sequence of selected activities performed by a business across time and space to complete a selected task. Each task has a start, selected inputs and selected operations performed on inputs, and an end. The task must fulfill the needs of the customer or organization by supplying merchandise, providing services, or performing procedures.

A block diagram of a business process is shown below in **Figure 6.3.**

Figure 6.3   Business Process

Business processes can be of three types:

- *Management processes*
  A management process is the process of planning and administering any type of activity. Typical management processes include project management.

- *Operational processes*
  An operational process is the process of planning and administering a particular type of operation in a business. Typical operational processes in businesses are manufacturing and purchasing.

- *Supporting processes*
  Supporting processes are processes that support operational processes. Examples include accounting, which supports sales operations, and recruiting, which supports human resources operations.

Business Process Modeling (BPM)

Business Process Modeling (BPM) is the study and analysis of existing processes and the act of modifying them in order to improve the efficiency and the quality of the process.

Components of a BPM

A business process model specifies the following components:

1. Objective of the task to be completed.
2. Predefined inputs to the process.
3. Operations to be performed on the inputs using various operators.
4. Defined outputs based on the operations performed in step 3.
5. Generated reports related to the completion of the task.

UML Model of a Business Process

The main objectives or advantages of a BPM are as follows.

1. Study the current process (for a particular activity) and identify its shortcomings or other issues that need to be resolved.
2. Design a new process that is more efficient, simpler, and faster, and, perhaps with the help of BPM tools and computers, explore the possibility of its automation.
3. Interaction with other processes—In industry, all processes are linked with other processes. BPM software can predict if the modification of a process will have an adverse effect on other linked processes.
4. Cost analysis—Whenever a process is modified, the company may have to incur additional costs, such as buying new equipment or training employees to use it. BPM can compare, contrast, and identify the benefits of switching or not switching to the new process.

Business Strategies and Total Quality Management (TQM)

All industries use quality control (QC) techniques on raw materials used in manufacturing their products, from the beginning of the manufacturing process to the end. Quality control ensures that the raw materials meet the product's specifications. If the raw material does not meet the required specifications, then it is not used. On the other hand, if the finished product does not meet the required product specifications, then the product is not sold or shipped to customers.

Total Quality Management (TQM) is a business management tool with one objective: all the departments of an organization must collectively operate in a manner that meets the customers' needs, maximizes the company's profits, and meets the company's goals and objectives.

Most companies apply Total Quality Management (TQM) tools to their products or services to ensure that all the products or services meet minimum standards or exceed the set standards. TQM is essential for the existence of a company.

Basic principles of TQM

1. Fulfill the minimum requirements of a customer.
2. Improve the quality of products or services on a constant basis to keep the customer satisfied.
3. Maintain the quality of current product or services provided, if the customer is satisfied.
4. Maintain good relationships with customers, the suppliers of raw materials and other products or services used.
5. Use BPM to continuously improve business processes.

Use of TQM tools

TQM tools are used to collect and analyze all types of data related to an organization and its products or services. The data is used for improving the efficiency and quality of the organization and its products or services. The basic information provided by TQM tools about an organization includes:

- Identifying the customer and their needs.

- Knowing the competition.

- Understanding organizational hierarchical structure.

- Providing statistics on the company's performance.

- Deploying staff, their work responsibilities, and their performance to achieve company objectives.

- Identifying positive and negative business practices that affect the quality of the products or services.

- Analyzing the organization's finances and financial status in the market.

- Identifying measures to improve productivity, processes, and quality of products.

Below is a list of various tools used in TQM.

- Line graph
  In a line graph, various points of intersections are plotted between the X axis and the Y axis on a graph and those points are then joined with a line. A line graph shows the relationship between two variables on a graph. The line graph example below (Figure 6.4) shows the days of the week represented on the x-axis and the corresponding daytime temperatures on the y-axis.

Figure 6.4   Line Graph of Weekday Temperatures

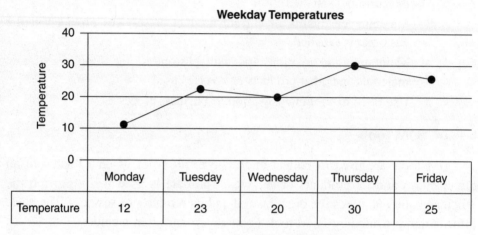

Days of the Week

- *Scatter plots*
  A scatter plot is similar to a line chart (graph) but it has no line. The points of intersection between the X axis and the Y axis are shown on the graph, but are not connected with a line. The information found in Figure 6.4 above is shown in scatter plot format below in Figure 6.5.

- *Run charts*
  A run chart displays process performance over a period of time. A control chart is a special type of run chart used to determine if a manufacturing or business process is running in control or out of control. The control chart shows the time on the x-axis and the run value on the y-axis. A center line (average line) shows the run value for a process when it has been running in a stable condition. An upper line shows the upper run value limit and a lower line shows the lower run value limit. If the process goes below the lower run limit or above the upper run limit, the process becomes unstable. The upper, lower, and average lines are statistical controls in running of a process.

  When a process is in control, it is running consistently. When it is out of control, the process is running inconsistently due to some factors.

- *Histograms or bar charts*
  Histograms or bar charts work on the same principle as that of a run chart, but the run data values are plotted as a height. Like a run chart, there is an average height bar for the average run, an upper-height bar for the upper control limit, and a lower-height bar for the lower control limit.

Figure 6.5   Scatter Plot of Weekday Temperature

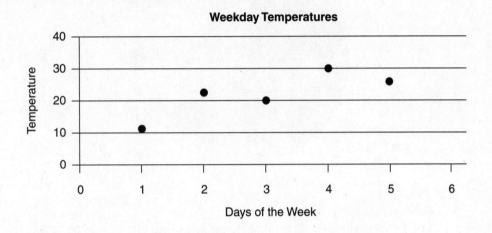

Figure 6.6   Bar Chart of Weekday Temperature

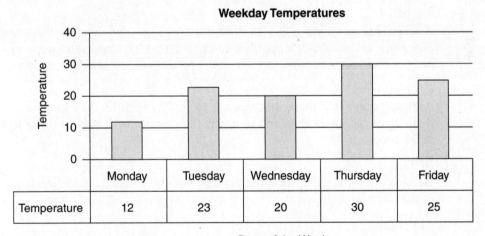

- *Pie charts*
  Pie charts are used to analyze data for one aspect of an entire operation. For example, Figure 6.7 shows the pie chart representing the percentages of expenditures on hardware, software, and other supplies.

Figure 6.7   Pie Chart—IT Expenses

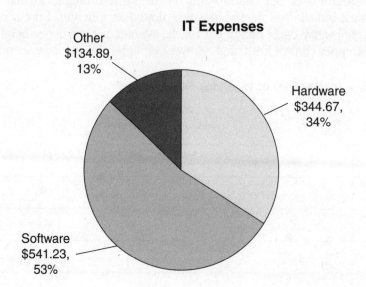

- *Pareto charts*
  The Pareto principle states that if you can eliminate problems that constitute a small percentage (i.e., 25%) of a large operation, then it will have an overall greater impact, increase profits and save money. Pareto charts are used to display the application of the Pareto principle.

- *Checklist*
  A checklist contains a list of things or objects that are relevant to processes or any other operation to ensure that all important steps or actions have been taken to complete the process or intended operation.

- *Check sheets*
  A check sheet is a form that is used to collect specific quantitative or qualitative repetitive data and interpret the data immediately in order to make decisions.

- *BPM*
  BPM is one of the quality management tools and was discussed earlier in this chapter.

- *Flowcharts*
  Flowcharts are maps or graphical representations of a process. There are many symbols used to construct a flowchart. The more common symbols are shown below in Figure 6.8, which illustrates the process of finding out if an input number is an even number or an odd number (Figure 6.9).

Figure 6.8   Flowchart Symbols and their Meaning

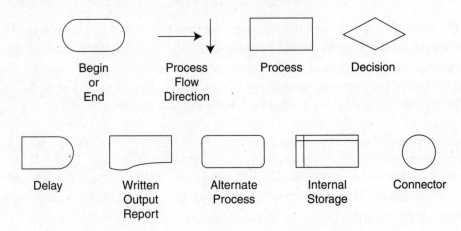

Begin
or
End

Process
Flow
Direction

Process

Decision

Delay

Written
Output
Report

Alternate
Process

Internal
Storage

Connector

Figure 6.9   Flowchart to Test if Number Is Even or Odd

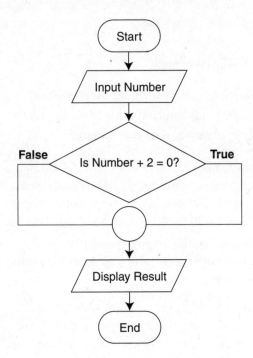

Start

Input Number

False   Is Number + 2 = 0?   **True**

Display Result

End

6.13 BUSINESS STRATEGIES AND E-COMMERCE

In a broad sense, e-commerce is any activity that takes place over digital communication channels, digital networks, and the Internet. The activities can be the electronic transfer of funds, purchasing and selling of merchandise, selling of goods and services, and so on. E-commerce involves the use of SCM, EDI, OLTP, and other systems that have been discussed earlier.

E-commerce is a part of e-business and can be divided into three categories:

- Business to Business (B2B), where the business takes place between wholesalers, governments, manufacturers, banks, farms, and organizations.

- Business to Consumers (B2C), where the business takes place between the wholesaler and a consumer.

- Consumer to Consumer (C2C), where the business takes place between two consumers.

Advantages of E-Commerce

In today's fast moving and electronically connected world, the concept of e-commerce is becoming advantageous for both the vendor and the consumer. Listed below are a few advantages of e-commerce.

- *Entry into global market*
  E-commerce can expand into global markets with a minimum of expense. In globalization, companies form partnerships with foreign companies leading to increased global marketing opportunities.

- *Target particular groups of customers*
  Companies can target a particular group of customers, even if they live in remote locations.

- *Decreased operational costs and increased profits*
  With the increased use of the Internet, e-commerce allows for increased cost effectiveness. Orders are created, processed, and confirmed online. This lowers mailing and printing costs of the organization.

- *Promotional advertisements on the Web*
  Companies sell their merchandise through their Websites. Therefore, the cost of promotional material drops. Companies can advertise their products or services through e-mail.

- *Lowers cost for customers*
  Since there is no middleman, companies can sell the same product at a lower cost than brick-and-mortar stores.

Shopping Carts for E-Commerce

Shopping Cart Software

A shopping cart is online software that is used by customers for online purchases of products from a website. Similar to shopping carts in grocery stores, online shopping cart software is used by most vendors conducting online businesses.

Once the customer goes on the website of the vendor, the shopping cart software opens the home page and is ready to take the customer's order. The customer can then view complete details of all the products the vendor is selling. He can add and remove items from the online shopping cart, the same way he does in his shopping cart at a grocery store. Once the customer has selected the products he wants to buy, he inputs his credit information and receives a confirmation number for the purchase.

Categories of Shopping Cart Software: Licensed and Hosted

Licensed software is bought and downloaded by the vendor for a one-time fee, and is then installed on any Web server meeting the software requirements. The source code of the software can be accessed and modified to meet the vendor's application requirements. On the other hand, hosted software is only provided to the vendor by a hosted service provider or application service provider. It is not downloaded and the vendor pays a monthly fee for its usage. In some cases, the host may charge a certain percentage of sales as commission. Hosted software cannot be modified, but the host provides updates, security features, and patches on a continuous basis.

6.14   COMPUTER THREATS

Hackers

Just like robbers who break into a home or a business to steal, hackers are people who write computer programs that can unlawfully break ("hack") into computer systems and computer networks, causing damage to computer hardware and software or data and information stored in a computer system. Hackers also steal personal data and information stored in a computer system and use it for their personal advantage. Identity theft often starts with hackers getting information from "secure" computer databases.

Hackers often use social engineering techniques to gain confidential information about a company from an employee of the company. Rather than breaking into a computer system, the hacker manipulates the victim into divulging information or confidential company secrets.

This leaked information can be lethal to a company's operations.

Types of Hackers

Listed below are the basic types of hackers: black-hat hackers, white-hat hackers, and script kiddies.

- *Black-hat hackers*
  Black-hat hackers enter computer systems with the intention of causing damage or destroying information. They also steal information for personal gains.

- *White-hat hackers*
  White-hat hackers enter computer systems to prove that computer systems are vulnerable to outside attacks. They do not want to cause any kind of damage.

- *Script kiddies*
  Script kiddies are people who don't have knowledge of hacking, but use computer programs written by professional hackers or pre-built tools to hack computers.

Viruses

A virus is a computer program that, when executed, links with another computer program and causes damage to a computer's hardware, software, or data stored in the computer. There are many types of viruses that attack computers, including Trojan horses, encryption viruses, worms, boot-sector viruses, script and macro-viruses, and logical bombs.

Trojan Horses

A Trojan horse is a virus program that appears to be a useful program, but, behind the scenes, it may cause damage to information stored on the computer. The name comes from the Greek tale of the "Trojan Horse" in which a large wooden horse was delivered to Troy as a sign of peace. However, hidden inside the Trojan Horse were Greek soldiers who eventually killed the citizens of Troy. Once a Trojan horse virus enters a computer, it can take full control of the computer. The computer owner may not be aware of the malicious acts of the Trojan horse virus. Once compromised, the computer is referred to as a zombie computer.

Encryption Viruses

An encryption virus is a program that searches for personal files and encrypts the personal data stored on those files so that the data file cannot be read.

Worms

Worms are programs that travel between networks and that attach themselves to files. When executed, the worm causes damage to information or computers.

Boot-Sector viruses

Boot-sector viruses attach themselves to boot-sector programs located on the hard drive of a computer. A boot-sector virus can delete all of the content stored on a computer's hard drive when the computer is booted up.

Script viruses

Scripts are small files that contain a series of program statements which, when executed, cause damage to a computer. For example, in an e-mail, a link is provided to take you to a website. When the link is clicked, it will cause the script to run and then damage the computer.

Macro viruses

A macro is a series of commands and actions that help automate some tasks. A macro virus will replace a normal macro with the virus. Macro viruses are difficult to detect and can be spread throughout e-mail attachments, discs, networks, modems, and the Internet.

Logic bombs

A logic bomb is a piece of code that will set off a malicious function (such as deleting files) when certain conditions are met. Logic bombs are usually not detected by the user of the software.

Denial-of-service attack

A denial-of-service attack is an attempt to make a computer resource unavailable to its user. A denial-of-service attack generally prevents an Internet site or service from functioning efficiently or at all, temporarily or indefinitely.

6.15   COMPUTER ETHICS AND SOCIETY

Computer ethics deals with how computing professionals should make decisions about professional and social conduct. One of the most definitive codes of ethics has been set out by the Association for Computing Machinery (ACM). The code covers a core set of computer ethics from professional responsibility to the consequences of technology in society. According to computer ethics, it is both wrong and illegal to hack computers and spread viruses in computers.

When using a computer or computer networks, an individual should keep the following computer ethics in mind:

Software Piracy

Software piracy occurs when someone intentionally steals copyrighted software, copies it to sell for profit, or alters or erases the program.

Intellectual Property Rights

Intellectual property rights are the rights that the creator of intellectual property is entitled to for his original work. Intellectual property was discussed earlier.

Information Privacy Rights

Information privacy rights means that a person or a company has full rights to decide how much and what type of information about them can be collected and used. For example, a patient has the right to decide to whom his personal health information should be released.

Unauthorized Access and Use of Computers

Unauthorized use of a computer means that a person uses the computer and computer networks without the permission of the owner. An example of unauthorized use of a computer would be when an employee does not return a laptop given to him by his employer after leaving the company.

Altering Information and Information Accuracy

Altering information refers to the act of replacing actual information with wrong information or spreading wrong information over the Internet.

PRACTICE TEST 1

CLEP Information Systems and Computer Applications

Also available at the REA Study Center (*www.rea.com/studycenter*)

This practice test is also offered online at the REA Study Center. All CLEP exams are computer-based, and our test is formatted to simulate test-day conditions. We recommend that you take the online version of the test to receive these added benefits:

- **Timed testing conditions** – helps you gauge how much time you can spend on each question
- **Automatic scoring** – find out how you did on the test, instantly
- **On-screen detailed explanations of answers** – gives you the correct answer and explains why the other answer choices are wrong
- **Diagnostic score reports** – pinpoint where you're strongest and where you need to focus your study

PRACTICE TEST 1

CLEP Information Systems and Computer Applications

(Answer sheets appear in the back of the book.)

TIME: 90 Minutes
75 Questions

DIRECTIONS: Each of the questions or incomplete statements below is followed by five possible answers or completions. Select the BEST choice in each case and fill in the corresponding oval on the answer sheet.

1. Which of the following allows data to be input into a computer system and then converts it to machine language?

    (A) Communication device
    (B) Network device
    (C) Input device
    (D) Output device
    (E) Biometric access device

2. Which functions are performed by the arithmetic logic unit (ALU) during the execution of a computer program?

    I. Converts data into information and translates human language to machine language
    II. Oversees the functions performed by other components of a computer
    III. Performs math calculations using arithmetical and relational operators

    (A) I only
    (B) II only
    (C) III only
    (D) I and II only
    (E) I and III only

3. To attach various peripheral devices—such as a keyboard, printers, and speakers—to the system unit, you would use a

   (A) control unit
   (B) register
   (C) plug
   (D) expansion slot
   (E) ports

4. The correct sequence of CPU machine-cycle instructions would be:

   (A) decode instruction, execute instruction, store result in registers, fetch instruction
   (B) execute instruction, store result in registers, fetch instruction, decode instruction
   (C) fetch instruction, decode instruction, execute instruction, store result in registers
   (D) store result in registers, fetch instruction, decode instruction, execute instruction
   (E) decode Instruction, fetch instruction, execute instruction, store result in registers

5. All of the following are various data types that can be handled by a computer EXCEPT

   (A) numerical data
   (B) audio (sound) data
   (C) operational data
   (D) pictorial data
   (E) text data

6. Which of the following gives commands (instructions) to the physical components of a computer in order to complete a specific task?

   (A) Hardware
   (B) Input Device
   (C) Software
   (D) Data
   (E) Output Device

7. What is the correct order of sequence that a computer performs to complete a specific task?

    (A) Storage, Process, Input, Output
    (B) Input, Output, Process, Storage
    (C) Input, Process, Output, Storage
    (D) Storage, Output, Input, Process
    (E) Input, Storage, Process, Output

8. A pair of digits that a computer can understand would be

    (A) 0, 8
    (B) 1, 8
    (C) 0, 1
    (D) 0, 256
    (E) 1, 256

9. Which of the following are designed specifically to perform complex tasks extremely fast?

    (A) Desktop computers
    (B) Mainframe computers
    (C) Mobile computers
    (D) Supercomputers
    (E) Laptop computers

10. What kind of memory is used by computers to store all programs, documents, and instructions while the computer is in use?

    (A) Storage, permanent
    (B) Storage, temporary
    (C) RAM, permanent
    (D) RAM, temporary
    (E) RAM, virtual

11. Which of the following are created when a disk is formatted and prepared for use and data storage?

    (A) Tracks, storage, sectors, RAM
    (B) Tracks, root directory, RAM, cache
    (C) Tracks, sectors, a file allocation table (FAT), a root directory
    (D) A file allocation table (FAT), a root directory, virtual memory, RAM
    (E) RAM, virtual memory, registers, storage

12. What is the correct sequence of units of memory, measured from lowest to highest?

    (A) Megabyte, byte, kilobyte, gigabyte, terabyte, petabyte
    (B) Byte, kilobyte, megabyte, gigabyte, terabyte, petabyte
    (C) Gigabyte, terabyte, petabyte, byte, kilobyte, megabyte
    (D) Byte, megabyte, kilobyte, gigabyte, terabyte, petabyte
    (E) Petabyte, terabyte, gigabyte, megabyte, kilobyte, byte

13. Telecommunications is the

    I.   use of a communication medium, such as telephone lines and computer hardware, to transfer data between two computers
    II. use of communication software to transfer data between two computers
    III. use of computer hardware, computer software, and a communication medium to transfer data between two computers

    (A) I only
    (B) II only
    (C) III only
    (D) I and II only
    (E) II and III only

14. What Wi-Fi signals are used to connect computers and other devices wirelessly and use the Internet for data transmission?

    (A) Analog signals
    (B) Digital signals
    (C) Cellular signals
    (D) Radio signals
    (E) Infrared light waves

15. The communication hardware that is used to transfer data between computers connected through the Internet is (are) the

    I.   modem
    II. Network Interface Card (NIC)
    III. Network Interface Controller

(A) I only
(B) II only
(C) III only
(D) I and II only
(E) I, II, and III

16. A network node is

    I.   any electronic device that is able to send data to another computer on the network.
    II. a device that converts an analog signal to a digital signal and vice-versa.
    III. any electronic device that is able to receive data from another computer on the network.

(A) I only
(B) II only
(C) III only
(D) I and III only
(E) I, II, and III

17. Which form below is used by laser-beam technology to write data on an optical disk?

(A) Crest and Trough
(B) Peak and Land
(C) Pit and Land
(D) Lit and Pit
(E) Peak and Lit

18. What are the three basic components of a computer?

    (A) A motherboard, a power supply unit, and a monitor
    (B) A power supply unit, a monitor, and a keyboard
    (C) A system unit, a power supply unit, and a keyboard
    (D) A monitor, a keyboard and mouse, and a system unit
    (E) A keyboard with mouse, a system unit, and a central processing unit (CPU)

19. The number systems that are used by a computer to represent and process data are the

    (A) binary number system, computer number system, octal number system, and decimal number system
    (B) computer number system, hexadecimal number system, octal number system, and decimal number system
    (C) binary number system, ASCII number system, hexadecimal number, and decimal number system
    (D) ASCII number system, binary number system, hexadecimal number system, and decimal number system
    (E) binary number system, octal number system, hexadecimal number system, and decimal number system

20. Which code uses an eight-digit binary coding system to represent 256 characters in computer systems?

    I.   EBCDIC Code
    II. ASCII Code
    III. Unicode

    (A) I only
    (B) II only
    (C) III only
    (D) I and II only
    (E) II and III only

21. Data that has been processed, organized, and is important to you is called

    (A) digital data
    (B) organized data
    (C) information
    (D) process
    (E) metadata

22. How much information can one byte hold?

   (A) A pixel
   (B) A bit
   (C) One digital picture
   (D) A character
   (E) A page

23. The "brain" of a computer that is used to process data is called the

   (A) modem
   (B) RAM
   (C) data processing card
   (D) central processing unit (CPU)
   (E) motherboard

24. Which of the following is approximately one billion bytes of information?

   (A) Megabyte
   (B) Petabyte
   (C) Kilobyte
   (D) Terabyte
   (E) Gigabyte

25. Which specially designed computer chips reside inside other operating devices?

   (A) Mainframe computers
   (B) Wearable computers
   (C) Embedded computers
   (D) Laptop computers
   (E) Mobile computers

26. Which of the following has its own group of machine-language instructions for a CPU?

   (A) Databases
   (B) Instruction set
   (C) Devices
   (D) Machine language
   (E) Program

27. Which of the following computer languages is formed by the binary digits 0 and 1 only?

    (A) Programming language
    (B) Assembly language
    (C) Machine language
    (D) High-level language
    (E) Java language

28. All of the following functions are performed by system software EXCEPT

    (A) coordinating instructions between computer application software and computer hardware devices
    (B) managing computer users, all the other software, and computer hardware known as computer resources
    (C) adding charts, graphs, and pictures to a stored file
    (D) controlling the operations in a computer
    (E) managing the booting of the computer

29. Which of the following is used to communicate with the operating system (a type of system software)?

    I.   Command-driven interface (used in old computers having Microsoft Disk Operating System, MS DOS)
    II. Graphical user interface (GUI)
    III. Menu driven interface

    (A) I only
    (B) II only
    (C) III only
    (D) I and II only
    (E) I, II, and III

30. Which of the following are types of operating systems used in computers?

    I.   Windows Vista and Windows 7
    II. Macintosh
    III. Open Source

    (A) I only
    (B) II only
    (C) III only
    (D) I and II only
    (E) I, II, and III

31. Which of the following in spreadsheet software represents the intersection of rows and columns to form a box that allows data to be entered?

(A) Address
(B) Cell
(C) Value
(D) Worksheet
(E) Formula bar

32. Which of the following in a spreadsheet uses an equation with arithmetical operators, cell addresses (references), and values entered in cells?

(A) Function
(B) Operation
(C) Formula
(D) Number
(E) Workbook

33. In PowerPoint presentations you can combine

   I.   text
   II. photographs, graphics, and charts
   III. sound

(A) I only
(B) II only
(C) III only
(D) I and III only
(E) I, II, and III

34. When using application software programs such as Word, Excel, and PowerPoint you may

   I.   link an Excel chart with a Microsoft Word document and a PowerPoint presentation
   II. insert command buttons and hyperlinks in PowerPoint slides
   III. perform spell check and use search and replace

(A) I only
(B) II only
(C) III only
(D) I and II only
(E) I, II, and III

35. Which of the following is the correct sequence of terms in a database hierarchy?

(A) Field names, records, file, database, character
(B) Records, file, database, character, field names
(C) Database, character, field names, records, file
(D) Character, field names, file, records, database
(E) Character, database, field names, records, file

36. A package (bundle) of programs that interact with each other, share a common interface, and allow the user to select specific programs to install is called a

(A) software suite
(B) package program
(C) integrated software package
(D) database
(E) spreadsheet

37. Which of the following are types of keys used in relational database packages to establish relationships between two or more tables?

    I.   Primary key or composite primary key
    II. Foreign key
    III. Relational key

(A) I only
(B) II only
(C) III only
(D) I and II only
(E) I, II, and III

38. Which of the following types of relationships may exist between tables in a relational database?

    I.   One-to-one
    II. One-to-many
    III. Many-to-many

(A) I only
(B) II only
(C) III only
(D) I and II only
(E) I, II, and III

39. An application program that looks for information, gets it, and makes a website viewable is called a

    (A) Web searcher
    (B) Web browser (or browser)
    (C) Web viewer
    (D) Web page
    (E) client program

40. All of the following are search engines EXCEPT

    (A) Bing
    (B) Google
    (C) MSN Search
    (D) VeriSign
    (E) Dogpile

41. Which of the following forms a computer system in an office?

    I.   Hardware
    II. Software
    III. Users

    (A) I only
    (B) II only
    (C) III only
    (D) I and II only
    (E) I, II, and III

42. The required parts of an e-mail message are the

    I.   message header
    II. message body
    III. subject header

    (A) I only
    (B) II only
    (C) III only
    (D) I and II only
    (E) I, II, and III

43. All of the following may be used to bring together company personnel from different geographical locations to discuss matters affecting the company EXCEPT

   (A) audioconferencing
   (B) tableconferencing
   (C) videoconferencing
   (D) tele-conferencing
   (E) Web conferencing

44. Which of the following constitutes computer-based information?

   I. Computer hardware and software
   II. Procedures, information, and data
   III. Networked computers

   (A) I only
   (B) II only
   (C) III only
   (D) I and III only
   (E) I, II, and III

45. An expert system, which collects and stores experiences and knowledge of human experts and is used to simulate human reasoning, is best described as a

   (A) computer information system
   (B) office automation system
   (C) decision support system
   (D) statistical analysis system
   (E) database management system (DBMS)

46. Which of the following in geographical information systems (GIS) uses vectors to express any object?

   I. Points
   II. Lines
   III. Polygons

   (A) I only
   (B) II only
   (C) III only
   (D) I and II only
   (E) I, II, and III

47. Which best expresses the business intelligence system to collect facts about business, and integrates, interprets, stores, and manages information to make sound business decisions?

    (A) Computerized intelligent system
    (B) Decision support system
    (C) Expert system
    (D) Computer information system
    (E) Database management system (DBMS)

48. The set of rules followed for the exchange of formatted messages and data related to purchases of goods and services between two networked computers is called

    (A) data exchange
    (B) electronic data interchange (EDI)
    (C) file transfer protocol (FTP)
    (D) telephone data exchange
    (E) HTTP

49. Which of the following uses FTP, HTTP, Telnet, modems, and e-mails for the exchange of data and formatted messages?

    (A) Telephone data exchange
    (B) Telecommunications
    (C) Electronic data interchange (EDI)
    (D) Computer information systems
    (E) EDI methodology

50. Which of the following are advantages of Enterprise Resource Planning (ERP)?

    I.   Reduced operational costs
    II. Improved efficiency
    III. Capability of making better decisions

    (A) I only
    (B) II only
    (C) III only
    (D) I and III only
    (E) I, II, and III

51. Which of the following connects businesses with the objective of acquiring raw materials, processing them for conversion into finished products, and delivering finished products to customers?

    (A) Delivery management
    (B) Supply chain management (SCM)
    (C) Customer resource management (CRM)
    (D) Product management
    (E) Total quality management (TQM)

52. A network node that is capable of sending, receiving, and forwarding data between computers on a network is called a

    (A) sending device
    (B) receiving device
    (C) magnetic device
    (D) electronic device
    (E) storage device

53. A protocol that allows you to transfer a file from a Web server on one computer to another is called

    (A) HTTP
    (B) COM
    (C) WWW
    (D) FTP
    (E) HTML

54. Which of the following describes "www." in a Uniform Resource Locator (URL)?

    (A) Protocol
    (B) Second-level domain name
    (C) Third-level domain name
    (D) Top-level domain name
    (E) Fourth-level domain name

55. All of the following are parts of a Uniform Resource Locator (URL) EXCEPT

   (A) top-level domain name
   (B) http://protocol
   (C) World Wide Web
   (D) second-level domain name
   (E) hyperlinks

56. Which of the following is related to Web technology?

   I.   Creating Web pages and websites
   II. Delivering Web pages on a client computer
   III. Creating networks for websites

   (A) I only
   (B) II only
   (C) III only
   (D) I and II only
   (E) I, II, and III

57. Which of the following creates a structured document using markup language?

   (A) Home site
   (B) Home page
   (C) Web page
   (D) Website page
   (E) URL locator

58. Which of the following is used to write an information tag when creating a Web page using HTML, where tags are written inside a pair of angled brackets (< >)?

   I.   First Tag, Last Tag
   II. Home Tag, Last Tag
   III. Opening Tag, Closing Tag

   (A) I only
   (B) II only
   (C) III only
   (D) I and II only
   (E) I, II, and III

59. Data can be defined as numbers, text, sound, or video that has not been

    (A) processed
    (B) saved
    (C) printed
    (D) sorted
    (E) entered

60. The process to remove redundant data or unwanted information from a pool of information is called

    (A) copying
    (B) filtering
    (C) sending
    (D) merging
    (E) saving

61. Which of the following describes the act of writing instructions for a computer that will solve a specific problem?

    I.   Information design
    II. Operating system development
    III. Software development

    (A) I only
    (B) II only
    (C) III only
    (D) I and III only
    (E) I, II, and III

62. Which of the following statements describes the "system implementation phase" of the system development life cycle (SDLC)?

    (A) All of the written programs of different modules are combined into a single complete system and are ready for testing.
    (B) The problem to be solved is clearly stated.
    (C) All the programs to solve a particular problem are completely written or coded.
    (D) The system is delivered and installed on the user's computer.
    (E) The system is continuously maintained.

63. Which of the following specifies building a working model of a system before building a large system?

    (A) Object modeling technique
    (B) Prototype
    (C) Waterfall system development model
    (D) Rapid application development
    (E) Iterative process

64. Some advantages of Rapid Application Development (RAD) are that

    I.   it saves time and money
    II. its end users are involved in all stages of the system development
    III. the system is built one segment at a time and is tested while it is being built

    (A) I only
    (B) II only
    (C) II and III only
    (D) I and II only
    (E) I, II, and III

65. Which of the following terms is (are) used when creating something new such as an information system, a product, or a new building?

    I.   Process
    II. Project
    III. Planning

    (A) I only
    (B) II only
    (C) II and III only
    (D) I and II only
    (E) I, II, and III

66. Which of the following represents processing data and converting it into useful information?

    (A) Batch processing
    (B) Transaction processing
    (C) Information processing
    (D) Online processing
    (E) Real-time processing

67. Which of the following allows people to use computer hardware and software to communicate with various computers and issue commands to enable computers to perform various tasks or operations?

    (A) Computer-user interface
    (B) Data communications
    (C) Transmission protocols
    (D) Information processing
    (E) IPOS cycle

68. Which of the following is used to define sets of rules, conditions, and guidelines for communication between different organizations when using computer hardware and software manufactured by different vendors?

    (A) Protocols
    (B) Standards
    (C) Requirements
    (D) System integration
    (E) ASCII Code

69. The system that developers use as a support or tool to create new systems, support other programs, or to write new application programs is called

    (A) data modeling tools
    (B) system development life cycle (SDLC)
    (C) rapid application development (RAD)
    (D) software development kit (SDK)
    (E) unified modeling language (UML)

70. Which of the following has set specification standards for Internet mark-up languages such as HTML, XHTML, CSS, and XML that are used in webpage design?

    (A) Institute of Electrical and Electronic Engineers (IEEE)
    (B) World Wide Web 3 (W3) Consortium
    (C) Association for Computing Machinery (ACM)
    (D) National Institute of Standards and Technology (NIST)
    (E) The American National Standards Institute (ANSI)

71. The detailed and finite set of instructions written in human language that specifically mentions what a computer must do in order to solve a particular problem or perform a particular task is called

    (A) a pseudocode
    (B) a data structure
    (C) programming logic
    (D) an algorithm
    (E) a computer program

72. Which of the following programming logics are used when writing a computer program?

    I.   Decision
    II. Looping
    III. Assembly

    (A) I only
    (B) II only
    (C) III only
    (D) I and II
    (E) I, II, and III

73. The following pseudocode lists some steps of logic in part of a computer program. After the execution of the steps, what will be the value of the variable NUM?

    ```
    SET NUM = 75
    WHILE NUM >= 10
        SET NUM = NUM - 15
    END WHILE
    ```

    (A) 65
    (B) 45
    (C) 30
    (D) 10
    (E) 15

74. Which of the following are event-driven programming languages?

      I.   Visual Basic

      II. C++

      III. Java

(A) I only
(B) II only
(C) I and III only
(D) II and III only
(E) I, II, and III

75. Which of the following describes Boolean data type in programming languages and is used to represent the result of testing an expression in selection control structure?

(A) Yes, No
(B) Positive, Negative
(C) Addition, Subtraction
(D) True, False
(E) Division, Multiplication

76. The file type where data stored in a file is an exact replica of data stored internally within the computer system (also known as an unformatted file) is called a

(A) text file
(B) program file
(C) binary file
(D) data file
(E) personal file

77. A scheme to organize data of varied types so that data can be efficiently entered, stored, sorted, retrieved, and manipulated by a computer program is known as a

(A) looping control structure
(B) data structure
(C) metadata
(D) decision control structure
(E) sequential control structure

78. Which of the following in object-oriented programming (OOP) is used to create user-defined data types by collecting a number of data fields of built-in data types of programming language and methods to perform operations on those data fields as one unit?

(A) Abstract data type (ADT)
(B) Numerical data type
(C) Encapsulation
(D) Object instantiation
(E) Inheritance

79. A method in object-oriented programming (OOP) that is called automatically when an object of a class is created and provides initial values to data fields of the created object is called the

(A) static method
(B) accessor method
(C) destructor method
(D) mutator method
(E) constructor method

80. What is the name of a file structure in which folders are arranged in a scheme that resembles a family tree with folders related to one another, from top to bottom, where the bottom file is used to store actual data or information?

(A) Sequential file structure
(B) Network file structure
(C) Hierarchical file structure
(D) Indexed file structure
(E) One-dimensional array structure

81. A collection of items of different data types that is better dealt with as Abstract Data Type (ADT) is called a

(A) two-dimensional array
(B) one-dimensional array
(C) multi-dimensional array
(D) heterogeneous array
(E) class

82. Which of the following types of situations use the linked list data structure in place of an array?

        I.   When inserting data items
        II. When deleting data items
        III. When sorting data Items

(A) I only
(B) II only
(C) I and II only
(D) II and III only
(E) I and III only

83. A technique used to create a database structure that collects data at its point of origin, organizes that data to store it efficiently, and is easily accessible in order to make business decisions and produce reports would be

(A) data management
(B) data maintenance
(C) metadata
(D) data modeling
(E) data integrity

84. A place where data has been collected, stored, and used for archival and security purposes is known as

(A) a data mart
(B) a data warehouse
(C) data mining
(D) data indexing
(E) data storage

85. Which of the following database models can be seen as a group of records that are joined in a 1:M relationship, where one record can have more than one parent?

(A) Relational
(B) Hierarchical
(C) Object oriented
(D) Network
(E) Hybrid

86. Which of the following represents where data processing takes place at the end of a certain time period?

      I.   Batch
      II. Transaction
      III. Online transaction

(A) I only
(B) II only
(C) III only
(D) I and II only
(E) I, II, and III

87. What attributes in a field of a database table must be specified?

      I.   Name
      II. Size (length)
      III. Data type

(A) I only
(B) II only
(C) III only
(D) II and III only
(E) I, II, and III

88. Study the following table.

Books

Title	Quantity	Price
Introduction to Computers	56	109.99
Java Programming	24	125.00
C++ Programming	98	69.00
Web Page Design	110	49.00

A user entered the following Oracle SQL command.
Select Title, Quantity, Price
From Books
Where Quantity >= 98 OR Price < 49;

How many rows will be displayed based on the given criteria?

(A) None
(B) One
(C) Two
(D) Three
(E) Four

89. What do we call the type of file access in which the data is read in the same order as the data was written to the file?

  I. Random access
  II. Sequential access
  III. Mixed access

(A) I only
(B) II only
(C) III only
(D) I and II only
(E) I, II, and III

90. A collection or a sequence of characters in which each character occupies one byte of memory space is known as a

(A) string
(B) queue
(C) stack
(D) tree
(E) list

91. Which of the following allows you to process, transmit, store, and view data in a digital (computer readable) form using the Internet or a computer network?

  I. E-commerce
  II. E-bay
  III. E-business

(A) I only
(B) II only
(C) III only
(D) I and III only
(E) I, II, and III

92. Which of the following are viruses that are executed when certain logical conditions are satisfied?

   (A) Boot-sector viruses
   (B) Logical bombs
   (C) Macro viruses
   (D) Worms
   (E) Trojan horses

93. The type of privacy that is related to storing an employee's work-related activities on his/her employer's computer system is known as

   (A) informational privacy
   (B) organizational privacy
   (C) occupational privacy
   (D) physical privacy
   (E) financial privacy

94. When a person creates or invents something new, which of the following protects his/her ownership of, or rights to, that creation?

   (A) Intellectual property rights
   (B) Real estate property rights
   (C) Artificial intelligence
   (D) Invention property rights
   (E) Copyright

95. Software whose source code is made available openly to the public to copy it, make changes to it, and redistribute the modified source code without paying any fees is known as

   (A) Open Source Initiative (OSI)
   (B) Linux technology
   (C) object code
   (D) open source
   (E) system software

96. Why is it important to set up a computer system that is ergonomically correct?

    I.   It reduces neck and eyestrain.
    II.   It prevents bodily injuries.
    III. It is a federal law.

(A) I only
(B) I and II only
(C) I and III only
(D) II and III only
(E) I, II, and III

97. A group of people who communicate electronically with each other in their profession is known as a

    I.   Virtual Private Network (VPN)
    II.   Virtual Memory
    III. Virtual Team

(A) I only
(B) II only
(C) III only
(D) I and II only
(E) II and III only

98. Which of the following is a procedure to list all the assigned tasks a person has to perform in his place of work, keeping in mind the organizational objectives, the individual worker's requirements, as well as health issues?

(A) Job rotation
(B) Job specification
(C) Job enrichment
(D) Job evaluation
(E) Job design

99. All of the following are benefits of outsourcing EXCEPT

(A) due to lowering their operation costs, companies can have a competitive edge over their competitors
(B) when a company chooses to outsource, it minimizes its operational risks because talented IT people will be handling operations
(C) by outsourcing services, companies can grow and expand as the demand for their services increases
(D) when a company outsources, it may have to share some of its trade secrets with outsourced vendors who might use the system for personal advantage and undermine the company's operations
(E) some portion of the money saved through outsourcing can be utilized in research and development of new technology in order to make IT more efficient

100. Which of the following is used to protect data when being transported between computers so that it cannot be intercepted, altered, or stolen by hackers?

(A) Computer access control
(B) Authentication techniques
(C) Chain of trust techniques
(D) Cryptographic techniques
(E) Firewall hardware devices

PRACTICE TEST 1

Answer Key

1.	(C)	34.	(E)	67.	(A)
2.	(E)	35.	(D)	68.	(B)
3.	(E)	36.	(A)	69.	(D)
4.	(C)	37.	(D)	70.	(B)
5.	(C)	38.	(E)	71.	(D)
6.	(C)	39.	(B)	72.	(D)
7.	(C)	40.	(D)	73.	(E)
8.	(C)	41.	(D)	74.	(C)
9.	(D)	42.	(D)	75.	(D)
10.	(D)	43.	(B)	76.	(C)
11.	(C)	44.	(E)	77.	(B)
12.	(B)	45.	(C)	78.	(A)
13.	(C)	46.	(E)	79.	(E)
14.	(D)	47.	(A)	80.	(C)
15.	(E)	48.	(B)	81.	(D)
16.	(D)	49.	(E)	82.	(C)
17.	(C)	50.	(E)	83.	(D)
18.	(D)	51.	(B)	84.	(B)
19.	(E)	52.	(D)	85.	(D)
20.	(D)	53.	(D)	86.	(A)
21.	(C)	54.	(C)	87.	(E)
22.	(D)	55.	(E)	88.	(C)
23.	(D)	56.	(D)	89.	(B)
24.	(E)	57.	(C)	90.	(A)
25.	(C)	58.	(C)	91.	(C)
26.	(B)	59.	(A)	92.	(B)
27.	(C)	60.	(B)	93.	(C)
28.	(C)	61.	(C)	94.	(A)
29.	(E)	62.	(C)	95.	(D)
30.	(D)	63.	(B)	96.	(B)
31.	(B)	64.	(E)	97.	(C)
32.	(C)	65.	(B)	98.	(E)
33.	(E)	66.	(C)	99.	(D)
				100.	(D)

PRACTICE TEST 1

Detailed Explanations of Answers

1. **(C)** By definition, an input device is the only device that allows data to be input into a computer system and then converts it to machine language.

2. **(E)** The arithmetic logic unit (ALU), a part of the central processing unit (CPU) in a computer system, is a hardware chip that converts data into information, translates human language to machine language, and performs math calculations using arithmetical and relational operators during the execution of a computer program. The control unit, which is another component of the CPU, oversees the functions performed by other components of a computer.

3. **(E)** Ports are used to connect peripheral devices, such as a keyboard, printers, speakers, and microphones, to the system unit. These ports can be on the front or back of the system unit. Most modern peripheral devices, such as digital cameras and printers, are connected to the system unit using USB ports.

4. **(C)** The correct sequence of CPU machine-cycle instructions is fetch instruction, decode instruction, execute instruction, and store result.

5. **(C)** Operational data is not a data type. All the others are data types.

6. **(C)** A software program, by definition, is a sequence of instructions given to a computer to complete a specific task.

7. **(C)** The correct sequence in the IPOS cycle is Input, Process, Output, and Storage.

8. **(C)** 0 (zero) and 1 (one) are the two binary digits of computer machine language.

9. **(D)** Supercomputers are designed specifically to perform complex tasks extremely fast. Many are used by government or federal agencies, such as the Internal Revenue Service (IRS), to store and process large amounts of data.

10. **(D)**   In computers, RAM (random access memory) is the temporary working memory. All programs, documents, and instructions are stored in RAM while the computer is being used.

11. **(C)**   Tracks, sectors, a file allocation table (FAT), and a root directory are all created when a disk is formatted to store data on it.

12. **(B)**   Byte, kilobyte, megabyte, gigabyte, terabyte, petabyte is the correct sequence of units of memory, measured from lowest to highest.

13. **(C)**   Use of computer hardware, computer software and a communication medium to transfer data between two computers defines telecommunications. Any computerized system requires the use of hardware as well as software for its operations.

14. **(D)**   Wi-Fi is a wireless network that uses radio signals to connect computers and other devices, and uses the Internet for data transmission. Analog signals and digital signals are handled by modems when data is sent between computers using telephone lines.

15. **(E)**   A modem, a Network Interface Card, and a Network Interface Controller are all required to transfer data between computers connected through the Internet.

16. **(D)**   Any electronic device that is able to send data to or receive data from another computer on the network is a network node. An example would be a fax machine, which can send and receive a document.

17. **(C)**   Laser beam technology writes data on an optical disk in the form of Pit and Land.

18. **(D)**   A monitor, a keyboard with a mouse, and a system unit are the three basic components of a computer. The motherboard, the central processing unit (CPU), and a power supply unit are components found inside the system unit.

19. **(E)**   A binary number system, an octal number system, a hexadecimal number system, and a decimal number system are four number systems used by computers to represent and process data.

20. **(D)**   Both EBCDIC code and ASCII code use an 8 digit binary coding system to represent 256 characters in computer systems. A unicode system incorporates characters from other languages, such as Chinese and Greek, and goes beyond 256 characters.

21. **(C)** Information is data that has been processed, organized, and is important to you. The computer stores data in a digital form. Organized data means that the data has been sorted alphabetically or numerically. Digital data is the data stored in a computer system in a digital (0, 1) form, and process shows the steps used to manipulate data and convert it into information.

22. **(D)** A byte holds one character of data.

23. **(D)** The central processing unit (CPU) is the "brain" of a computer and is used to process data.

24. **(E)** A gigabyte is approximately one billion bytes of information.

25. **(C)** Embedded computers are specially designed computer chips that reside inside other operating devices. For example, a digital microwave has an embedded computer.

26. **(B)** Each CPU in a computer system has its own group of machine language instructions known as an instruction set. An instruction set has two parts—OpCode and Operands.

27. **(C)** A computer understands only machine language that is formed by using the binary digits 0 and 1. Programming language is used to write programs in order to solve a particular computer problem. Assembly language uses symbols and is one level away from machine language. An assembler is a program that translates assembly language instructions into machine language instructions. High-level language uses keywords that are close to human language. A compiler translates high-level instructions into machine language instructions.

28. **(C)** System software does not add charts, graphs, and pictures to a stored file. Application software, such as Excel, adds charts, graphs, and pictures to a stored file.

29. **(E)** A user communicates with the operating system by using command driven interfaces, graphical user interfaces (GUI), and menu driven interfaces.

30. **(D)** Types of operating systems include Windows Vista, Windows 7, and Macintosh. Linux and UNIX are open-source operating systems.

31. **(B)** In spreadsheet software, the intersection of rows and columns that forms a box is known as a cell. Each cell has an address (location) and is used to enter a formula.

32. **(C)** In a spreadsheet, an equation using arithmetical operators, cell addresses (references), and values entered into cells, is known as a formula. Functions are built-in formulas not created by the user. Operations, such as adding or subtracting values in different cells, are performed on values (numbers) stored in those cells.

33. **(E)** Text, photographs, graphics, charts, and sound can all be used in PowerPoint presentations.

34. **(E)** All of the functions listed are possible when using application software such as Word, Excel, and PowerPoint.

35. **(D)** In databases, the correct sequence of terms in a database hierarchy is character, field names, file, records, and database.

36. **(A)** A software suite, by definition, is a package (bundle) of programs that interact with each other, share a common interface, and allow the user to choose specific program(s) to install. An integrated software package contains the basic features of various application programs, but all the programs in the package must be installed. A database package is one type of application program that is usually included in a software suite.

37. **(D)** A primary key (or composite primary key) and a foreign key are the types of keys used in relational database packages, which establish relationships between two tables.

38. **(E)** All of the relationships listed are types of relationships between tables in a relational database.

39. **(B)** A Web browser is an application program that looks for information, gets it, and makes a website viewable. A Web page is one page of a website on the Internet.

40. **(D)** Bing, Google, MSN Search and Dogpile are all search engines. VeriSign certifies that a website has a Secure Socket Layer (SSL) certificate, indicating that any transaction on the website will be secure.

41. **(D)** Hardware and software form the basis of a computer system in an office. Users use the computer system, but are not a part of the system.

42. **(D)** A message header and a message body are the required parts of an e-mail message. A subject header is optional.

43. **(B** Audioconferencing, videoconferencing, tele-conferencing, and Web conferencing are all conferencing techniques that help to gather company personnel from all over the world to discuss company business.

44. **(E)** Computer-based information is a collection of computer hardware and software, procedures, information and data, and networked computers.

45. **(C)** An expert system is a collection of specialized decision support systems that collect and store experiences and knowledge of human experts in various fields, and is used to simulate human reasoning to solve a specific problem.

46. **(E)** Geographical information systems (GIS) use vectors to express an object as points where a city or an object may be shown as a point on a map, lines to quantify the distance or the height of an object, and polygons to indicate a two-dimensional object.

47. **(A)** A computerized intelligent system is a business intelligence system that collects facts about business, and that integrates, interprets, stores, and manages information to make sound business decisions.

48. **(B)** Electronic data interchange (EDI) is a set of rules used to exchange formatted messages and data related to purchases of goods and services between two networked computers. Data exchange is the process of converting source data into target format. The target format is an exact representation of the source format. File transfer protocols (FTP) are sets of rules that allow the transferring of a file from a Web server to another computer.

49. **(E)** The EDI methodology uses FTP, HTTP, Telnet, modems, and e-mails for exchange of data and formatted messages.

50. **(E)** Some advantages of Enterprise Resource Planning (ERP) are reduced operational costs, improved efficiency, and capability of making better decisions. Another advantage is that it enables the delivery of the right product at the right time.

51. **(B)** Supply chain management is the management of interconnected businesses that have the objectives of acquiring raw materials, processing raw materials for conversion into finished products, and delivering the finished products to customers. Delivery management is an integrated plan used to organize, manage, and supervise staff, procedures, equipment, and technology in order to deliver merchandise to clients at the right place, at the right time and in the proper condition. Customer resource management (CRM) is an integral part of supply chain management, in which the sales, marketing, and customer service departments operate together with the objective of meeting the customers' requirements in terms of supply of goods and services. Product management involves product planning and product

marketing and has to do with the manufacturing of a product or creation of services, based on the current or future demand of the product in the market. Product marketing deals with the questions of what product to sell in the market, at what price, and how to promote its sales. Product management is an ongoing process and is done for the entire lifecycle of the product.

52. **(D)**   A network node is any electronic device that is capable of sending, receiving, and forwarding data between computers on a network. The term *electronic* means that data must be in binary code (0 and 1) format.

53. **(D)**   FTP (file transfer protocol) allows the copying of a file from one host computer to another host computer on the Internet.

54. **(C)**   In a Uniform Resource Locator (URL), the portion labeled "www." is a third-level domain name.

55. **(E)**   All are parts of a URL, except for hyperlinks.

56. **(D)**   Creating Web pages and websites as well as delivering Web pages to a client computer are related to Web technology.

57. **(C)**   Markup language is used to create a structured document known as a Web page.

58. **(C)**   When using HTML to create a Web page, the information tag has an opening tag and a closing tag written inside a pair of angled brackets (<>).

59. **(A)**   Data can be defined as numbers, text, sound, or video that has not been processed.

60. **(B)**   Filtering is the process of removing redundant data or unwanted information from a pool of information.

61. **(C)**   Generally, the act of writing instructions which, when followed by a computer will solve a specific problem, is known as software development. By definition, software is a set of instructions written with the purpose of solving a specific problem.

62. **(C)**   The system implementation phase of the system development life cycle (SDLC) happens when all the programs used to solve a particular problem are actually written or coded. The system integration phase happens when all the written programs of different modules are combined into a single complete system and are ready for testing. The system requirement phase happens when the problem to be solved is clearly stated. The system installation phase happens when the system is delivered and installed on

the user's computer. In the system maintenance phase, continuous maintenance of the system is done.

63. **(B)** A prototype is a working model of a system that is constructed before building a large system. The object modeling technique is used to identify objects in a system and the relationship between them. The waterfall model is a sequential development process that employs a "top down" approach in the software development life cycle (SDLC). The Rapid Application Development (RAD) is system development methodology that uses an iterative process and that incorporates prototype methodology to develop a system one segment at a time. The iterative process is the process in which the same sets of instructions are repeated again and again.

64. **(E)** The Rapid Application Development (RAD) saves time and money, involves the end users at all stages of development, and is built and tested one segment at a time.

65. **(B)** "Project" is the term used whenever something new is created such as an information system, a product, or a new building.

66. **(C)** Processing data and converting it into useful information is known as information processing. Batch processing, transaction processing, and real-time processing are three types of information processing methods.

67. **(A)** A computer-user interface allows people to use computer hardware and software to communicate with and issue commands to computers, in order to perform various tasks or operations. Data communications has to do with transmission of data over communication channels using computers. Transmission protocols are rules and regulations that a user has to follow when sending or receiving data over communication channels, when information is processing, and when it is converting data into useful information.

68. **(B)** Standards in computer technology define sets of rules, conditions, and guidelines for communication between different organizations using computer hardware and software from different vendors. Protocols, such as HTPP and FTP, are rules for communications between computers over the Internet when exchanging data or a file. Requirements, in general, are conditions that need to be satisfied in order to perform certain operations. System integration is one of the phases in software development, and ASCII code is the machine language of a computer system.

69. **(D)** A software development kit (SDK) is used as a support or tool to create new systems, to support other programs, or to write new application programs. Data modeling tools are used during the development of an information system by providing the definition and format of data and describing how data is represented and accessed. The system development life cycle (SDLC) is a systematic and organized way to develop an information system (IS) by specifying problem analysis, design, implementation, testing, and support (maintenance) of the IS. Rapid Application Development (RAD) is an approach used in system development and is not a tool. The unified modeling language (UML) is used to model an object-oriented system, describing a system in terms of objects.

70. **(B)** The W3 Consortium has set specification standards for Internet markup languages that are used in Webpage design. Examples include HTML, XHTML, CSS, and XML. The Institute of Electrical and Electronic Engineers (IEEE) sets the standards for all types of hardware used in computers. The Association for Computing Machinery, or ACM, is a learned society for computing. The National Institute of Standards and Technology (NIST), formerly known as the National Bureau of Standards (NBS), is a measurement standards laboratory, which is a non-regulatory agency of the United States Department of Commerce. The American National Standards Institute (ANSI) is a private, non-profit organization that oversees the development of voluntary consensus standards for products, services, processes, systems, and personnel in the United States. The organization also coordinates U.S. standards with international standards so that American products can be used worldwide.

71. **(D)** An algorithm is a detailed and finite set of instructions written in human language that specifically mentions what a computer must do in order to solve a particular problem or perform a particular task. A pseudo-code is one way of writing computer algorithm in human language readable form, but it is more structured and simpler than human language, which then can be used as a basis to write an actual computer program. Data structure is a scheme used to structure (arrange or organize) data so that a variety of data types can be entered, stored, sorted, retrieved, and manipulated by a computer program efficiently. Programming logic is a method that involves human thinking to give correct and valid mathematical reasons (logic) in a step-by-step manner when writing a computer program that will perform a particular task or solve a particular problem.

72. **(D)** Decision and looping are programming logics. Assembly programming is a computer programming language, not a programming logic.

73. **(E)** After the execution of the following steps, the value of the variable NUM will be 15. Solution:

- Starting value for variable NUM is 75, which is greater than or equal to 10 as specified in WHILE loop test condition;

- Inside the loop, NUM is decreased by 15 every time WHILE loop executes. The last value that a variable NUM stores until NUM is greater than or equal to 10 is 15. This is arrived at as follows:

NUM = 75 − 15 = 60 Satisfies the WHILE test condition   NUM >= 10

NUM = 60 − 15 = 45 Satisfies the WHILE test condition   NUM >= 10

NUM = 45 − 15 = 30 Satisfies the WHILE test condition   NUM >= 10

NUM = 30 − 15 = 15 Satisfies the WHILE test condition   NUM >= 10

NUM = 15 − 15 = 0   Does not satisfy the test condition   NUM >= 10

74. **(C)** Visual Basic and Java are event-driven programming languages.

75. **(D)** In programming language, the Boolean data type is used to represent the result of testing an expression in selection control structure as True or False.

76. **(C)** The data stored in a binary file is an exact replica of data stored internally within the computer system and is also known as an unformatted file.

77. **(B)** Data structure is a scheme to structure data so that data of varied types can be efficiently entered, stored, sorted, retrieved, and manipulated by a computer program. A looping control structure is a computer programming control structure where the same set of statements is executed a certain number of times. Metadata, also known as a data dictionary, contains descriptions and examples of all the terms in any computer-based system. Decision control structure and sequential control structure are program-writing logics.

78. **(A)** In object-oriented programming (OOP), abstract data type (ADT) is used to create user-defined data types, by collecting a number of data fields of built-in data types of programming language and methods in order to perform operations on those data fields as one unit.

79. **(E)**   The constructor method is a method in object-oriented programming (OOP) that is called automatically when an object of a class is created and provides initial values to data fields of the created object.

80. **(C)**   A hierarchical file structure is a file structure in which folders are arranged in a scheme that resembles a family tree. Folders at the top are related to one another, and the bottom file is used to store actual data or information.

81. **(D)**   A collection of items of different data types, known as a heterogeneous array, are better dealt with as an abstract data type (ADT).

82. **(C)**   The linked list data structure is used in place of an array only when data items need to be inserted or deleted from an array.

83. **(D)**   Data modeling is a technique used to create a database structure, which collects data at its point of origin, organizes that data to store it efficiently, and makes it easily accessible in order to make business decisions and produce reports.

84. **(B)**   A data warehouse is a place where data can be collected, stored, and used for archival and security purposes.

85. **(D)**   In a network database model, the database can be seen as a group of records that are joined in a 1:M relationship, where one record can have more than one parent.

86. **(A)**   In batch processing, processing of data takes place at the end of a certain time period.

87. **(E)**   Each field in a table of a database must have a name, size (length), and a data type for the field.

88. **(C)**   Two rows will be displayed. Two rows meet the test criteria of "Quantity >= 98," and none of the rows meets the test criteria of "Price < 49," and the use of the "OR" operator between two test criteria gives a total of two rows. The "OR" operator adds the rows that meet the test criteria.

89. **(B)**   Sequential access takes place when the data is read in the same order that the data was written to the file.

90. **(A)**   In computer programming, a string is a collection or a sequence of characters, where each character occupies one byte of memory space.

91. **(C)** E-business is the activity that allows you to process, transmit, store, and view data in a digital (computer readable) form using the Internet or a computer network.

92. **(B)** Logical bombs are viruses that are executed when certain logical conditions are satisfied.

93. **(C)** The storing of an individual's activities during the duties of their profession on a computer system relates to occupational privacy.

94. **(A)** Intellectual property rights protect the ownership and the rights of the creator of a new product.

95. **(D)** Open source is software whose source code is made available openly to the public to copy it, make changes to it, and redistribute the modified source code without paying any fees.

96. **(B)** It is important to set up a computer system that is ergonomically correct so that users have reduced neck and eye strain as well as no bodily injuries.

97. **(C)** A virtual team is a group of people, who communicate electronically with each other in their profession.

98. **(E)** Job design is a procedure that lists all the assigned tasks that a person has to perform in his place of work, by keeping in mind the organizational objectives, the individual worker's requirements, as well as health issues.

99. **(D)** When a company outsources, it may have to share some of its trade secrets with outsourced vendors, who might use the information for their personal advantage and undermine the company's operations.

100. **(D)** Cryptographic techniques are used to protect data when it is being transported between computers so that it cannot be intercepted, altered, or stolen by hackers.

PRACTICE TEST 2

CLEP Information Systems and Computer Applications

Also available at the REA Study Center (*www.rea.com/studycenter*)

This practice test is also offered online at the REA Study Center. All CLEP exams are computer-based, and our test is formatted to simulate test-day conditions. We recommend that you take the online version of the test to receive these added benefits:

- **Timed testing conditions** – helps you gauge how much time you can spend on each question
- **Automatic scoring** – find out how you did on the test, instantly
- **On-screen detailed explanations of answers** – gives you the correct answer and explains why the other answer choices are wrong
- **Diagnostic score reports** – pinpoint where you're strongest and where you need to focus your study

PRACTICE TEST 2

CLEP Information Systems and Computer Applications

(Answer sheets appear in the back of the book.)

TIME: 90 Minutes
75 Questions

DIRECTIONS: Each of the questions or incomplete statements below is followed by five possible answers or completions. Select the BEST choice in each case and fill in the corresponding oval on the answer sheet.

1. Which of the devices listed below keeps track of the movements of a product?

    (A) Bar code reader
    (B) Joystick
    (C) RFID tag
    (D) Optical mark reader
    (E) Image scanner

2. Which of the following is used in a computer system to represent any number as a *hexadecimal* number?

    (A) Digits 0, 1
    (B) Digits 0 to 9 and alphabet letters A to F
    (C) Digits 0 to 7
    (D) Digits 0 to 9
    (E) Digits 0 to 100

3. A hard disk

    (A) is a nonvolatile storage device
    (B) writes (saves) data at a slower speed than a flash drive, a CD, or a DVD
    (C) is a volatile storage device
    (D) has a smaller storage capacity than a flash drive, a CD, or a DVD
    (E) is always sold as an internal hard drive

4.   Which of the following is an 8 bit binary number representation of the decimal 103?

(A) 01001111
(B) 10001110
(C) 01100111
(D) 01111011
(E) 01100011

5.   All of the following are true about cell phones EXCEPT:

(A) A cell phone has an input device.
(B) A cell phone has an output device.
(C) A cell phone stores the telephone numbers of contacts on a built-in hard drive.
(D) A cell phone has a built-in processor.
(E) A cell phone has an operating system known as Symbian.

6.   Which of the following fits the following statement? "It is a handheld computing device that stores information such as telephone numbers, addresses, photos, games, and songs. It can also be used as an appointment book; it has a built-in calculator; and it can be synchronized with a desktop computer."

(A) Laptop computer
(B) Personal Digital Assistant (PDA)
(C) Portable Media Player (PMP)
(D) Wearable computer
(E) Global Positioning System (GPS)

7.   Which input device uses special characteristics and patterns of human body parts for authentication purposes, by storing them in a database?

(A) Input device for the handicapped
(B) Scanning input device
(C) Gaming input device
(D) Biometric input device
(E) Audio input device

8. A temporary and volatile working memory of a computer is its

    (A) storage
    (B) read-only memory (ROM)
    (C) virtual memory
    (D) random access memory (RAM)
    (E) cache memory

9. The component of a computer system that manages all the operations taking place in the computer is its

    (A) arithmetic logic unit (ALU)
    (B) central processing unit (CPU)
    (C) control unit
    (D) system unit
    (E) power supply unit

10. Which of the following is a device in a computer that provides information, translates machine language to human language and allows a user to see, read, or hear the data and information that is entered into the computer system?

    (A) Input device
    (B) Communication device
    (C) Storage device
    (D) Network device
    (E) Output device

11. The data type that a businessperson uses to create a Web advertisement with a musical background is called a(n)

    (A) audio data type
    (B) picture data type
    (C) numerical data type
    (D) audio/video data type
    (E) text data type

12. Which of the following lists the comparison operators used in a computer program?

      I. $+, -, *, /, \%$
      II. $>, >=, <, <=, !=$
      III. AND, OR, NOT

(A) I only
(B) II only
(C) III only
(D) I and II only
(E) I, II and III

13. Which of the following is the type of battery used to power a laptop?

      I.   Lithium Ion
      II. Ni-Metal Hydride (NiMH)
      III. Sodium Ion

(A) I only
(B) II only
(C) I and II only
(D) II and III only
(E) I, II, and III

14. Which type of computer would someone use if installing a computerized digital thermostat in his or her house?

(A) Mobile computer
(B) Desktop computer
(C) General purpose computer
(D) Wearable computer
(E) Special purpose computer

15. In computer binary language, each special character, numerical digit, and letter of the alphabet typed on a keyboard is made up of a unique combination of eight

(A) kilobytes
(B) bytes
(C) bits
(D) characters
(E) megabytes

16. When data is sent over the Internet, it is separated into small pieces known as

    (A) fragments
    (B) bits
    (C) kilobytes
    (D) bundles
    (E) packets

17. "A message sent over a network between two devices, subdivided into units, where each unit stores binary data, has a header, and a body of its own" is called a

    I.   Packet
    II. Frame
    III. Segment

    (A) I only
    (B) I and II only
    (C) II and III only
    (D) I and III only
    (E) I , II, and III

18. Where are the CPU and the memory located in a computer system?

    (A) Expansion boards
    (B) Motherboard
    (C) Storage device
    (D) Output device
    (E) Communication device

19. Which of the following describes the network architecture used in most homes?

    (A) Client/Server LAN
    (B) Peer-to-peer WAN
    (C) Peer-to-peer LAN
    (D) Client/Server WAN
    (E) Computer network

20. Which of the following refers to the design of a network?

(A) Network type
(B) Network architecture
(C) Network server
(D) Network communication
(E) Network devices

21. The ability of an operating system to control the activities of a number of programs at the same time is called

(A) mult-programming
(B) multi-processing
(C) simul-programming
(D) multi-user
(E) multi-tasking

22. Which application program listed below will calculate the sum and the average of five numbers using a built-in predefined function?

(A) Database
(B) Word processing
(C) Spreadsheet
(D) Presentation
(E) Business intelligence system

23. All of the following statements are true for an operating system EXCEPT that it

(A) allows users to interface with the computer
(B) manages memory (RAM)
(C) manages storage devices
(D) manages the Central Processing Unit (CPU)
(E) allows users to check spelling

24. A word-processing program has all of the following features EXCEPT

(A) spelling and grammar check
(B) mail merge
(C) disk formatting
(D) search and replace
(E) inserting headers and footers in a document

25. Which of the following operations can be done in a database?

> I. Edit records
> II. Sort records
> III. Link records

(A) I only
(B) II only
(C) III only
(D) I and II only
(E) II and III only

26. Which of the following are parts of a search engine?

> I. Spider
> II. Indexer
> III. Search engine program

(A) I only
(B) II only
(C) III only
(D) I and III only
(E) I, II and III

27. All of the following are required when sending or receiving e-mail EXCEPT a(n)

(A) modem
(B) Network Interface Card (NIC)
(C) printer
(D) Web browser
(E) e-mail account with an e-mail service provider

28. Which of the following are types of objects handled by a geographic information system (GIS)?

> I. Image object
> II. Discrete object
> III. Continuous value object

(A) I only
(B) II only
(C) I and II only
(D) II and III only
(E) I, II, and III

29. All of the following are managed by a CRM EXCEPT

    (A) the customer's personal information
    (B) the customer's relationship with other customers
    (C) the customer's purchasing history
    (D) response to the customer's inquiries
    (E) providing a high level of customer service

30. The name of the page that a person first sees when searching a website on the Internet is called a(n)

    (A) end page
    (B) first page
    (C) home page
    (D) Web page
    (E) primary page

31. Which of the following terms describes a file being sent via the Internet to a home computer from another computer?

    (A) Uploading a file
    (B) Getting a file
    (C) Receiving a file
    (D) Downloading a file
    (E) Saving a file

32. The protocol that determines the path that each e-mail should follow when it is sent over the Internet is called

    (A) HTTP
    (B) FTP
    (C) SMTP
    (D) IMAP
    (E) TCP/IP

33. Which of the following describes the portion labeled ".com" in a URL?

    (A) Protocol
    (B) Top-level domain
    (C) Domain name
    (D) Host
    (E) FTP

34. Which of the following is NOT a protocol?

    (A) HTTP
    (B) FTP
    (C) HTML
    (D) TCP/IP
    (E) IMAP

35. A computer language that creates a structured document using metadata concepts and also creates user-defined tags is

    (A) XML
    (B) HTML
    (C) C++
    (D) Java
    (E) JavaScript

36. Which type of computer delivers a requested Web page to a Web browser and then displays it on the computer's monitor?

    (A) Home computer
    (B) Client computer
    (C) Server computer
    (D) Network computer
    (E) Embedded computer

37. What does "<html> . . .<\html>" indicate when designing a Web page?

    I. The start and the end of the Web page
    II. The start and the end of a text paragraph within a Web page
    III. The start and the end of an ordered list within a Web page

    (A) I only
    (B) II only
    (C) III only
    (D) I and II only
    (E) I, II, and III

38. Which of the following represents the minimum required parts of a machine language instruction set?

      I.   OpCode
      II. Operands
      III. Operator

(A) I only
(B) II only
(C) III only
(D) I and II only
(E) II and III only

39. All of the following are functions of a network operating system EXCEPT

(A) managing the flow of information on the network
(B) managing network security
(C) managing the peripheral devices on the desktop
(D) managing the hardware on the network
(E) providing file management on the network

40. Which of the following describes the type of relationship that exists when more than one row in one table matches more than one row in a second table and vice-versa?

      I.   1:M type of relationship
      II. 1:1 type of relationship
      III. M:N type of relationship

(A) I only
(B) II only
(C) III only
(D) I and II only
(E) I and III only

41. What is the term used to describe how a group of people can work together in one location to attain their company's objectives?

(A) Cooperative work environment
(B) Conferences in office systems
(C) Audioconference
(D) Web conference
(E) Videoconference

42. Which of the following employs a combination of tools (data warehousing, data mining, decision support systems, data marts, and online analytical processing [OLAP]) for its operations and helps to make important business decisions?

(A) Expert systems
(B) Business intelligence systems (BIS)
(C) Computer information systems (CIS)
(D) Decision support systems (DSS)
(E) Supply chain management (SCM)

43. All of the following are true for browser plug-ins EXCEPT that they

(A) are additional software installed to provide additional capabilities and features to a Web browser
(B) deliver audio, video, and 3D animation on demand
(C) view multimedia files directly in a Web browser
(D) design or create Web pages
(E) run Java Applets and access PDF files on the World Wide Web

44. A network in which some of its parts use the Internet, but data is encrypted before sending it to the Internet, indicating that it is a private network, is known as a

(A) Local Area Network (LAN)
(B) Wide Area Network (WAN)
(C) Virtual Private Network (VPN)
(D) Value Added Network (VAN)
(E) Metropolitan Area Network (MAN)

45. A single computing system that combines and coordinates all business operations and stores information in a single system so it can be shared by all departments and all levels of management is called a(n)

(A) enterprise-wide information system
(B) computer information system (CIS)
(C) business intelligence system (BIS)
(D) expert system (ES)
(E) decision support system (DSS)

46. Which of the following takes inputs and converts them from one form into another form by following a sequence of steps?

(A) Planning
(B) Project
(C) Process
(D) Filtering
(E) Merging

47. Which of the following types of media is (are) formed when text, audio, video, animation, and still images are combined into one?

   I.   Multimedia
   II. Communication media
   III. Hypermedia

(A) I only
(B) II only
(C) III only
(D) I and II only
(E) II and III only

48. In which phase of the system development life cycle (SDLC) are the needs of the new system analyzed to meet the objectives of an organization?

(A) System design
(B) System implementation
(C) System requirement analysis
(D) System testing
(E) System installation

49. Which software consists of automated tools and methods used to support various activities in the system development life cycle (SDLC)?

   I.   C++
   II. Java
   III. Computer-aided software engineering (CASE)

(A) I only
(B) II only
(C) III only
(D) I and II only
(E) I, II, and III

50. Which system processes data the moment it is generated?

      I.   Batch processing system
      II. Real-time processing system
      III. Transaction processing system

(A) I only
(B) II only
(C) III only
(D) I and II
(E) I, II, and III

51. Which interface is used when an instruction is typed into a computer on a DOS prompt by using a keyboard?

(A) GUI interface
(B) Hardware interface
(C) Mouse/keyboard interface
(D) Command line interface
(E) Software interface

52. Which of the following enables computers that use hardware/software from different vendors to communicate with each other?

      I.   Standards in computer technology
      II. Communication protocols
      III. User interface design

(A) I only
(B) II only
(C) III only
(D) I and II only
(E) I and III only

53. In object-oriented programming (OOP), which of the following describes the type of action performed by an object?

(A) Attributes
(B) Methods
(C) Behavior
(D) Unified model language
(E) Process

54. Which of the following describes a way to sort (arrange) data stored in a database?

   I. Alphabetically
   II. Numerically
   III. In Groups

(A) I only
(B) II only
(C) III only
(D) I and II
(E) I, II, and III

55. What is the correct sequence of steps in the waterfall model of system development?

(A) Design, requirement analysis, integration, testing, maintenance, installation, implementation.
(B) Requirement analysis, design, implementation, integration, testing, installation, maintenance.
(C) Requirement analysis, design, implementation, testing, integration, installation, maintenance.
(D) Requirement analysis, design, testing, implementation, integration, installation, maintenance.
(E) Design, requirement analysis, testing, implementation, integration, installation, maintenance.

56. A scientific approach to initiate, plan, organize, manage, staff, and complete a task successfully would be called

(A) database management
(B) corporate resource management
(C) project management
(D) supply chain management
(E) business management

57. The duties of a project manager include

      I.   task needs
      II. individual needs
      III. team needs

(A) I only
(B) II only
(C) III only
(D) I and III only
(E) I, II, and III

58. Which user interface is used when a user selects only one choice or no choice from a number of listed choices?

(A) Check box
(B) Dialog box
(C) Option button
(D) Keyboard
(E) Dialog window

59. Which type of programming can be described as follows: "In the Windows XP model, a group of individuals work together freely by sharing ideas, giving suggestions, and applying all steps of SDLC at every stage of system development"?

(A) Object-oriented programming (OOP)
(B) Extreme programming
(C) C++ programming
(D) Java programming
(E) Visual Basic programming

60. All of the following are true for Rapid Application Development (RAD) EXCEPT:

    (A) RAD is a system development methodology and incorporates prototype methodology to develop a system one segment at a time.
    (B) RAD is a Joint Application Development (JAD) in which both developers and users are involved in all stages of development.
    (C) RAD uses the "time boxed" concept, in which the project is divided into a number of parts, and each part must be completed by its own deadline date.
    (D) RAD is a sequential process.
    (E) RAD uses already developed and tested software when building a new system.

61. Which of the following is a way of writing a computer algorithm in human language readable form, which is more structured and simpler than human language and can be used as a basis to write a computer program?

    (A) Data structure
    (B) Programming logic
    (C) Algorithm
    (D) Computer program
    (E) Pseudocode

62. Which programming logic would be used to print weekly payroll checks for ten employees who work forty hours per week at the rate of $10.00 an hour and get paid overtime if they work more than forty hours?

    I.   Looping programming logic
    II. Sequential programming logic
    III. Decision programming logic

    (A) I only
    (B) II only
    (C) III only
    (D) I and III only
    (E) I, II, and III

63. In OOP, which of the following will exhibit a certain state of the object?

   (A) Attributes or characteristics
   (B) Methods
   (C) Behavior
   (D) Class
   (E) Object instantiation

64. The method in OOP that will change or modify the state of an object is known as the

   (A) static method
   (B) accessor method
   (C) destructor method
   (D) mutator method
   (E) constructor method

65. A file in which the data is accessed and processed in a serial manner from beginning to end, and in the order the data was written during the creation of the file is called

   (A) sequential file structure
   (B) network file structure
   (C) hierarchical file structure
   (D) indexed file structure
   (E) one-dimensional array structure

66. All of the application programs that are NOT part of the operating system are installed and stored, by default, in the

   (A) text file
   (B) data file
   (C) digital file
   (D) audio file
   (E) program file

67. Which of the following will be an array subscript for a one-dimensional array with six integer elements in C++?

    I.   1, 2, 3, 4, 5, 6
    II. 0, 1, 2, 3, 4, 5
    III. 2, 3, 4, 5, 6, 7

(A) I only
(B) II only
(C) III only
(D) I and II only
(E) II and III only

68. A technique used to manage data stored in a computer's memory as a resource for an organization is known as

(A) data warehousing
(B) data mining
(C) data modeling
(D) database administration
(E) data management

69. Which of the following means that "an individual or an organization can determine who can see the data, what part of the data can be seen, how the data will be used, and where the data will be used"?

(A) Data privacy
(B) Data security
(C) Data indexing
(D) Data mart
(E) Data maintenance

70. A flexible and commonly used method to reduce the number of times a user accesses a database when searching for data is called

(A) data privacy
(B) data security
(C) data indexing
(D) data mart
(E) data maintenance

71. Which of the following database models represents data that is stored in tables, where the tables are made up of matrices of M number of columns (attributes) and N number of rows (records)?

(A) Network database model
(B) Hierarchical database model
(C) Object-oriented database model
(D) Relational database model
(E) Hybrid database model

72. The storage of the same data in different locations in a database which could lead to data inconsistency is known as

    I.   data corruption
    II. data redundancy
    III. data loss

(A) I only
(B) II only
(C) III only
(D) I and II only
(E) II and III only

73. Which of the following is used to create a table structure inside a database?

    I.   Data creation language (DCL)
    II. Data manipulation language (DML)
    III. Data definition language (DDL)

(A) I only
(B) II only
(C) III only
(D) I and III only
(E) I, II, and III

74. All of the following are true for queue data structure EXCEPT

(A) new data items are added at the end of a list
(B) items are removed from the beginning of the list
(C) the front of the queue is called the *head*
(D) the end of the queue is called the *tail*
(E) the queue works on a concept known as "Last In, First Out" (LIFO)

75. Which of the following describes the storage of information that provides details of characteristics of the data as well as the relationships between the data stored in a database?

      I.   Metadata
      II. Data mart
      III. Data dictionary

(A) I only
(B) II only
(C) III only
(D) I and III only
(E) II and III only

76. All of the following are true for a database administrator EXCEPT:

(A) Provides support services to end users that are dealing with data and information usage
(B) Handles the procedures for backup and recovery of the data stored in a computer's memory
(C) Provides support services to end users when they want to print a document
(D) Provides for data integrity of the data stored in a computer system
(E) Provides for data security and the privacy of the data stored in a computer system

77. All of the following are true for data stored in a data warehouse EXCEPT that it

(A) can be updated only once a week
(B) can be centralized
(C) can be decentralized, based on the department or mode of operation
(D) can be subject oriented
(E) is never removed

78. Which interface takes place when starting an event such as saving a file in programming languages like Visual Basic and Java?

      I.   Command-driven interface
      II. Menu-driven interface
      III. Graphical user interface

(A) I only
(B) II only
(C) III only
(D) I and III only
(E) I, II, and III

79. All of the following are true for inheritance in OOP EXCEPT

(A) an existing class is known as the base or parent class having some data members and some member functions

(B) a newly created class from an existing base class is known as a child class or a derived class

(C) a child class inherits all data members and member functions of its base class

(D) a child class can add its own data members

(E) a child class can be created from two or more base classes, under a concept known as *Multiple Inheritance*

80. Which of the following are valid statements for STACK data structure?

      I.   It is a data structure in which data items are removed from the top of the stack and added to the top of the stack.
      II. It is a data structure in which data items are added to the top of the stack and removed from the bottom of the stack.
      III. It is a data structure in which data items are removed from the top of the stack and added to the bottom of the stack.

(A) I only
(B) II only
(C) III only
(D) I and II only
(E) II and III only

81. How many combinations of binary 0s and 1s can be displayed by a group of 8 bits?

    (A) 8
    (B) 16
    (C) 4
    (D) 128
    (E) 256

82. A customer purchases a television online using his credit card. The television is shipped to his home address. Which of the following type of transaction took place after the delivery of the television?

    I.   Batch processing
    II. Transaction processing
    III. Mixed-batch and transaction processing

    (A) I only
    (B) II only
    (C) III only
    (D) I and II only
    (E) I, II, and III only

83. All of the following statements are TRUE about a relation (table) inside a database EXCEPT

    (A) A relation in a database is an entity (noun) and is created by organizing data in M number of columns and N number of rows.
    (B) The data about an entity is collected using column names (field names), where each column describes a particular attribute about the entity.
    (C) Each column in a table must have a distinct name and the value stored in that column must be an allowed value for that column.
    (D) Every entity must have a column name that can be selected as a primary key (PK).
    (E) Each row (record) in a table stores the data for all the columns (attributes) in that table and forms an instance of that table.

84. Which of the following finds the location of a data item or a record stored in the memory directly from the PK value, rather than looking for a PK value in the index table and then searching the corresponding record in a data file?

    I.   Hashing
    II. Indexing
    III. Sorting

(A) I only
(B) II only
(C) III only
(D) I and II only
(E) II and III only

85. The structured query language (SQL) that is used to create database objects and to perform various operations on database tables is known as

    I.   data definition language (DDL)
    II. data manipulation language (DML)
    III. data control language (DCL)

(A) I only
(B) II only
(C) III only
(D) I and II only
(E) I, II and III

86. Which of the following offers protection from Internet identity theft by verifying the authenticity of websites that hide their true URL addresses?

(A) antivirus software
(B) software firewall
(C) antispyware
(D) antispam software
(E) antiphishing software

87. Which of the following is an entity whose details are known only to its owner, is used for commercial purposes and economic gains, and whose details are kept secret from the public?

    (A) Patent
    (B) Trademark
    (C) Copyright
    (D) Trade secret
    (E) Symbols

88. All of the following are types of virtual groups EXCEPT

    (A) task
    (B) interest
    (C) command
    (D) role
    (E) global

89. Which of the following job-design methods mentions the skills, education, experience, and any other requirement that a candidate must fulfill when applying for a particular position in a company?

    (A) Job enlargement
    (B) Job rotation
    (C) Job specification
    (D) Job evaluation
    (E) Job enrichment

90. All of the following are advantages of insourcing EXCEPT:

    (A) The company creates more jobs for the domestic market.
    (B) The creation of more jobs in the domestic market helps the economy.
    (C) Many local talented IT people, trained according to domestic standards, can be used to provide IT service operations locally.
    (D) The outsourced vendor may not provide the same quality of service that a local company can provide.
    (E) The IT people hired when insourcing have a higher level of technical expertise than the IT people hired when outsourcing.

91. A collection of techniques, strategies, or practices used to identify, collect, and organize knowledge to meet a company's objectives by increasing their competitive edge in the market, profits, productivity, and market share is known as

     I.   Total Quality Management
     II. Knowledge Management
     III. Database Management

(A) I only
(B) II only
(C) III only
(D) I and III only
(E) II and III only

92. The process in which employees of various companies and governments do business using information technology that includes multinational investment is called

     I.   Nationalization
     II. Globalization
     III. Trade Liberalization

(A) I only
(B) II only
(C) III only
(D) I and II only
(E) II and III only

93. Which of the following is the study and modification of existing business strategies, business processes, technology, hierarchical organizational structure, and computer informational systems that improve a business's performance, market share, profit, and a company's competitive edge in the market?

    I.   Business Process Modeling (BPM)
    II. Total Quality Management (TQM)
    III. Business Process Reengineering (BPR)

(A) I only
(B) II only
(C) III only
(D) I and II only
(E) I, II and III

94. All of the following are flowchart symbols EXCEPT

(A) start and end
(B) input and output
(C) conditional or decision
(D) pointers
(E) connectors

95. Which type of software is used when a customer makes real-time, online purchases of products from a Website?

(A) E-commerce
(B) Shopping cart
(C) Application
(D) AutoCAD
(E) Business

96. All of the following are types of hackers EXCEPT

(A) black hat
(B) white hat
(C) script kiddies
(D) Trojan horses
(E) cybercriminals

97. Which of the following are classifications of e-commerce?

> I. Business to Business (B2B)
> II. Retailer to Consumer (R2C)
> III. Business to Consumer (B2C)

(A) I only
(B) II only
(C) III only
(D) I and III only
(E) I, II, and III

98. Which of the following describes the type of privacy where organizations or government agencies don't want to reveal their trade secrets or any other activities to non-intended entities or persons, especially to business competitors?

(A) Informational privacy
(B) Organizational privacy
(C) Occupational privacy
(D) Physical privacy
(E) Financial privacy

99. The protocol that is used to send personal messages securely over the Internet is known as

(A) HTTP
(B) FTP
(C) TCP/IP
(D) SHTTP
(E) ICMP

100. A chart or graph that displays process performance over a period of time is called a

(A) line graph
(B) scatter plot
(C) run chart
(D) histogram or bar chart
(E) pie chart

PRACTICE TEST 2

Answer Key

1.	(C)	34.	(C)	67.	(B)
2.	(B)	35.	(A)	68.	(E)
3.	(A)	36.	(C)	69.	(A)
4.	(C)	37.	(A)	70.	(C)
5.	(C)	38.	(D)	71.	(D)
6.	(B)	39.	(C)	72.	(B)
7.	(D)	40.	(C)	73.	(C)
8.	(D)	41.	(A)	74.	(E)
9.	(C)	42.	(B)	75.	(E)
10.	(E)	43.	(D)	76.	(C)
11.	(D)	44.	(C)	77.	(A)
12.	(B)	45.	(A)	78.	(C)
13.	(C)	46.	(C)	79.	(D)
14.	(E)	47.	(A)	80.	(A)
15.	(C)	48.	(C)	81.	(E)
16.	(E)	49.	(C)	82.	(C)
17.	(E)	50.	(B)	83.	(D)
18.	(B)	51.	(D)	84.	(A)
19.	(C)	52.	(A)	85.	(E)
20.	(B)	53.	(C)	86.	(E)
21.	(E)	54.	(E)	87.	(D)
22.	(C)	55.	(B)	88.	(D)
23.	(E)	56.	(C)	89.	(C)
24.	(C)	57.	(E)	90.	(E)
25.	(D)	58.	(C)	91.	(B)
26.	(E)	59.	(B)	92.	(B)
27.	(C)	60.	(D)	93.	(C)
28.	(D)	61.	(E)	94.	(D)
29.	(B)	62.	(E)	95.	(B)
30.	(C)	63.	(A)	96.	(D)
31.	(D)	64.	(D)	97.	(D)
32.	(C)	65.	(A)	98.	(B)
33.	(B)	66.	(E)	99.	(D)
				100.	(C)

PRACTICE TEST 2

Detailed Explanations of Answers

1. **(C)** An RFID tag is the device that tracks the movement of a product.

2. **(B)** Digits 0 to 9 and alphabet letters A to F represent a hexadecimal number system. Digits 0, 1 represent a binary number system. Digits 0 to 7 represent an octal number system. Digits 0 to 7 represent an octal number system. Digits 0 to 9 represent a decimal number system. Digits 0 to 100 do not represent any number system.

3. **(A)** A hard disk is a nonvolatile storage device.

4. **(C)** 01100111 is an 8-bit binary number representation of the decimal 103.

5. **(C)** Cell phones do not store phone numbers of contact persons on a built-in hard drive. Cell phones store numbers on a read-only memory (ROM) chip.

6. **(B)** The statement describes a PDA.

7. **(D)** A biometric input device uses special characteristics and patterns of human body parts for authentication purposes, by storing them in a database.

8. **(D)** Random access memory (RAM) is the temporary and volatile working memory of a computer. You can perform reading and writing operations using RAM, and its contents are deleted when the computer is turned off.

9. **(C)** The control unit manages all the operations that take place in a computer.

10. **(E)** By definition, an output device is a device that provides information to people, that translates machine language to human language, and that

allows the user to see, read, or hear the data and information that was entered into the computer system.

11. **(D)** The Audio/Video data type is the data type that would be used by a businessperson to create an appealing Web advertisement with a musical background.

12. **(B)** $>, >=, <, <=$, and $!=$ are comparison operators used in computer programs. $+, -, *, /$, and $\%$ are a list of arithmetical operators used in computer programs. AND, OR, and NOT are logical operators used in computer programs.

13. **(C)** Lithium-ion batteries are used in newer laptops and Ni-metal hydride (NiMH) batteries are used in older laptops. Sodium ion batteries are not used in laptops.

14. **(E)** A computerized digital thermostat in a house is an embedded computer. All embedded computers are special purpose computers, as they perform a special task, such as controlling room temperature with a thermostat.

15. **(C)** The binary language used by a computer for each special character, each numerical digit, and each letter of the alphabet typed on a keyboard is made up of eight bits.

16. **(E)** Data sent over the Internet is separated into packets.

17. **(E)** A packet, frame, or a segment describes a message that is sent over a network subdivided into units, where each unit stores binary data, has a header, and a body of its own.

18. **(B)** The motherboard is where the CPU and the memory are located, in a computer system.

19. **(C)** A peer-to-peer Local Area Network (LAN) is the network architecture used in most homes.

20. **(B)** Network architecture refers to the design of a network.

21. **(E)** Multitasking is the ability of an operating system to control the activities of a number of programs at the same time.

22. **(C)** A spreadsheet is an application program that will calculate the sum and average of five numbers that use a built-in formula known as function average.

23. **(E)** An operating system does not allow users to check their spelling.

24. **(C)** A word-processing program cannot format a disk.

25. **(D)** Databases can edit and sort records. Database link tables store records, but the records are not linked.

26. **(E)** Spider, indexer, and a search-engine program are all parts of a search engine.

27. **(C)** A printer is not required when sending or receiving e-mail.

28. **(D)** Discrete and continuous value objects are handled by the geographic information systems (GIS). Image objects are graphical elements used to create objects in an application software window.

29. **(B)** CRM, or customer relationship management, has nothing to do with a customer's relationship with another customer.

30. **(C)** The first page seen on a website is called a home page. A Web page is any other page on the website.

31. **(D)** *Downloading* is the terminology used to describe the process of transferring a file that has been sent to a home computer from another computer over the Internet. Saving a file is the process of storing a file on the hard disk of a computer.

32. **(C)** SMTP is the protocol that determines the path that each e-mail may follow when it is sent over the Internet.

33. **(B)** ".com" is a top level domain.

34. **(C)** HTML is not a protocol. HTML is a markup language used to create a Web page.

35. **(A)** XML is the markup language used to create a structured document that uses metadata concepts and that creates user-defined tags. The HTML

language is used to create Web pages, but does not allow the creation of user-defined tags. C++ and Java are programs used to write computer programs, but not for creating Web pages. JavaScript codes are placed into HTML codes.

36. **(C)**   A server computer delivers a requested Web page to a Web browser, which then displays it on the computer's monitor. The computer requesting a Web page is known as a client computer. Any computer connected to a network is known as a network computer. An embedded computer is a computer that is built inside another product, such as a thermostat.

37. **(A)**   <html> . . . . . .<\html> indicates the start and the end of a Web page.

38. **(D)**   An OpCode and Operands are the minimum required parts of a machine language instruction set.

39. **(C)**   The network operating system does not manage the peripheral devices on the desktop.

40. **(C)**   M:N is the type of relationship when more than one row in one table matches more than one row in a second table and vice-versa.

41. **(A)**   The term *cooperative work environment* describes a group of people working together in one location to attain the company's objectives.

42. **(B)**   A business intelligence system (BIS) employs a combination of tools such as data warehousing, data mining, decision support systems, data marts, and online analytical processing for its operations to help make important decisions.

43. **(D)**   Browser plug-ins do not design or create Web pages.

44. **(C)**   A virtual private network (VPN) is a network in which some parts of the network use the Internet, but where the data is encrypted before being sent to the Internet, indicating that it is a private network.

45. **(A)**   An enterprise-wide information system is a computer system that combines and coordinates all business operations and stores the information in a single system that can be shared by all departments and all levels of management.

46. **(C)** Process is the act of taking inputs and converting them from one form into another form by following a sequence of steps.

47. **(A)** Multimedia is formed when text, audio, video, animation, and still images are combined.

48. **(C)** The system requirement analysis phase of the system development life cycle (SDLC) is the phase when the needs of the new system are analyzed to meet the objectives of an organization.

49. **(C)** Computer-aided software engineering (CASE) software consists of automated tools and methods used to support various activities in the system development life cycle (SDLC). C++ and Java are programming languages used to write computer programs.

50. **(B)** The real-time processing system processes data at the moment that it is generated.

51. **(D)** Command line interface takes place when a user types an instruction (command) into a computer on a DOS prompt, by using a keyboard.

52. **(A)** Standards in computer technology enable computers that use hardware/software from different vendors to communicate with each other and exchange data and information.

53. **(C)** In object-oriented programming (OOP), behavior describes the type of action performed by an object.

54. **(E)** Data stored in a database can be sorted alphabetically, numerically, or by group.

55. **(B)** Requirement analysis, design, implementation, integration, testing, installation, and maintenance is the correct sequence of steps in the waterfall model of system development.

56. **(C)** Project management is a scientific approach for initiating, planning, organizing, managing, staffing and completing a task successfully.

57. **(E)** A project manager is responsible for task needs, individual needs, and team needs.

58. **(C)**   An option button is the interface that allows a user to select only one choice (option) or no choice (option) from a number of listed choices.

59. **(B)**   Extreme programming is the type of programming in which individuals work together to share ideas, give suggestions, and apply all the steps of SDLC at every stage of system development.

60. **(D)**   RAD is an iterative process.

61. **(E)**   Pseudocode is a way of writing a computer algorithm in human language readable form, which is more structured and simpler than human language. It can be used as a basis to write a computer program.

62. **(E)**   All three programming logics would be used to print weekly payroll checks for ten employees who normally work forty hours a week at the rate of $10.00 an hour and get paid overtime if they work more than forty hours.

63. **(A)**   In OOP, the attributes or characteristics of an object will exhibit a certain state of the object.

64. **(D)**   The mutator method in OOP will change or modify the state of an object.

65. **(A)**   A sequential file structure happens when the data is accessed and processed in a serial manner from its beginning to its end and in the order that the data was written during the creation of the file.

66. **(E)**   A program file stores all the application programs that are not part of the operating system.

67. **(B)**   0, 1, 2, 3, 4, 5 will be the array subscript for a one-dimensional array with six integer elements in C++. Array subscripts start from 0 in C++.

68. **(E)**   Data management is the technique used to manage the data stored in a computer's memory, as a resource for an organization.

69. **(A)**   Data privacy means that an individual or an organization determines who, what, how, and where the data can be seen and used.

70. **(C)** Data indexing is a flexible and commonly used method to reduce the number of times that a user accesses a database when searching for data.

71. **(D)** A relational database model stores data in tables that are made up of matrices of columns (attributes) and rows (records).

72. **(B)** Data redundancy is the storage of the same data in different locations of a database which could lead to data inconsistency.

73. **(C)** The data definition language is used to create a table structure inside a database.

74. **(E)** The queue data structure does not work on a concept known as "Last In, First Out" (LIFO). It works on a concept known as "First In, First Out" (FIFO).

75. **(E)** Metadata or a data dictionary is the storage of information that provides details of characteristics of data and the relationships between the data stored in a database. It is the storage of data about the data.

76. **(C)** A database administrator does not provide support services to end users when they need to print a document.

77. **(A)** The statement, "Data stored in a data warehouse can be updated only once a week" is false. Depending on the requirements, the data can be updated on any schedule such as: once a day, once a week, once a month, or once a year.

78. **(C)** Graphical user interface is the interface that takes place when starting an event such as saving a file in programming languages like Visual Basic and Java. The user needs to click on a "Save" command button to start an event. A command button on a form represents a graphical user interface.

79. **(D)** The newly created child class can add its own data members as well as the members' functions.

80. **(A)** The stack data structure is a kind of data structure wherein data items are removed from the top of the stack and added to the top of the stack.

81. **(E)** 256 (2^8) combinations of binary 0s and 1s can be displayed by a group of 8 bits. 0s and 1s represent binary digits with base 2.

82. **(C)**   The payment made for purchasing a television using a credit card is known as transaction processing, as the transaction must be completed for receipt of payment. The delivery of the television is batch processing.

83. **(D)**   "Every entity must have a column name that can be selected as a primary key (PK)" is a false statement. It is not a hard and fast rule to satisfy. It is a database requirement that some tables need to have at least one column name as a foreign key (FK) in order to establish relationships with common fields of other tables, where the same field is a PK to perform database processing.

84. **(A)**   Hashing finds the location of a data item or record, which is stored in the memory directly from the PK value, rather than looking for a PK value in the index table and then searching for the corresponding record in a data file.

85. **(E)**   DDL, DML, and DCL are all used to create database objects and perform various operations on database tables.

86. **(E)**   Antiphishing software offers protection from Internet identity theft by verifying the authenticity of websites that hide their true URL addresses.

87. **(D)**   A trade secret is an entity (such as a process, a design of a machine or equipment, a chemical formula, or an instrument) whose details are known only to its owner, are used for commercial purposes and economic gains, and whose details are kept secret from the public.

88. **(D)**   A role is not a type of virtual group.

89. **(C)**   A job specification is the job-design method that mentions the skills, education, experience, and any other requirement that a candidate must fulfill when applying for a particular position in a company.

90. **(E)**   The false statement is: "The IT people hired when insourcing have a higher level of technical expertise than the IT people hired when outsourcing."

91. **(B)**   Knowledge management is a collection of techniques, strategies, or practices to identify, collect and organize knowledge to meet a company's objectives by increasing its competitive edge in the market, profits, productivity, and market share.

92. **(B)**   Globalization is a process whereby employees of companies and governments of different nations cooperate with each other to do business using information technology that includes multinational investment.

93. **(C)**   Business Process Reengineering (BPR) is the study and modification of existing business strategies, business processes, technology, hierarchical organizational structure, and computer informational systems that improve business performance, market share, profit, and a company's competitive edge in the market.

94. **(D)**   There is no symbol labeled "pointers." There are symbols, known as arrows, which are used to indicate the "flow of control" in a process.

95. **(B)**   Shopping cart is online software that is used when a customer makes real-time, online purchases of products from a website.

96. **(D)**   A Trojan horse is a virus program and not a type of hacker.

97. **(D)**   There is no e-commerce classification known as retailer-to-consumer (R2C).

98. **(B)**   Organizational privacy describes the type of privacy where some organizations or government agencies don't want to reveal their trade secrets or any other activities to non-intended entities or persons, especially to competitors.

99. **(D)**   SHTTP is the protocol used to send personal messages securely over the Internet.

100. **(C)**   A run chart is a chart that displays process performance over a period of time.

ANSWER SHEETS

Practice Test 1
Practice Test 2

PRACTICE TEST 1

Answer Sheet

1. Ⓐ Ⓑ Ⓒ Ⓓ Ⓔ	35. Ⓐ Ⓑ Ⓒ Ⓓ Ⓔ	69. Ⓐ Ⓑ Ⓒ Ⓓ Ⓔ	
2. Ⓐ Ⓑ Ⓒ Ⓓ Ⓔ	36. Ⓐ Ⓑ Ⓒ Ⓓ Ⓔ	70. Ⓐ Ⓑ Ⓒ Ⓓ Ⓔ	
3. Ⓐ Ⓑ Ⓒ Ⓓ Ⓔ	37. Ⓐ Ⓑ Ⓒ Ⓓ Ⓔ	71. Ⓐ Ⓑ Ⓒ Ⓓ Ⓔ	
4. Ⓐ Ⓑ Ⓒ Ⓓ Ⓔ	38. Ⓐ Ⓑ Ⓒ Ⓓ Ⓔ	72. Ⓐ Ⓑ Ⓒ Ⓓ Ⓔ	
5. Ⓐ Ⓑ Ⓒ Ⓓ Ⓔ	39. Ⓐ Ⓑ Ⓒ Ⓓ Ⓔ	73. Ⓐ Ⓑ Ⓒ Ⓓ Ⓔ	
6. Ⓐ Ⓑ Ⓒ Ⓓ Ⓔ	40. Ⓐ Ⓑ Ⓒ Ⓓ Ⓔ	74. Ⓐ Ⓑ Ⓒ Ⓓ Ⓔ	
7. Ⓐ Ⓑ Ⓒ Ⓓ Ⓔ	41. Ⓐ Ⓑ Ⓒ Ⓓ Ⓔ	75. Ⓐ Ⓑ Ⓒ Ⓓ Ⓔ	
8. Ⓐ Ⓑ Ⓒ Ⓓ Ⓔ	42. Ⓐ Ⓑ Ⓒ Ⓓ Ⓔ	76. Ⓐ Ⓑ Ⓒ Ⓓ Ⓔ	
9. Ⓐ Ⓑ Ⓒ Ⓓ Ⓔ	43. Ⓐ Ⓑ Ⓒ Ⓓ Ⓔ	77. Ⓐ Ⓑ Ⓒ Ⓓ Ⓔ	
10. Ⓐ Ⓑ Ⓒ Ⓓ Ⓔ	44. Ⓐ Ⓑ Ⓒ Ⓓ Ⓔ	78. Ⓐ Ⓑ Ⓒ Ⓓ Ⓔ	
11. Ⓐ Ⓑ Ⓒ Ⓓ Ⓔ	45. Ⓐ Ⓑ Ⓒ Ⓓ Ⓔ	79. Ⓐ Ⓑ Ⓒ Ⓓ Ⓔ	
12. Ⓐ Ⓑ Ⓒ Ⓓ Ⓔ	46. Ⓐ Ⓑ Ⓒ Ⓓ Ⓔ	80. Ⓐ Ⓑ Ⓒ Ⓓ Ⓔ	
13. Ⓐ Ⓑ Ⓒ Ⓓ Ⓔ	47. Ⓐ Ⓑ Ⓒ Ⓓ Ⓔ	81. Ⓐ Ⓑ Ⓒ Ⓓ Ⓔ	
14. Ⓐ Ⓑ Ⓒ Ⓓ Ⓔ	48. Ⓐ Ⓑ Ⓒ Ⓓ Ⓔ	82. Ⓐ Ⓑ Ⓒ Ⓓ Ⓔ	
15. Ⓐ Ⓑ Ⓒ Ⓓ Ⓔ	49. Ⓐ Ⓑ Ⓒ Ⓓ Ⓔ	83. Ⓐ Ⓑ Ⓒ Ⓓ Ⓔ	
16. Ⓐ Ⓑ Ⓒ Ⓓ Ⓔ	50. Ⓐ Ⓑ Ⓒ Ⓓ Ⓔ	84. Ⓐ Ⓑ Ⓒ Ⓓ Ⓔ	
17. Ⓐ Ⓑ Ⓒ Ⓓ Ⓔ	51. Ⓐ Ⓑ Ⓒ Ⓓ Ⓔ	85. Ⓐ Ⓑ Ⓒ Ⓓ Ⓔ	
18. Ⓐ Ⓑ Ⓒ Ⓓ Ⓔ	52. Ⓐ Ⓑ Ⓒ Ⓓ Ⓔ	86. Ⓐ Ⓑ Ⓒ Ⓓ Ⓔ	
19. Ⓐ Ⓑ Ⓒ Ⓓ Ⓔ	53. Ⓐ Ⓑ Ⓒ Ⓓ Ⓔ	87. Ⓐ Ⓑ Ⓒ Ⓓ Ⓔ	
20. Ⓐ Ⓑ Ⓒ Ⓓ Ⓔ	54. Ⓐ Ⓑ Ⓒ Ⓓ Ⓔ	88. Ⓐ Ⓑ Ⓒ Ⓓ Ⓔ	
21. Ⓐ Ⓑ Ⓒ Ⓓ Ⓔ	55. Ⓐ Ⓑ Ⓒ Ⓓ Ⓔ	89. Ⓐ Ⓑ Ⓒ Ⓓ Ⓔ	
22. Ⓐ Ⓑ Ⓒ Ⓓ Ⓔ	56. Ⓐ Ⓑ Ⓒ Ⓓ Ⓔ	90. Ⓐ Ⓑ Ⓒ Ⓓ Ⓔ	
23. Ⓐ Ⓑ Ⓒ Ⓓ Ⓔ	57. Ⓐ Ⓑ Ⓒ Ⓓ Ⓔ	91. Ⓐ Ⓑ Ⓒ Ⓓ Ⓔ	
24. Ⓐ Ⓑ Ⓒ Ⓓ Ⓔ	58. Ⓐ Ⓑ Ⓒ Ⓓ Ⓔ	92. Ⓐ Ⓑ Ⓒ Ⓓ Ⓔ	
25. Ⓐ Ⓑ Ⓒ Ⓓ Ⓔ	59. Ⓐ Ⓑ Ⓒ Ⓓ Ⓔ	93. Ⓐ Ⓑ Ⓒ Ⓓ Ⓔ	
26. Ⓐ Ⓑ Ⓒ Ⓓ Ⓔ	60. Ⓐ Ⓑ Ⓒ Ⓓ Ⓔ	94. Ⓐ Ⓑ Ⓒ Ⓓ Ⓔ	
27. Ⓐ Ⓑ Ⓒ Ⓓ Ⓔ	61. Ⓐ Ⓑ Ⓒ Ⓓ Ⓔ	95. Ⓐ Ⓑ Ⓒ Ⓓ Ⓔ	
28. Ⓐ Ⓑ Ⓒ Ⓓ Ⓔ	62. Ⓐ Ⓑ Ⓒ Ⓓ Ⓔ	95. Ⓐ Ⓑ Ⓒ Ⓓ Ⓔ	
29. Ⓐ Ⓑ Ⓒ Ⓓ Ⓔ	63. Ⓐ Ⓑ Ⓒ Ⓓ Ⓔ	96. Ⓐ Ⓑ Ⓒ Ⓓ Ⓔ	
30. Ⓐ Ⓑ Ⓒ Ⓓ Ⓔ	64. Ⓐ Ⓑ Ⓒ Ⓓ Ⓔ	97. Ⓐ Ⓑ Ⓒ Ⓓ Ⓔ	
31. Ⓐ Ⓑ Ⓒ Ⓓ Ⓔ	65. Ⓐ Ⓑ Ⓒ Ⓓ Ⓔ	98. Ⓐ Ⓑ Ⓒ Ⓓ Ⓔ	
32. Ⓐ Ⓑ Ⓒ Ⓓ Ⓔ	66. Ⓐ Ⓑ Ⓒ Ⓓ Ⓔ	99. Ⓐ Ⓑ Ⓒ Ⓓ Ⓔ	
33. Ⓐ Ⓑ Ⓒ Ⓓ Ⓔ	67. Ⓐ Ⓑ Ⓒ Ⓓ Ⓔ	100. Ⓐ Ⓑ Ⓒ Ⓓ Ⓔ	
34. Ⓐ Ⓑ Ⓒ Ⓓ Ⓔ	68. Ⓐ Ⓑ Ⓒ Ⓓ Ⓔ		

PRACTICE TEST 2

Answer Sheet

1. Ⓐ Ⓑ Ⓒ Ⓓ Ⓔ
2. Ⓐ Ⓑ Ⓒ Ⓓ Ⓔ
3. Ⓐ Ⓑ Ⓒ Ⓓ Ⓔ
4. Ⓐ Ⓑ Ⓒ Ⓓ Ⓔ
5. Ⓐ Ⓑ Ⓒ Ⓓ Ⓔ
6. Ⓐ Ⓑ Ⓒ Ⓓ Ⓔ
7. Ⓐ Ⓑ Ⓒ Ⓓ Ⓔ
8. Ⓐ Ⓑ Ⓒ Ⓓ Ⓔ
9. Ⓐ Ⓑ Ⓒ Ⓓ Ⓔ
10. Ⓐ Ⓑ Ⓒ Ⓓ Ⓔ
11. Ⓐ Ⓑ Ⓒ Ⓓ Ⓔ
12. Ⓐ Ⓑ Ⓒ Ⓓ Ⓔ
13. Ⓐ Ⓑ Ⓒ Ⓓ Ⓔ
14. Ⓐ Ⓑ Ⓒ Ⓓ Ⓔ
15. Ⓐ Ⓑ Ⓒ Ⓓ Ⓔ
16. Ⓐ Ⓑ Ⓒ Ⓓ Ⓔ
17. Ⓐ Ⓑ Ⓒ Ⓓ Ⓔ
18. Ⓐ Ⓑ Ⓒ Ⓓ Ⓔ
19. Ⓐ Ⓑ Ⓒ Ⓓ Ⓔ
20. Ⓐ Ⓑ Ⓒ Ⓓ Ⓔ
21. Ⓐ Ⓑ Ⓒ Ⓓ Ⓔ
22. Ⓐ Ⓑ Ⓒ Ⓓ Ⓔ
23. Ⓐ Ⓑ Ⓒ Ⓓ Ⓔ
24. Ⓐ Ⓑ Ⓒ Ⓓ Ⓔ
25. Ⓐ Ⓑ Ⓒ Ⓓ Ⓔ
26. Ⓐ Ⓑ Ⓒ Ⓓ Ⓔ
27. Ⓐ Ⓑ Ⓒ Ⓓ Ⓔ
28. Ⓐ Ⓑ Ⓒ Ⓓ Ⓔ
29. Ⓐ Ⓑ Ⓒ Ⓓ Ⓔ
30. Ⓐ Ⓑ Ⓒ Ⓓ Ⓔ
31. Ⓐ Ⓑ Ⓒ Ⓓ Ⓔ
32. Ⓐ Ⓑ Ⓒ Ⓓ Ⓔ
33. Ⓐ Ⓑ Ⓒ Ⓓ Ⓔ
34. Ⓐ Ⓑ Ⓒ Ⓓ Ⓔ

35. Ⓐ Ⓑ Ⓒ Ⓓ Ⓔ
36. Ⓐ Ⓑ Ⓒ Ⓓ Ⓔ
37. Ⓐ Ⓑ Ⓒ Ⓓ Ⓔ
38. Ⓐ Ⓑ Ⓒ Ⓓ Ⓔ
39. Ⓐ Ⓑ Ⓒ Ⓓ Ⓔ
40. Ⓐ Ⓑ Ⓒ Ⓓ Ⓔ
41. Ⓐ Ⓑ Ⓒ Ⓓ Ⓔ
42. Ⓐ Ⓑ Ⓒ Ⓓ Ⓔ
43. Ⓐ Ⓑ Ⓒ Ⓓ Ⓔ
44. Ⓐ Ⓑ Ⓒ Ⓓ Ⓔ
45. Ⓐ Ⓑ Ⓒ Ⓓ Ⓔ
46. Ⓐ Ⓑ Ⓒ Ⓓ Ⓔ
47. Ⓐ Ⓑ Ⓒ Ⓓ Ⓔ
48. Ⓐ Ⓑ Ⓒ Ⓓ Ⓔ
49. Ⓐ Ⓑ Ⓒ Ⓓ Ⓔ
50. Ⓐ Ⓑ Ⓒ Ⓓ Ⓔ
51. Ⓐ Ⓑ Ⓒ Ⓓ Ⓔ
52. Ⓐ Ⓑ Ⓒ Ⓓ Ⓔ
53. Ⓐ Ⓑ Ⓒ Ⓓ Ⓔ
54. Ⓐ Ⓑ Ⓒ Ⓓ Ⓔ
55. Ⓐ Ⓑ Ⓒ Ⓓ Ⓔ
56. Ⓐ Ⓑ Ⓒ Ⓓ Ⓔ
57. Ⓐ Ⓑ Ⓒ Ⓓ Ⓔ
58. Ⓐ Ⓑ Ⓒ Ⓓ Ⓔ
59. Ⓐ Ⓑ Ⓒ Ⓓ Ⓔ
60. Ⓐ Ⓑ Ⓒ Ⓓ Ⓔ
61. Ⓐ Ⓑ Ⓒ Ⓓ Ⓔ
62. Ⓐ Ⓑ Ⓒ Ⓓ Ⓔ
63. Ⓐ Ⓑ Ⓒ Ⓓ Ⓔ
64. Ⓐ Ⓑ Ⓒ Ⓓ Ⓔ
65. Ⓐ Ⓑ Ⓒ Ⓓ Ⓔ
66. Ⓐ Ⓑ Ⓒ Ⓓ Ⓔ
67. Ⓐ Ⓑ Ⓒ Ⓓ Ⓔ
68. Ⓐ Ⓑ Ⓒ Ⓓ Ⓔ

69. Ⓐ Ⓑ Ⓒ Ⓓ Ⓔ
70. Ⓐ Ⓑ Ⓒ Ⓓ Ⓔ
71. Ⓐ Ⓑ Ⓒ Ⓓ Ⓔ
72. Ⓐ Ⓑ Ⓒ Ⓓ Ⓔ
73. Ⓐ Ⓑ Ⓒ Ⓓ Ⓔ
74. Ⓐ Ⓑ Ⓒ Ⓓ Ⓔ
75. Ⓐ Ⓑ Ⓒ Ⓓ Ⓔ
76. Ⓐ Ⓑ Ⓒ Ⓓ Ⓔ
77. Ⓐ Ⓑ Ⓒ Ⓓ Ⓔ
78. Ⓐ Ⓑ Ⓒ Ⓓ Ⓔ
79. Ⓐ Ⓑ Ⓒ Ⓓ Ⓔ
80. Ⓐ Ⓑ Ⓒ Ⓓ Ⓔ
81. Ⓐ Ⓑ Ⓒ Ⓓ Ⓔ
82. Ⓐ Ⓑ Ⓒ Ⓓ Ⓔ
83. Ⓐ Ⓑ Ⓒ Ⓓ Ⓔ
84. Ⓐ Ⓑ Ⓒ Ⓓ Ⓔ
85. Ⓐ Ⓑ Ⓒ Ⓓ Ⓔ
86. Ⓐ Ⓑ Ⓒ Ⓓ Ⓔ
87. Ⓐ Ⓑ Ⓒ Ⓓ Ⓔ
88. Ⓐ Ⓑ Ⓒ Ⓓ Ⓔ
89. Ⓐ Ⓑ Ⓒ Ⓓ Ⓔ
90. Ⓐ Ⓑ Ⓒ Ⓓ Ⓔ
91. Ⓐ Ⓑ Ⓒ Ⓓ Ⓔ
92. Ⓐ Ⓑ Ⓒ Ⓓ Ⓔ
93. Ⓐ Ⓑ Ⓒ Ⓓ Ⓔ
94. Ⓐ Ⓑ Ⓒ Ⓓ Ⓔ
95. Ⓐ Ⓑ Ⓒ Ⓓ Ⓔ
95. Ⓐ Ⓑ Ⓒ Ⓓ Ⓔ
96. Ⓐ Ⓑ Ⓒ Ⓓ Ⓔ
97. Ⓐ Ⓑ Ⓒ Ⓓ Ⓔ
98. Ⓐ Ⓑ Ⓒ Ⓓ Ⓔ
99. Ⓐ Ⓑ Ⓒ Ⓓ Ⓔ
100. Ⓐ Ⓑ Ⓒ Ⓓ Ⓔ

Glossary

algorithm—A detailed and finite sequence of instructions or steps, written in a natural human language through the drawing of charts or the writing of pseudocode, to precisely specify what a computer program must do in order to complete a specific task or problem.

alphanumeric data—A type of data that has a mixture of alphabet letters and numbers.

anti-phishing software—Programs that verify the authenticity of websites that hide their true URL address.

anti-spam software—Programs that protect computers from unwanted (junk) e-mail.

anti-spyware—Protects computers from spyware programs that collect information from computers without the user's knowledge.

anti-virus software—Provides security and protection against viruses, Web attacks, and identity theft by inspecting websites to make sure they are genuine. Helps to secure and monitor a computer's home network. Installed to protect computers from attacks by viruses such as Trojan horses, encryption viruses, worms, boot-sector viruses, script and macro-viruses, and logical bombs.

applications architect—Computer professional who designs components of applications, including interfaces, middleware, and infrastructure, and complies with employer's design standards.

arithmetic/logic unit (ALU)—A device that performs required arithmetical and logical operations to complete a particular task in a computer system by executing all the instructions required.

ASCII—Stands for American Standard Code for Information Interchange. A coding system that uses 8 binary digit patterns consisting of 0s and 1s, which represent up to 256 different characters.

attributes—Characteristics that describe the selected element, for instance the part of an HTML tag that tells the location of a file.

audio data—Any type of data that involves sound.

audio input devices—Input devices that create new sounds or capture and store sounds in a computer system.

audio ports—A port that connects audio devices, such as headphones or microphones, to a computer.

audio/video data—A type of data that consists of moving images.

authentication techniques—Used to control access to data stored in computers.

biometric input devices—Input devices that collect information from characteristics of the human body, such as finger prints and voice patterns, for identification purposes.

bit—the smallest unit of data that a computer can perform an operation on.

black-hat hackers—Black-hat hackers enter computer systems with the intention of causing damage or destroying information. They also steal information for personal gains.

branch—The entire side of a node, including all child nodes.

business systems analyst—Computer professional responsible for guiding, aligning, and accurately communicating business needs and processes with IT solutions for various types of customers.

cable modems—Digital modems that send and receive data over the Internet using cable television networks.

cache memory—Memory that stores and quickly accesses data or instructions that the computer uses frequently.

cartography—The design and printing of maps or visual representations of spatial data used in GIS.

cell phone—A mobile computing device that has its own operating system. They usually have input hardware, processing hardware, output hardware, and storage hardware.

centralized data warehouse—One centralized location where all company data is stored.

chain of trust techniques—Used to ensure that all software installed on computers is authentic software carrying a seal of authenticity and purchased from authorized distributors or sellers of software.

character—The smallest unit of meaningful information.

checklist—A list of things or objects that are relevant to processes or any other operation. Its purpose is to ensure that all important steps or actions have been taken to complete the process or intended operation.

check sheets—A check sheet is a form that is used to collect specific quantitative or qualitative repetitive data and interpret the data immediately in order to make decisions.

chief technology officer—Computer professional responsible for setting the firm's overall technology standards and practices, making recommendations and explaining technology solutions to senior management through presentations and advocacy, managing the implementation of data systems and monitoring their effectiveness in meeting business unit needs, providing leadership and managing staff, creating reports in functional areas such as systems operations, LAN/WAN architecture, and hardware and software support.

class—a collection of similar or identical objects.

clear history—Clears a computer's Internet search history.

cluster (allocation unit)—A group of two to eight sectors that store information.

coaxial cables—Copper cables that have two parallel physical channels. Each channel can carry a signal.

command driven interface—An interface in which the user types commands and command prompts.

comment tag—HTML code used to write comments describing the action of the HTML code on the webpage.

communication—The transferring of data or information from one computer to another.

communication protocols—A set of rules that computers follow when they communicate over a network or the Internet.

composite primary keys—Two columns that together uniquely identify a record in a table.

computer access controls—Protection that deals with the physical security of buildings and rooms where computers storing data and computer networks are located.

computer audits—Using computers to automate or simplify the audit process in the financial sector. They are also used for fraud detection and for continuous monitoring to acquire and analyze business data.

computer database administrator—Computer professional who designs, writes, and takes care of computer database systems so that the right person can get the right information at the right time. They also write programs to perform queries to extract useful information and to produce reports as necessary. They watch over the system to ensure that users do not tamper with the information or the structure of the database.

computer hardware engineer—Computer professional who designs, develops, tests, and supervises the manufacture of computer hardware.

computer intrusion detection—A system used to monitor all activities taking place in a computer system or network.

computer programmer—Computer professional who converts software program design into a logical series of instructions that the computer can follow.

computer scientist—A scientist who studies and uses the theoretical foundations of information and computation and their application in various computer systems.

computer security specialist—Responsible for assisting with the administration of the information system's security.

computer software engineer—Computer professional who designs and develops various types of software, including computer games, business applications, operating systems, network control systems, and middleware; they apply the theories and principles of computer science and mathematical analysis to create, test, and evaluate the software applications and systems that make computers work.

connectivity port—A port that allows a computer to access networks.

control unit—The part of the CPU that manages all the operations of the computer system.

CPU registers—Storage areas of the CPU that are used only by the CPU.

cryptographic technique—Protects data being transported between computers so that it cannot be intercepted, altered, or stolen by hackers.

cylinder—A vertical section of a track that passes through all the platters in a hard disk.

data—A collection of text, numbers, images, audio, and video that has not been processed.

databases—Used in knowledge management to store large amounts of information. The stored information can be organized according to the specific requirements of an organization in making decisions to improve a company's operations.

data browsing—The process of going through various files of a database and reading each record in a file to search for a particular kind of information.

data consistency—The same value for a particular piece of data appears in different places in a database.

data corruption—Stored data that has been damaged and is unreadable.

data integrity—Ensuring that data stored in a database is accurate (no inconsistencies) and that, when processed, it yields the same results all the time.

data loss—Data that was input and is stored on a storage medium can no longer be retrieved.

data maintenance—A technology that allows information or data to be kept accurate and up to date. It is also used to determine the percentage of errors an organization can tolerate in a database.

data mining—An automatic process that searches and analyzes data stored in a database from different angles and converts it into useful information.

data modeling—The technique used to create a database structure that allows data to be collected at its point of origin. It organizes that data in a manner that stores it efficiently and with easy accessibility to make business decisions and produce reports and allows data to be manipulated.

data structure—A scheme to structure (arrange or organize) data so that data of varied types can efficiently be entered, stored, sorted, retrieved, and manipulated by a computer program. Provides different ways of storing and using all the varying data type values discussed above in a computer system.

data warehouse—A place where data that has been collected (integrated) from various databases is housed for archival and security purposes.

database administration—An important part of data management in an organization. Work performed by a database administrator.

database management system—A program that performs all the actual operations inside a database.

decentralized data warehouse—Storage of data in regionally based warehouses.

decision programming logic—Also known as selection programming logic, selects one choice from a number of different operations that can be performed based on the outcome of some test condition applied to a variable such as a test score.

dial-up modems—Electric devices that convert digital signals to analog signals.

digital media specialist—Computer professional who works with computer technology to promote a company, cause, or idea. Digital media specialist jobs are found in both the private and public sectors where a message or idea needs to be conveyed to the public quickly.

digital pen—An input device used to convert handwriting and drawings into data that a computer can use.

domain—A collection of values of the same data type that are allowed for a particular column in a table.

dot pitch—The distance between the centers of two pixels.

doubly linked list—Data in which each data item has one backward pointer to point to the previous data item and one forward pointer to point to the next data item in the list.

DSL modems—Modems that send and receive digital data signals using a DSL data communication medium.

EBCDIC—Stands for Extended Binary-Coded Decimal Interchange Code. A coding system that uses 8 binary digit patterns consisting of 0s and 1s, which represent up to 256 different characters.

economic growth—The financial success incurred by creating new products, creating more jobs, etc.

elements—The basic items used to build a webpage.

empty tags—HTML tags that contain no information.

enterprise content management—The techniques and strategies used to acquire, organize, manage, warehouse, and deliver content and documents related to an organization and its processes.

entity—A place, person, thing, or any other item about which we can collect data or information.

ethernet port—A port that connects a computer to another computer, a local network, or a modem.

event—Signal to a program that something has happened or occurred and the program must perform some operation to deal with the occurrence of that event.

exclusive rights—Copyrights, patents, names, etc., which, in terms of the law, give exclusive rights to the owner of the intellectual property for its use.

expansion cards (adapter cards)—Devices added to a computer system to provide increased functionality.

expansion slots—Openings in the motherboard where users can insert extra expansion cards to increase the abilities of a computer.

explicit knowledge—Knowledge that is communicated in a systematic way using methods such as collecting data, writing formulas, designing operational manuals, etc. It is stored in computers and it is easily shared.

fax machines—Output devices that can send or receive printed information using telephone lines.

fiber optic cables—Cables that are made from transparent fiberglass or plastic.

field—The smallest piece of data that a database user can read from a database table.

file—A collection of identical types of records.

file transfer protocol (FTP)—A set of rules that allow files to be transferred from one computer to another.

filtering—The process of removing redundant or unwanted data from a pool of information.

firewall hardware devices—Devices, such as routers, that when attached to computers are configured to act as firewalls by keeping unused logical ports closed.

firewire port—A digital device that allows for a faster transfer of information.

flowcharts—Flowcharts are maps or graphical representations of a process.

gaming input devices—Devices—such as joysticks, steering wheels, track balls, and game pads—that input information for games.

geo-coding scheme—A process that determines location by stating the longitude, latitude, and elevation of an object.

global positioning system (GPS)—A system that uses information from satellites to give real-time information about a location.

graphical user interface (GUI)—An interface in which the user clicks on an icon that represents a particular operation.

graphics data—A type of data that includes drawings, pictures, and charts.

graphics port—A port that connects a monitor to a computer. It can also be called a video port.

hard disk platter—Plates made up of a rigid material, such as aluminum, that make up the hard disk and store data magnetically.

hardware security—Logins and passwords used to access computers and data.

head—The first data item in a list.

helpdesk support specialist—Computer professional who handles software and hardware issues. Helpdesk support staff resolve issues and decide when to create work tickets for issues that can't be solved by phone or e-mail and that require a visit to the user's workspace.

heterogeneous array—A collection of items of different data types.

histograms—Also called bar charts. There is an average height bar for the average run, an upper-height bar for the upper control limit, and a lower-height bar for the lower control limit.

homogenous two-dimensional array—A collection of data items of the same data type that is stored in a rows and columns format

hypermedia link—A link that connects an HTML document with a multimedia file when a user clicks on it.

hypertext link—Text on one webpage of a website that links to another page of the website when a user clicks on it.

hypertext transfer protocol (HTTP)—A protocol that allows files to transfer from a webserver to an individual computer so the files can be viewed with web-browsing software.

imaging and video input devices—Input devices that input images and video into computer language in a process known as digitizing.

implicit knowledge—Knowledge that is not written or stored in computers, but is instead acquired through experience and observation. People usually pass this knowledge onto others through word of mouth.

incident reporting—Checking for signs of possible violations or imminent threats of violations to computer security policies.

index—An arrangement to sort or arrange data used to access the records in a data file (table).

index key—A sorted data field in a table that is used to access data in a data file.

information—Processed data that can help users make decisions and answer questions.

information systems manager—Computer professional who plans, coordinates, and directs research and design for the computer–related activities of firms.

input—The entering of data into a computer.

instance—An entity that exists distinctly in the world. Object-Oriented Programming perceives everything as an instance, where every instance has a unique identity, displays some state, and exhibits some behavior.

interface—People talking and communicating using human language.

Internal modems—Modems located inside computer systems and connected to system boards.

internet message access protocol (IMAP)—A protocol that accesses e-mail messages from e-mail servers and allows users to view them.

internet protocol (IP) address—The address a computer user enters in the address window of an Internet browser.

internet security suites—A number of programs built into one collection, such as anti–virus, anti–spyware, and firewall programs to keep information and systems safe.

ISDN modems—Modems that send and receive digital data using an ISDN data communication medium.

iterative process—A process that is repeated until a required outcome is reached.

keyboard—An input device that allows the user to enter text and numerical data into a computer.

knowledge management—A variety of techniques, strategies, or practices that identify, collect, and organize knowledge to meet a company's objectives by increasing the competitive edge of the company, its profits, productivity, and market shares.

laptop computers—Portable, thin, lightweight, and easy-to-carry computers that can have the same power and capabilities as desktop computers.

large-format printers—Printers that accommodate paper with widths of up to sixty inches.

laser printers—Printers that print quickly and accurately.

lead applications developer—Computer professional who manages software development teams on the designing, developing, coding, testing, and debugging of applications.

line graph—Various points of intersections are plotted between the X axis and the Y axis on a graph and those points are then joined with a line. A line graph shows the relationship between two variables on a graph.

linked list—A data structure that, when storing records or data items, uses an additional field (known as a pointer) in a record to store the link (reference or address) to the next data item or record in the list.

local area networks (LAN)—Networks that connect computers that are in the same room or building.

looping programming logic—The same sets of statements are repeated a certain number of times. Also known as repetition or iterative programming logic.

magnetic storage devices—Devices commonly used to store data, information, and instructions.

management processes—The process of planning and administering any type of activity.

manager of technical services—Computer professional who manages help desk operations and support service; manages staff with regards to hiring, training, scheduling work assignments, and conducting evaluations; monitors response times, evaluates user satisfaction levels and makes recommendations for improvement in services; evaluates and manages technical support systems hardware and software and makes recommendations regarding upgrades or changes; and negotiates, writes, and reports on internal and external service level agreements.

messaging administrator—Computer professional who controls e–mail and groupware systems, including associated servers, operating systems, and backup and recovery programs; also fixes system problems and attends to service requests.

menu driven interface—An interface in which users click menu choices to perform functions.

metadata—The storage of information that provides a detailed explanation of the characteristics of the data and the set of relationships between data stored inside the database.

method—A set of programming statements that can perform some action on the data fields of an object in order to change the state of that object; input values in data fields when creating a new object; and display the current value stored in the data fields of a particular object. Also known as a sub-routine.

mobile printers—Small, lightweight printers that print from mobile devices, such as laptop computers and smart phones.

modem—A device that connects digital signals and analog signals.

monetary incentives—The creator of the intellectual property is given exclusive rights to use it and receive monetary gains for its use.

mouse—An input device that allows the user to make a selection of data or choose an operation.

multifunction office machines—Machines that do a number of tasks, including printing, scanning, copying, and faxing.

network and computer systems administrator—Designs, installs, and supports an organization's computer systems. This person is responsible for LANs, WANs, network segments, Internet and intranet systems.

network architect—Designers of computer networks. They set up, test, and evaluate systems such as local area networks (LANs), wide area networks (WANs), the Internet, intranets, and other data communications systems.

network community—The use of e–mail and Web logs in computer networks to encourage people to communicate their implicit knowledge through those and store it in databases.

network data model—Databases organized as a group of records that are joined in a 1:M relationship; one record can have more than one parent.

network engineer—Designers of computer networks. They set up, test, and evaluate systems such as local area networks (LANs), wide area networks (WANs), the Internet, intranets, and other data communications systems.

network manager—Performs direct day–to–day operations and maintenance of the firm's networking technology; collaborates with network engineers, architects, and other team members on the implementation, testing, deployment, and integration of network systems.

node—Each location in a tree, or data item in a list.

numerical data—A type of data that is made up of only numbers and can be used to perform arithmetical operations to generate numerical output.

object—A noun representing an entity that exists distinctly in the world. Object Oriented Programming perceives everything as an object, where every object has a unique identity, displays some state, and exhibits some behavior.

object-oriented analysis (OOA)—A software engineering approach that analyzes the functional requirements of a system.

object-oriented analysis and design (OOAD)—A software engineering approach that models a system as a group of interacting objects.

operating system (OS)—Software that manages the hardware and other software on a computer. It is the first software that is installed on a computer.

operational processes—The process of planning and administering a particular type of operation in a business. Typical operational processes in businesses are manufacturing and purchasing.

organizing—Sorting or arranging the data alphabetically, numerically, or into groups.

output—Results that are presented after data has been processed.

packet—An entity that stores one unit of binary data.

packet body—The part of the packet that contains the actual information. It is also called the payload.

packet footer—The part of the packet that contains a sequence of bits that indicate the end of the message. This part of the packet is optional.

packet header—The part of the packet that gives information about the packet, such as the destination IP address.

packet switching—The act of turning the original message into smaller packets and transmitting them on the Internet.

parallel ports—A port that sends two or more bits of data at a time, making them faster than serial ports.

parent node—The node at the top of a tree, also called a root node.

Pareto charts—Used to display the application of the Pareto principle, which states that if you can eliminate problems that constitute a small percentage (i.e., 25%) of a large operation, then it will have an overall greater impact, increase profits, and save money.

personal digital assistants (PDAs)—Handheld devices that carry personal information—such as phone numbers, addresses, and events—in a digital form.

photo printers—Printers that print high-quality black-and-white or color photos.

pie charts—Used to analyze data for one aspect of an entire operation.

pixel—A picture or element that is represented by a single point, or dot, on any digital image.

pointer—An added data field in a record (data item) that points to the location of the next record in the list.

portable media players (PMPs)—A mobile electronic device that stores, plays, and supports digital audio, video, and image files.

primary key—A column name that uniquely identifies a row or a record in a table.

procedure—A sequence of instructions that tells the computer to perform a specific task.

process—A program that follows a series of instructions to perform a specific action.

processing—Converting data or information from one form to another form by following a series of steps.

programming—The act of creating and writing a computer program to perform a particular task.

programming language—A sequence of instructions used to create a computer program.

progress of human beings—Improvement in terms of saving time, money, and natural resources; having a better living style; and promoting better health.

project—A specific task undertaken to create or build something new, such as an information system.

proxy software—Makes a computer's Internet surfing anonymous.

pull technology—Research system in which information is collected from outside sources or experts when a company realizes there is a need for improvement in the company's operations.

push technology—Research system that uses products and services, such as PointCast and BackWeb, that push information into a computer based on the selection criteria.

queue—a data structure in which new data items are added at the end of the list while other items are removed from the beginning of the list.

random access memory (RAM)—Memory that stores all the data, instructions, programs, and documents that are accessed while the computer is being used.

RAM (Random Access Memory)—Storage that can record and erase data multiple times.

relation—Also called a file, or a collection of identical types of records.

resolution—The detail of an image that is expressed in the number of pixels arranged vertically by the number of pixels arranged horizontally.

run charts—Graphics that display process performance over a period of time.

scatter plots—Similar to a line chart (graph) but with no line. The points of intersection between the X axis and the Y axis are shown on the graph, but are not connected with a line.

script kiddies—Script kiddies are people who don't have knowledge of hacking, but use computer programs written by professional hackers or pre–built tools to hack computers.

sector—Pie-shaped arcs that make up the tracks in a hard disk.

secure socket layer—Protocol used by institutions for transmitting private information over the Internet.

serial port—A port that sends one bit of data at a time.

siblings—Nodes with the same parent nodes.

simple mail transfer protocol (SMTP)—A protocol that determines which path an e-mail message will follow.

singly linked list—Each data item points to the next data item in the list without pointing backward.

software firewall—Installed to protect attacks on computer networks or computers that are using networks or the Internet. Personal firewalls close all open logical ports on computers to protect computers from attackers when using the Internet.

software tools—Software, such as groupware (used in collaborative technologies), social software (such as wikis) and databases can be used collectively to help KM.

sound card (audio card) devices—A device that allows a computer to output sound signals.

speaker ports—A port that connects speakers to a computer.

spreadsheet—A program that is similar to an accounting ledger book. It is also known as a worksheet.

stack—A data structure in which the data items are removed from the top of a list and inserted only at the top of a list.

storage—The saving of data, programs, or output for future use.

storing—The process of saving collected data on a storage device or disk.

string—A collection or a sequence of characters in which each character occupies one byte of memory space

structure—How data or information is stored in a computer system.

sub-tree—Also called a branch, the entire side of a node, including all child nodes.

supporting processes—Processes that support operational processes.

systems administrator—Computer professionals who have in–depth technical knowledge of systems hardware and software as well as of operating systems. They should have experience installing operating system software, patches, and upgrades; analyzing, troubleshooting, and resolving system hardware, software, and networking issues; configuring, optimizing, fine-tuning, and monitoring operating system software and servers; and performing system backups and recovery.

systems programmer—Computer professionals responsible for the installation, maintenance, implementation, and tuning of UNIX and other operating systems' hardware and software along with other as-

sociated components. They support various Web servers, and perform troubleshooting, performance, and capacity tuning.

table—Graphic in which data is stored in a rows and columns format. In a table, the column represents data fields and the rows represent records by providing data for each of the fields in a table.

tail—indicates the end of data items in a list.

technical writer—Writes technical materials such as equipment or product manuals, appendices, and operating and maintenance instructions. A technical writer knows how to use software such as Author IT, Photoshop, and Framemaker.

text data—A type of data that includes alphabet letters, numerical digits, and special characters.

touch input devices—Devices—such as touch screens and touch sensitive pads—that users touch to input data.

tracks—Concentric circles that make up a hard disk.

transmission—Another word for *communication*. The transferring of data or information from one computer to another.

transmission control protocol/internet protocol (TCP/IP)—A protocol that routes files from one end of a network to the other end.

tree—List of data items

twisted-pair cables—Cable made up of two individual copper wires that are wrapped with insulation.

unicode—A universal coding system that represents characters from other languages and uses 16 binary digit (2 bytes) patterns to represent up to 65,536 different characters in computers.

unified modeling language (UML)—A language used to model an Object Oriented System.

unique index—An index key that points to a unique row in a data file.

uniform resource locator (URL)—A string of characters that specifies the unique address of a particular website and also specifies the type of transfer protocol to use when transferring the document over the Internet.

universal serial bus (USB)—A port that connects many different types of input, output, and peripheral devices, such as printers, keyboards, and external drives.

user interface—The part of a software program that allows users to communicate with the computer.

utility programs—Programs that perform routine maintenance-type tasks that are usually related to managing computer hardware devices and software programs.

virtual memory—RAM that stores programs that the computer is actively executing.

Web developer—Computer professional who plans and implements Web–based applications; and coordinates with the product development, marketing, product management and other teams to bring new applications online.

Web indexing—An alphabetical indexing system for a website or an Intranet.

Web programmer—Computer professional who provides technical guidance to the program manager and team members on the implementation and maintenance of a project's website; translates detailed website design into code, and programs, tests, debugs, and updates the website as required.

webmaster—A person who manages and maintains a website.

webpage—An electronic document on the Internet that stores data, including text, sound, and video.

webserver—A computer that stores the webpages of a particular website.

white-hat hackers—White-hat hackers enter computer systems to prove that computer systems are vulnerable to outside attacks. They do not want to cause any kind of damage.

wide area networks (WAN)—Networks that cover large areas. These networks may be used by large companies or organizations.

word processor—A program used to manipulate a text document.

Index

Notes

Notes

Notes

REA's Test Preps
The Best in Test Preparation

- *REA "Test Preps" are **far more** comprehensive than any other test preparation series*
- *Each book contains full-length practice tests based on the most recent exams*
- ***Every** type of question likely to be given on the exams is included*
- *Answers are accompanied by **full** and **detailed** explanations*

REA publishes hundreds of test prep books. Some of our titles include:

Advanced Placement Exams (APs)
Art History
Biology
Calculus AB & BC
Chemistry
Economics
English Language & Composition
English Literature & Composition
European History
French Language
Government & Politics
Latin Vergil
Physics B & C
Psychology
Spanish Language
Statistics
United States History
World History

College-Level Examination Program (CLEP)
American Government
College Algebra
General Examinations
History of the United States I
History of the United States II
Introduction to Educational Psychology
Human Growth and Development
Introductory Psychology
Introductory Sociology
Principles of Management
Principles of Marketing
Spanish
Western Civilization I
Western Civilization II

SAT Subject Tests
Biology E/M
Chemistry
French
German
Literature
Mathematics Level 1, 2
Physics
Spanish
United States History

Graduate Record Exams (GREs)
Biology
Chemistry
Computer Science
General
Literature in English
Mathematics
Physics
Psychology

ACT - ACT Assessment

ASVAB - Armed Services Vocational Aptitude Battery

CBEST - California Basic Educational Skills Test

CDL - Commercial Driver License Exam

COOP, HSPT & TACHS - Catholic High School Admission Tests

FE (EIT) - Fundamentals of Engineering Exams

FTCE - Florida Teacher Certification Examinations

GED

GMAT - Graduate Management Admission Test

LSAT - Law School Admission Test

MAT - Miller Analogies Test

MCAT - Medical College Admission Test

MTEL - Massachusetts Tests for Educator Licensure

NJ HSPA - New Jersey High School Proficiency Assessment

NYSTCE - New York State Teacher Certification Examinations

PRAXIS PLT - Principles of Learning & Teaching Tests

PRAXIS PPST - Pre-Professional Skills Tests

PSAT/NMSQT

SAT

TExES - Texas Examinations of Educator Standards

THEA - Texas Higher Education Assessment

TOEFL - Test of English as a Foreign Language

USMLE Steps 1,2,3 - U.S. Medical Licensing Exams

For information about any of REA's books, visit www.rea.com

Research & Education Association
61 Ethel Road W., Piscataway, NJ 08854
Phone: (732) 819-8880

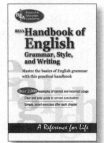